Democratization
through the looking-glass

MANCHESTER
UNIVERSITY PRESS

PERSPECTIVES ON DEMOCRATIZATION

The series presents critical texts on democratization processes and democratic theory. Written in an accessible style, the books are theoretically informed and empirically rich, and examine issues critical to the establishment, extension and deepening of democracy in different political systems and contexts. Important examples of successful democratization processes, as well as reasons why experiments in democratic government fail, are some of the issues analysed in the series. The books in the series make an important contribution to the ongoing debates about democracy, good governance and democratization.

series editors: SHIRIN M. RAI and WYN GRANT

already published

Funding democratization
PETER BURNELL and ALAN WARE (editors)

Democracy as public deliberation
MAURIZIO PASSERIN D'ENTRÈVES (editor)

Globalizing democracy
KATHERINE FIERLBECK

Terrorism and democratic stability
JENNIFER S. HOLMES

Democratizing the European Union
CATHERINE HOSKYNS and MICHAEL NEWMAN (editors)

Democracy in Latin America
GERALDINE LIEVESLEY

Democratization in the South
ROBIN LUCKHAM and GORDON WHITE (editors)

Mainstreaming gender, democratizing the state?
SHIRIN RAI (editor)

Democratization through the looking-glass

PETER BURNELL editor

MANCHESTER UNIVERSITY PRESS
Manchester and New York

distributed exclusively in the USA by Palgrave

Published by Manchester University Press
Oxford Road, Manchester M13 9NR, UK
and Room 400, 175 Fifth Avenue, New York, NY 10010, USA
www.manchesteruniversitypress.co.uk

Distributed exclusively in the USA by
Palgrave, 175 Fifth Avenue, New York,
NY 10010, USA

Distributed exclusively in Canada by
UBC Press, University of British Columbia, 2029 West Mall,
Vancouver, BC, Canada V6T 1Z2

British Library Cataloguing-in-Publication Data
A catalogue record for this book is available from the British Library

Library of Congress Cataloging-in-Publication Data applied for

ISBN   0 7190 6243 8   *hardback*

First published 2002

11 10 09 08 07 06 05 04 03   10 9 8 7 6 5 4 3 2 1

Typeset in Trump Medieval
by Graphicraft Limited, Hong Kong
Printed in Great Britain
by Biddles Ltd, Guildford and King's Lynn

Contents

Tables

Contributors

Tony Addison is Deputy Director, World Institute for Development Economics Research (United Nations University) Helsinki.

Shaun Breslin is a Professor in Politics in the Department of Politics and International Studies at the University of Warwick.

Peter Burnell is a Professor in the Department of Politics and International Studies at the University of Warwick.

Peter Calvert is Emeritus Professor of Comparative and International Politics at the University of Southampton and a Fellow of the Royal Historical Society.

Philip Cerny is a Professor in the Department of Government, University of Manchester.

Francisco E. González is a British Academy Post-doctoral Research Fellow, University of Oxford.

Jeremy Gould is a Senior Research Fellow with the Academy of Finland, based at the Institute of Development Studies, University of Helsinki.

Desmond King is Andrew W. Mellon Professor of American Government, University of Oxford and Fellow of Nuffield College and a Fellow of the British Academy.

Paul G. Lewis is a Reader in Central and East European Politics at the Open University.

John McEldowney is a Professor of Law in the School of Law, University of Warwick.

George Philip is a Professor in the Department of Government at the London School of Economics and Political Science.

Shirin M. Rai is Professor in the Department of Politics and International Studies at the University of Warwick.

Gurharpal Singh is the Nadir Dinshaw Chair in Inter-Religious Relations at the University of Birmingham, and previously the C. R. Parekh Chair in Indian Politics and Director of the Centre for Indian Studies at the University of Hull.

Roger Southall is Executive Director of the Democracy and Governance Research Programme, Human Sciences Research Council, Pretoria.

Alex Warleigh is Professor of International Politics and Public Policy at the University of Limerick.

Geoffrey Wood is Professor of Comparative Human Resource Management at Middlesex University Business School.

1

Perspectives

PETER BURNELL

The Looking-Glass for the Mind; or Intellectual Mirror (1792)
(*Oxford English Dictionary*, 2nd edn, 1989)

In the last decade or so democratization has been the focus
of a burgeoning political science literature. Democratization
is multifaceted and multidimensional. As both an idea and
a practical phenomenon it belongs exclusively to no single
discipline or branch of academic learning, and to no one
geographical area. The purpose of this book is to show how
our knowledge and understanding of democratization are
enriched by studying through the lens of multidisciplinarity
(Part I) and from a broadly-based comparative analysis – one
that is deeply informed by area studies that are themselves
comparative at the regional level (Part II). The volume takes
the form of authentic accounts by specialists of what their
own subject brings to the study of democratization. They
pose some distinctive questions, with the potential to uncover unique insights. Of course, some areas of interest are
bound to overlap, and there will be points of convergence
too: their identity will become clear also.

The book is addressed especially *but not only* to the
political science community, being an invitation to each one
of us to 'think outside the box' of the usual parameters that
shape our study of democratization. It aims to demonstrate
that by being receptive to multidisciplinarity and equipped
with a broadly-based geopolitical knowledge we should be
better placed to:

- address some of the gaps that political scientists recognize are present in the political science literature on
  democratization;

- pursue a more comprehensive understanding of demo-cratization as a process that takes a variety of forms and is not solely a political phenomenon;
- provide explanations of democratization that will more easily satisfy the criteria of coherence, consistency, and plausibility while making sense of the variety of experiences undergone by different societies at different times;
- anticipate the wider compass of democratization's consequences for the human condition at all levels;
- critically assess strategies for extending and 'deepening' democracy that have as their goal improvement in democracy's quality and its chances of being sustained;
- move in the direction of foretelling the future of democracy and democratization with greater accuracy.

While the underlying claims about the value of multi-disciplinarity and broadly-based area studies might seem far from heretical, they do face resistance – as is borne out by the literature. For example, on the spread of democracy Remmer's (1995: 105) view is that disciplinary traditions 'have created major barriers to the development of theory capable of comprehending new international realities', that is, theories fit for the purpose of 'integrating data drawn from both national and systemic levels of analysis'. The situation Remmer described then has not changed greatly, notwithstanding a welcome increase of attention to the international dimensions of democratization. Mair (1996: 317) noted the 'now virtual absence of comparative analyses with a global, or even cross-regional ambition'. More recently still it has been said 'democratisation studies would greatly profit from expanding its disciplinary and geographical constraints' (Kopecý and Mudde 2000: 517). This chapter, 'Perspectives', amplifies such sentiments, presenting reasons why students of politics should reject parochialism in their attempts to understand democratization.

Political studies as an open discipline

The proposition that comparative analysis will have most to offer when informed by a broadly-based knowledge of different regions hardly needs elaboration. For one thing there is Remmer's (1995: 107) reminder that the 'theoretical pay-off of research conceived within a traditional case study format has been limited'. For another, comparability 'is a quality that is not inherent in any given set of objects; rather it is a quality imparted to them by the observer's perspective' (Rustow 1968: 47). By limiting comparative analysis to areas of close proximity we risk creating an appearance of inter-regional differences that owes too much to the way regions are defined and to regionally-specific research agendas – 'an areal version of an old problem, that is, case selection determining the conclusions drawn' (Bunce 2000a: 721). By comparison the case for multidisciplinarity, though not idiosyncratic,[1] might seem less obvious, and so receives greater elaboration here.

Disciplines can be differentiated in terms of *what* they study – their substantive concerns – and *how* they study it – their methodologies, as well as in some cases by special purpose and the development of a distinctive 'jargon' or technical vocabulary. There is a long-established view that although politics may be defined in terms of the activity studied, it is not definable in terms of a singular method of study, let alone a unique method that it can call its own. Instead, politics is what might be called an 'open' discipline: it relies, uniquely so, on the methods and the modes of explanation of other branches of knowledge, and what is more without obvious sense of embarrassment or the urge to pretend otherwise. Thus, in the words of a Professor of Political Theory and Government, 'the suggestion that the student of politics is an eclectic is very well observed, for he draws on so many ways of analysis as seem to suit his purpose' (Greenleaf 1968: 1–2). Political science 'has always borrowed much more than it has lent' (Dogan 1996: 102),[2] perhaps lending support to the view that politics should not be called an autonomous discipline, for that very reason (Wiseman 1969: 96).

However, if it is in respect of its principal choice of subject matter that the study of politics most clearly stands out, then the precise identity of that subject or its core has itself been much debated. For Duverger 'the essence of politics, its real nature and true significance, is to be found in the fact that it is always and at all times ambivalent' (Duverger 1966: xiii). For political analysts who find the institutions of government to be far too narrow a focus – and that now means the great majority – bounded disciplinary perspectives are considered unhelpful to the investigation of the problems they want to focus on. Some go further than others: for instance Leftwich (1984: 159) travels beyond multidisciplinarity to say 'there is no contradiction (except in semantic terms) to say that the discipline of Politics must be interdisciplinary in its focus and its frameworks'.

Moreover, it is not just that the boundaries of the 'political' appear both porous and fuzzy once we have taken into account all the different views of what politics is; but that the different views each incline towards their own view of how politics should be studied. They generate different ideas about the relationships between politics and 'sister disciplines', and about which disciplines have the nearest blood ties and which ones have the most to offer the study of politics. For example there is Oakeshott's (1991) conviction that politics is a 'conversation with tradition'. This invites a particular kind of historical approach. Then there is the view that politics is essentially about reconciling interests, which leads towards rational choice theory and the statistical modelling of individual and group behaviour. In fact, although one implication shared by all the main ideas of what politics comprises is that democratic values and practices lie more or less close to the heart, they do this for different reasons. In consequence they give rise to their own questions and sense of priorities relevant to the range of issues that democratization is likely to provoke; and moreover they imply different ways of going about finding answers.

Among disciplines offering approaches that can be employed to advantage in the study of politics generally, and democratization specifically, the disagreements over method extend to arguments about what constitutes a satisfactory explanation. Thus in one corner lies the historians' search for qualitative information to supply context and identify the reasons and intentions, to get at the meaning and significance of ideas and events for the actors themselves both individually and as rooted in specific social contexts. This is a world where human agency is potentially very significant. And there may be a place for historical accident or chance too. In a different corner social scientists sift quantitative information, looking for 'forces' that in the view of some are analogous to causes; they hope to subsume the *explanandum* under a covering law or law-like generalization. Disciplines impose their own canons of acceptable forms of evidence and offer different frameworks of analysis, in addition to their own choice of starting-points, lead questions and principal concerns. How did something happen? Why did it happen? What brought it about? What are the consequences and why do they matter? How will it end? What is it, anyway? Are these questions interdependent or can they be answered separately? And all the time politics in the real world is moving on, and with it the study of politics develops as well. To dismiss the contributions that some other specialisms might make to understanding something like democratization simply on the grounds that they do not happen to coincide with *today's* fashions in political science would be short-sighted indeed.

Of course, the fruitfulness of applying several disciplines to the analysis of politics will vary across different kinds of political phenomena. But we should rule out any a priori assumption that mutually exclusive choices must be made. It is far more helpful to recognize that there can be different levels of explanation, some more immediate, some more 'fundamental'. And that variations in the degree of completeness can be quite legitimate; they can all be judged in relation both to the specific point of the inquiry and the existing knowledge and understanding of the inquirer.

Looking-glass – a 'mirror for looking at oneself'

The construction of democratization as a unit of study will reflect the intellectual standpoint of the inquirer. Put simply, the understanding we are likely to gain will be affected by where we are coming from and what we bring to the table. This will be just as true for area and country specialists as for analysts whose main intellectual training and vocabulary of discourse are in some field other than politics. We would not expect, say, Europeanists writing abut eastern

Europe and Africanists writing about southern Africa to make identical approaches to studying democratization; and regions differ in terms of which particular aspects of democratization they illuminate most sharply. Equally we would not expect the accounts by economists to duplicate those of, say, anthropologists – if not because of basic epistemological differences then because of variations in the conceptual lens and methodological apparatus they bring to bear. In principle, the contributors to this volume ask different questions, address different problems, will strike different emphases and offer their own concerns; but in practice there is also much to be gained from establishing where they touch at certain points and share similar observations and reflections.

However, there are caveats, which the following chapters will illustrate. First, we should not be surprised to find evidence of contestation over the precise nature of the preferred method or mode of explanation not just in political studies but in other disciplines and sub-disciplines as well. Like the study of politics, the other disciplines too are dynamic, and their approaches can even vary according to distinct national cultural and educational or professional institutional traditions. There are differences of time, place and circumstance that impact on the way political phenomena, including democracy, are viewed – and not just by political scientists. Second, even where there are shared convictions over a discipline's main parameters and substantive concerns, the meaning and significance of democratization may still be the subject of lively dispute. Indeed, the disagreements over the meaning and significance of something like democratization could be more vigorously contested inside a single discipline such as sociology or within a distinct geopolitical region than are the divisions that appear most clearly to set the disciplines or regions apart. After all, neither Marxism and dependency theory nor social constructivism and post-modernism have any respect for national or disciplinary boundaries. Put starkly, it is feasible that political researchers interested in democratization could gain more by collaborating with colleagues from other disciplines than by engaging with specialists from certain other branches of political science (Dogan 1996: 123–4).

Studying democratization

In Britain the academic study of politics began half a century ago from foundations in constitutional law, philosophy and history. In the years since, the study of politics and law seem to have grown apart, comparatively speaking, with few notable exceptions, such as in politics the writings of Drewry, who sees (1996: 201) 'a natural affinity between law and politics, which takes many forms'. Yet constitutional engineering in new democracies, the determination of procedures for institutionalizing the rule of law, and the pros and cons of judicial activism are but three notable areas where in principle political inquiries have much to learn from legal scholarship. Thus political scientists studying democratization appear much taken with the idea of judicial autonomy as part of the institutional architecture for ensuring the horizontal accountability of the executive – a seemingly necessary counterpart to the vertical accountability that legislatures and electorates seem only imperfectly to exact. But here (Chapter 7) McEldowney's approach from the side of legal studies highlights instead a growing tension between the principle of democratic accountability and the increase of judicial power. If, as some observers believe, the world is moving inexorably towards the elaboration of a right to democratic rule in international law, then both Drewry's point and McEldowney's cautioning could both take on even greater import.

The last fifteen years or so have seen the rise of the so-called 'new institutionalism' in social sciences generally and political science specifically. This stresses the relative autonomy of institutions, and rejects earlier reductionist tendencies that made political phenomena the dependent variable of other primarily social or economic forces. The 'new institutionalism' encourages us to revisit the arrangements that embed political behaviour in rules, norms, expectations and traditions. One implication is that not only legal analysts, but possibly anthropologists too should be consulted for their insights into the complexities of 'crafting' democratic institutions appropriate to individual societies. Anthropological studies shed light on the world of *informal* practice of customs and conventions that can

profoundly affect the working of formally democratic arrangements, especially at the 'microphysical' level. Traditionally,
the way the embedded neo-patrimonial and clientelistic
relationships of power complicate the transfer of Western-
style democracy to Africa has been paradigmatic. In Africa
Chabal and Daloz (1999: 9) say politics 'is not functionally
differentiated, or separated, from the socio-cultural considerations which govern everyday life . . . there is a constant
and dynamic interpenetration of the different spheres of
human experience, from the political to the religious'.[3]
But in Chapter 2, below, Gould goes further in examining
the perspectives that recent anthropological thinking contributes, including fundamental reservations about democratization both as explanatory tool and (even more so) as
normative ideal. On the other side, a political scientist's
view of the perspectives and dimensions of democratization
found in Africa is explored in Chapter 9, by Southall.

In this context political sociologists too should come into
their own, especially now that the idea of political culture
– a concept whose validity or usefulness political analysts
have often questioned in the past – has experienced major
rehabilitation in the politics literature on democratization.
There is a growing tendency to root variations in the success and failure of democratic experiments as much in the
values and attitudes of the people as in qualities of formal
institutional design. At the same time in the 'third world'
Kamrava (1995: 699) judges a democratic polity to be requi-
site for forging what is still clearly lacking in some societies:
a 'nationally cohesive political culture'. These are perspectives that offer alternatives to those grounded in levels
of economic development and the accompanying socio-
economic structure. That said, neither the contemporary
standing of the 'new institutionalism' nor the rediscovery
of political culture as a significant influence have diminished the amount of attention given to economic and socio-
economic factors in supporting long-term democratic trends.
On the contrary, it is in regard to the interaction among
all these variables and others besides that there is now
the most pressing need to improve our understanding. To
illustrate, from a feminist perspective Rai (Chapter 4) rightly
raises the issue of the *costs* of participation, for women.
Are the cultural impediments to political equality between

men and women and to greater female political participation more resistant to all-round improvements in material circumstances in some societies than in others – and if so, why? Similarly, is the persistence of neo-patrimonialism more debilitating for democratic progress when supported by large inflows of conditionality-based international economic aid, or would it be better if the underlying scarcity of domestic resources was allowed to persist?

Economists, with their fondness for the rigorous application of statistical techniques to the measurement of aggregate data, are, like sociologists, well equipped to investigate the social and economic *consequences* of democratization – consequences that in turn will have implications for the quality and sustainability of democracy. Chapter 3 by Addison shows that economics' fundamental commitment to a priori reasoning and a deductive approach creates no blind spot to the political significance of distributive concerns, while noting that whether or not society is a democracy might matter less for economic growth than whether it is highly polarized. Yet, unsurprisingly, it is in the sociological literature reviewed by Wood (Chapter 8) that we find the most recurrent concern with the political impact of such forces as absolute and relative poverty, together with the rise of corporate financial and economic power. Here, recognition of the role played by the likes of social movements (discussed in a South Asian context by Gurharpal Singh in Chapter 14) offers a valuable corrective to the elite-level focus that has typified much of the political science literature on democratic transition to date.

But whereas the search for evidence of statistical correlations is *de rigueur* in both economics and political sociology, a somewhat contrary orientation is implied by path dependence – another fashionable theory and approach. This draws attention to the kind of legacy left by the previous political regime and its impact on the dynamics of change, with the outcomes seen to be influenced by the manner in which change comes about and the route that is taken. Here the accumulation of historical evidence portraying in detail the 'inner' connections of temporal processes looks to be most relevant. This will incline research towards case-studies of the origins and genesis of change. What is perhaps surprising, then, is that it was in economics (more accurately, economic geography) where the idea emerged that a richer appreciation of the role of historical processes in generating variations in political life would be gained if we applied the idea of increasing returns. The idea of 'increasing returns' maintains that the *sequence* of events can have specific consequences ('democratization backwards' is a striking example).[4] But its main value is said to lie in challenging the continuing supremacy in political science of the functionalist approach, which, in seeking to explain all institutions by referring to their performance in serving some particularly useful purpose, can offer only a partial insight (Pierson 2000: 263–4).

Finally, in an increasingly seamless world, where the boundaries between the domestic and the international are becoming broken and indistinct, it is now generally accepted that the international context and the influence of transboundary forces must be included when trying to comprehend 'domestic' events. The limitations of trying to make sense of national democratization trends in purely endogenous terms are becoming ever more apparent. This is especially true of democratic transformation in some of the former Soviet bloc states, explored by Lewis (Chapter 10). In that region a strong desire to be admitted to full membership of the European Union (EU) has driven the tempo of political and economic reform, even though a democratic deficit lies at the core of the EU's own arrangements. At the global level the title of an essay in international relations (IR) theory 'Why is there no international democratic theory?' (H. Smith 2000) speaks volumes, and exposes the limitations of traditional approaches based on realist assumptions.[5]

Similarly, the foreign policy of democracy-promotion by the West offers a research agenda that has yet to be fully explored through the prism of 'alternative' IR approaches that maintain that theory constructs reality.[6] But one thing is certain: it is important to examine whether and how the institutions of regional and global governance can themselves be democratized. The European Union, an obvious test case, is explored by Warleigh (Chapter 12); more specifically, the significance of both the European Court of Justice and the European Court of Human Rights for Britain's parliamentary democracy is considered by McEldowney in

Chapter 7. Moreover Cerny explains (Chapter 6) why the consequences of globalization, broadly conceived, for democratic self-governance could hardly be less significant. The point is valid regardless of whether we view the global political economy's dissemination of capitalism as on balance dangerous to liberal democracy or instead as something that can be more constructive, for instance by lending impetus to a project of democratization more radical than that in operation in 'really existing democracy'. Of course, Cerny's presentation could be construed as taking up a position on one side of a particularly vigorous debate, namely one that could be summed up as 'hyper-globalist'. It should be read as an example of international political economy (IPE) theorizing, and is not necessarily representative of every position that IPE scholars adopt towards the topic. Nevertheless, given the enormity of the issues, arcane questions about whether international relations constitutes a separate discipline (and foreign policy analysis just a sub-section of that), or instead refers to just one specialized dimension of political studies, hardly seem important.

Why democratization?

The benefits to be gained from multidisciplinarity and by drawing on a wide range of area studies are not peculiar to the study of democratization. There are other political and social phenomena that offer themselves as prime candidates, nationalism and globalization (and their interconnections) being obvious examples. So why does this volume privilege democratization? Democracy combines unprecedented worldwide interest with an ancient lineage, democracy's roots being in the ancient Greek *polis* and classical political philosophy. Democracy remains to this day a strongly contested idea, occupying a large literature in social and political philosophy that needs no elaboration here. Moreover the politics of democratization too is more than a struggle for democracy – it is a struggle about the very nature of democracy (Luckham and White 1996: 277). That makes democratization an essentially value-laden project, a realm where no discipline can claim a monopoly on wisdom. And it is no mere coincidence that disciplines other than politics have construed democratization as a social process or as an economic process well before politics discovered the 'third wave'. They see its relevance to a variety of 'sites' other than just government or the political system, such as the family or the workplace, and situated not just at the national but at local and international levels too. Political democracy may *never* acquire the sort of unparalleled global legitimacy that premature claims to the end of history at one time appeared to suggest. But, if the Nobel prize-winning economist Amartya Sen (1999: 3) is right in saying that the rise of democracy is the most important occurrence of the twentieth century, then the case for *using all available means* to raise the levels of understanding now looks unanswerable.

That said, there is a special reason why political scientists, especially observers of international politics, should be sympathetic to the idea that the subject of democratization is a prime candidate for the approach taken in this book: the systematic study of politics has itself been a notable beneficiary of democratization. Huntington, widely known as author of *The Third Wave. Democratization in the Late Twentieth Century* (1991), said 'where democracy is strong, political science is strong; where democracy is weak, political science is weak' (Huntington 1988: 7). His claim is borne out by the evidence, as can be seen in the expansion of political studies in the post-communist countries, fed by scholars branching out from hitherto politically safer disciplines, such as history, sociology and philosophy. Thus democratization has left its mark not simply on the world of politics but quite specifically on the study of politics (*as well as on other disciplines too*). That means decisions about whose politics are worth studying and about the practical possibilities too: for instance, Russia's opening up to public attitude surveys, and innovations like David Beetham's 'democratic audit'. Lewis (Chapter 10) shows how studies of central and eastern Europe are extending the conceptual sensitivity and the aspiration to general theories grounded in data analysis that have been well established traits in the comparative political science of Western Europe, even if the achievements so far are modest. And organizations such as Freedom House (established in 1941), a Washington, DC-based, non-profit non-governmental body whose annual surveys of freedom in the world are cited in a number of the chapters in this book, have acquired greatly increased international prominence.[7]

The literature on democratization has also added new words to our politics vocabulary, such as 'transitology' and 'consolidology', together with a large assortment of terms to depict states of near-but-not-quite democracy, or 'democracy with adjectives'. In a citation index 'low-intensity democracy' (Gills, Rocamora and Wilson 1993) is one such term that would feature very strongly. The study of democratization has provided a new arena for replaying recurring big debates in politics, such as those over the competing claims of voluntarism and determinism. At the same time it has promoted a revival of interest in some hitherto neglected terms, 'civil society', for example,[8] and not just among political scientists; analysts of international affairs are now beginning to consider how democracy's prospects could benefit from the emergence of global civil society. Newer concepts have come to the fore, such as 'social capital' (discussed by Gonzalez and King in Chapter 15). We have been led to re-examine such long-standing puzzles as the relationship between structure and agency in order to pinpoint who or what accounts for different stages or phases of democratic political change. Here, Karl's (1991: 5–8) idea of 'structured contingency' looks a particularly promising analytical suggestion and has been widely endorsed, but is far from simple to put into operation.

Democratization has changed both the curriculum and the political science profession in ways that go beyond merely repackaging, relabelling, or reshuffling, although there have been numerous examples of those things too.[9] And just as the spread of democratization inspires some thoughts that a universal study of politics, employing concepts, theories and empirical generalizations that are more or less universally valid, could be coming that much closer, so it has made the profession more cosmopolitan (Norris 1997). Intellectual communities in countries that were hitherto marginalized have entered the central flow, even if, as Blondel (2001: 4–5) claims, too much empirical political research is still country-based and not enough is oriented towards general comparative model-building. The academic study of politics is making its own distinctive contribution to 'globalization' in the form of a knowledge-based community that transcends national boundaries, assisted by democratization. Indeed Norris (1997: 30–1) argues this common node of study could be helping to bridge the methodological rift that has existed between European and American political science, although inter-collegial transatlantic collaboration still remains limited. The links between scholars and bureaucrats, and between academics and the media, have also increased as a result of public interest in democratization and the increase of international programmes and projects of democracy assistance. However, none of this is to claim that the general social standing of political scientists has increased, or that political studies now exerts greater influence on world events.

Everything has its limits

Politics has been defined *inter alia* as the art of the possible. This book is not an encyclopaedia and makes no pretence to be comprehensive; it has been selective in the choice both of disciplines and of the building-blocks for comparative politics. And while the chapters in each Part are arranged alphabetically, readers should make their own choice of starting-point; there is for instance no logical reason for starting with anthropological perspectives.

On the one side, the rationale for including Europe and North America is that democratization is unfinished business; in theory democracy could become weaker there, and, according to some critics that is precisely what is happening (the increase of judicial power in Britain being but one possible example). A significant literature on growing disaffection towards politicians and the established institutions of 'mature' democracies has brought to attention distinctive issues of both a theoretical and practical nature, not least the significance of social capital and civic trust. There is a growing crisis over the financing of political competition – its reputation for lack of integrity – which implies lessons for much newer democracies. The possibility that old democracies could be infused with new vitality by different kinds of participation, like those involving 'third sector' associations, and by experimenting with forms such as deliberative democracy, is a more positive contribution to the debate, and has resonance in emerging democracies.

On the other side, the omission of the Middle East and the Arab world from this collection owes more to pragmatic grounds. Democratization is generally reckoned to have made least headway there, and the outlook is unpromising (both the record and the prospects in black Africa now look more fragile too, compared with the early 1990s). Of course, in the broader scheme of things *any* region's omission is inexcusable. For our understanding of a phenomenon may well be assisted by comparisons with locations where it has not occurred, especially if there are some shared features with more successful newly democratizing countries – economic backwardness, for example. Ignoring a region like the Middle East clearly will not help us to predict if the countries there will ever successfully introduce democracy and if so how, when and what kind of democracy.

Turf wars over boundaries between disciplines and the demarcation of sub-disciplines can cause genuine confusion. International political economy is one example: is it a ward of international relations, a descendant of politics, or of economics, or an extension of political economy in the original sense of the late-eighteenth-century Scottish Enlightenment? Is it in the process of becoming a discipline in its own right? The inclusion of a chapter on the unique perspectives offered by gender and women's studies may well not be controversial, even though 'the majority of the mainstream democratization literature has remained gender-blind' (Waylen 2003: 157). After all, it has been said that 'if democracy (or lack of it) is something which transcends all human relations, then, surely, relations between the genders lie at the heart of democracy?' (Allison 1994: 100). Rai's call (in Chapter 4) to expand our definitions to encompass not only the public but the private sphere chimes with this, offering not so much a view within politics but a view of politics itself. And of course it is true that a case could be advanced for several other branches of knowledge – development studies, race (or racial) and ethnic (ethnicity) studies, and nationalism studies, and so on – that are not included here. But although these branches of inquiry are all institutionalized in the sense of having such things as

research institutes, university departments or teaching programmes and major journals devoted to them, it is less
obvious that they offer distinctive methods of inquiry or
techniques. Nor do they appear to offer their own *modes* of
explanation. Their *raison d'être* is to privilege certain issues, explanations and facets of the human condition precisely because other disciplines (political science included)
could have given them greater prominence but so far have
failed to do so. They are studies and are not (yet) generally
thought to possess the conventional status of disciplines.
Take each one in turn.

First, development studies might be held to offer great
purchase for examining the future prospects for democratization, given that not just the country long called the
world's largest democracy (India) but all of today's least
democratic countries are found in the developing world.
Furthermore, it is the changes that have taken place in
development thinking that help explain the growth of international democracy-promotion. But much more even than
political science, development studies draws on economics
and sociology (as well as on politics), to name but some of
its tributaries. China, of course, is the most dynamic large
economy in the developing world. Recent claims that
China's political evolution in the 1990s had unparalleled
significance for democratization trends worldwide (Youngs
2001: 165) look to be an exaggeration. Even so, as the most
populous country China could potentially make a dramatic
difference to surveys like Freedom House's annual review
of democracy and freedom in the world. Breslin's sceptical
account (in Chapter 11) shows that not just in China but in
East Asia more generally a historical perspective and recent
international economic developments should both be taken
into account when assessing democratic trends and possibilities. The other groups of countries that development
studies feature most prominently are typically found in
South Asia, Africa, and Latin America. All these regions
are already represented in this volume, with for instance
Philip (Chapter 13) explaining how the persistence of democracies *without* democratic consolidation is a distinguishing
feature of politics in Latin America today.

Second, there can be no disputing the claim that attempts
to establish democracy in multiethnic and multicultural

societies raise special questions about who constitutes the *demos* and the underlying sense of community. A discussion of the politics of identity becomes unavoidable. The growth in citizenship studies itself owes something to the spread of democracy, both as an emancipating trend and as a potentially destabilizing force in divided societies that previously were tightly controlled by highly centralized states. Innovative ideas of global citizenship are currently being advanced as part of the international studies agenda. But in principle there is no reason why other well-established fields of study such as anthropology and sociology cannot shed more light on these subjects (see for example Chapter 2). And here, relevant area studies are offered as a proxy (see for example the discussions of identity and ethnic and/or racial dimensions in Chapters 12, 14, and 15).

Lastly, there is the argument that the political science literature on democratization underestimates the importance of nation- and state-building, which betrays its origins in the study of Latin America and southern Europe. According to Kopecý and Mudde (2000) this shortcoming in the literature limits its ability to illuminate the more recent experience of democratization in such places as central and eastern Europe. Whatever the merits of that argument, the threat globalization now poses to nation and national identity even in established democracies is assessed in Chapter 6, by Cerny, who details the transient historical circumstances giving rise to the nation-states system that enabled, and perhaps necessitated, democracy as we know it. In any event, we can always turn to the historical literature on earlier 'waves' of democratization in Western Europe if we want to investigate nationalism's contribution to stimulating or subverting movements towards greater democracy, as Kopecý and Mudde (2000: 529) themselves admit. Thus it is self-evident that an understanding of the past should not necessarily compete with our interest in the present and our desire to foretell the future. Instead history should be viewed as a complementary source of revelation (see Chapter 5, by Calvert); the fact that previous 'waves' of democratization ended in democratic reversal only serves to sharpen the point. If prediction is the Grail of political science then the comparative historical method is at the very minimum a useful handmaiden. And for analysts with a more prescriptive intent, such as the democracy-promoters and their 'democracy trainers', history – including the failed attempts by Western powers to transfer democracy in previous decades – should be considered essential reading.

Notes

1 Comparative politics 'does not consist only in cross-national analysis. It is also necessarily a cross-disciplinary endeavor, because in comparative research we are crossing units (nations) and variables (numerical and nominal). . . . The relations between variables are often more important for theoretical explanations than the discovery of analogies and differences between nations'; 'Comparative politics across disciplines means first of all crossing history' (Dogan 1996: 122, 123).

2 Barry (1999: 435) claims that the political science profession 'is still more hospitable to those with doctorates outside the subject than its sister disciplines'.

3 'The vote is not primarily a token of individual choice but part of a calculus of patrimonial reciprocity based on ties of solidarity' (Chabal and Daloz 1999: 39). Political anthropology gained ground in studies of Third World politics as a critical reaction to 'a simplistic zero-sum view of tradition and modernity'; social anthropology followed on, evincing a desire to 'fill the gap in dependency theory' (Randall and Theobald 1998: 6). Dogan (1996: 117), however, argues that in post-colonial regions area studies have taken over the mantle of anthropology without respect for disciplinary boundaries.

4 'Democratization backwards' refers to the introduction of competitive elections before establishing the basic institutions of a modern state, such as the rule of law and the institutions of civil society (Rose and Shin 2001).

5 The study of international relations 'takes aspects of theory from all sorts of different places; but if you try to think of what IR has exported to any of the other disciplines, or indeed whether any of the other disciplines pay any attention to it at all, it's a much bleaker landscape' (Buzan 2001: 12).

6 But on the United States see Cox, Ikenberry and Inoguchi (eds) (2000). A sizeable literature exists on the 'democratic peace' hypothesis, which is said to warrant unambiguous support for the internationalization of democracy.

7 Freedom House's annual assessments of political rights and civil liberties around the world define democracy as, at minimum a political system in which people choose their authoritative leaders freely from among competing groups and individuals who are not chosen by the government. Democracies are judged to be either free or partly free (scores 1.0–3.0 = free; 3.0–5.5 = partly free; 5.5–7.0 = not free). Although this idea of democracy and the organization's methodology for scoring countries are challenged, especially by European social scientists, the assessments are widely used and there appears to be no superior, more generally accepted source of convenient data.

8 However, reputations have not fared equally: the renewed prominence of Alexis de Toqueville (author of *Democracy in America*, 1835 and 1840) undoubtedly reflects the preponderant American displacement in the political science of democratization. By comparison John Stuart Mill's *On Liberty* (1859) and *Considerations on Representative Government* (1861) are rarely mentioned.

9 Among the more visible signs of democratization's impact on academia are a stream of major conferences and workshops (for example IPSA's sixteenth World Congress in 1994 was on 'Democratization'; the Political Studies Association in Britain chose 'The Challenge of Democracy in the 21st Century' for its 50th annual conference, in 2000); specialized book series on democratization (three in Britain alone); new book titles (web sites list several hundred titles in English containing the keyword 'democratization' and several thousand containing the keyword 'democracy'); the publication of encylopaedias of democracy (in the US, 1995) and democratic thought (in Britain, 2001); dedicated new journals, most notably the *Journal of Democracy* (the first issue each year publishes the latest Freedom House assessments) and *Democratization*, publishing many issues each year (in total well over 1,000 articles to date); and numerous 'special issues' of many longer-established journals and area studies periodicals. There are many special 'Centres' or 'Institutes' of research into democratization scattered around the globe; and universities have constructed graduate programmes and customized undergraduate modules on democratization.

Part I
Disciplines

2
Anthropology

JEREMY GOULD

There is no self-evident consensus on what constitutes genuine anthropology. For some, anthropology is defined by its fieldwork-based methodology; for others, it is its non-reductionist commitment to fleshing out complex causalities from the empirical foliage of thick description. For others still, anthropology is simply a general social science of non-Western societies.

This writer's understanding of the anthropological enterprise revolves around the need for a self-reflective perspective on the nature and use of normative discourse in social interaction. My empirical work highlights the use of normative argument to legitimize the exercise of power. The focus on normative discourse highlights the realm of narrative practices, but to become meaningful these must be situated – and studied empirically – within the concrete matrices of social action. The demand for self-reflection implies incessant interrogation of one's own relationship to the value-claims of the observed actors. Although no transcendental authority is claimed for this version of anthropology, it reflects concerns common to the endeavours in the discipline.

There is, similarly, no fixed definition of democratization. As a non-specialist I reflect here on the uses of democratization most prevalent in my own observations of external pressures for state reform in some southern and eastern African countries. Hence the writer's exposure to the rhetoric of democratization stems largely from the normative discourse of Western governments and transnational agencies concerning desirable modes of institutional practice – what they often refer to as 'good governance' – in the political systems of the region. This understanding of democratization relates specifically to a programmatic agenda of state reform promoted by transnational actors and enforced via conditions associated with foreign aid and, more recently, debt relief.

Donor-endorsed versions of democratization claim to be grounded in a liberal notion of inalienable individual rights. This encompasses, among other things: political pluralism (the freedom to form political parties); free and regular elections; an unconstrained (and privately-owned) media; and the separation of powers among the branches of the state. To some extent, the transnational narrative of democratization also includes demands for decentralizing state authority and for greater freedom of participation for 'civil society' in political processes. Of late, demands for 'pro-poor' policies on the part of the state have been incorporated as well.

The juxtaposition of a normative-instrumental political agenda with an adamantly non-normative intellectual tradition obviously works against efforts to identify areas of synergy between the two. The ensuing tale, in other words, is not about how anthropological insights might best be harnessed in the service of Bretton Woods-endorsed campaigns for state reform in highly indebted countries. Instead, the intention is to link this analysis of anthropology and democratization to a broader narrative about the tension between instrumental interests and reflexivity. This theme is not specific to the study of political change, but it comes into quite distinct focus when viewed through the eyes of an anthropologist contemplating efforts to reform the postcolonial African state.

The normative enigma of democratization

The notion of democratization has, at best, an uneasy status in the anthropological vocabulary. For a number of reasons, both extra-scientific and scholarly, many anthropologists have been ambivalent about democratization and hesitant to embrace democratization as an explanatory tool, let alone as a normative ideal for passing judgement on the maturity of polities and political processes. Part of the reason for this can be found in the normative character of 'democratization' as a research agenda. Where the die-hard liberal protagonist claims that anthropology 'has abandoned its claim to truth and is given over to an insidious relativism' (see Shils 1992: 183), the anthropologist would ask: Where does the liberal certainty in its universal truth reside? And to the accusation that such relativism 'undermines democratic values and gives the young little reason to believe that [anthropology] can contribute anything to the betterment of society' (Shils 1992: 183), an anthropologist might respond that it is precisely through self-reflection based on the contemplation of alternative versions of 'betterment' that society can best agree upon means to address pressing problems.[1]

One source of the aloofness with which anthropologists observe the rhetoric of democratization is the left-leaning liberal political sensibility endemic to the anthropological community. The core of this sensibility gelled in the radical ferment of the 1960s, when various versions of 'radical' and 'Marxist' anthropology gained academic currency. Anthropologists publicly voiced scepticism about (and overt opposition to) all aspects of Western dealings with the Third World committed in the name of democracy. Noted anthropologists, from Claude Lévi-Strauss to Eric Wolf, expressed indignation over imperialist interventions ranging from the assassination of Patrice Lumumba in the Congo to United States aggression in parts of Southeast Asia. Anthropologists were well situated to experience the ambivalence of democratization. University campuses teemed with opposition to Western interventions in the Third World. The destructive consequences of these interventions – both military and technical – were becoming increasingly apparent. Like many other social groups, anthropologists found themselves in sympathy with popular demands for greater democracy at home as a protest against heinous deeds committed in the name of democracy abroad. Thus the American legal anthropologist Laura Nader (1969: 293) argued that anthropologists needed to 'study up' to reveal the workings of power relations within American society in order to achieve greater 'democratic relevance' for the discipline.

However not all anthropologists were radical or Marxist. Many members of the profession, including the young Clifford Geertz (1963), became involved in the post-colonial project of modernization. Interestingly, democratic politics did not play a significant role in the discourse of modernization, either. The advice of the Columbia University anthropologist Conrad Arensberg to American development 'technicians' abroad is telling:

> The overseas American will have to learn the particular distinctions of the country where he [sic] is working; he will be compelled to accept the local definitions of differences to some extent if he wishes his projects to succeed. It may be possible to gradually introduce some democratic procedures into these countries, but the individual worker will probably be wasting his time and ensuring the failure of his program if he demands an immediate acceptance of democratic methods. (Arensberg and Niehoff 1964: 41–2)

Beyond the ideological skirmishes of the Cold War and the profession's instinctive aversion to universalizing value claims, it is evident that democratization is a troublesome notion for anthropology. This is because, generally speaking, 'anthropologists . . . have a problem with politics' (Spencer 1997: 3). That is not to say that anthropologists have ignored political analysis. They incessantly probe the exercise of power as it is played out via dense social matrices of intense and intimate interaction. They have been particularly keen to unravel the puzzling mesh of continuity and rupture in the reproduction and transformation of power relations over time. Anthropology's fascination with the microphysics of power, and the way that power participates in the negotiation of subjectivity, both predate current articulations of these issues that sociologists and others might more commonly associate with the French philosopher Michel Foucault.

Central to anthropological research on politics is a rich literature on 'local political arenas' (defined below). But this work has rarely concerned the politics of mainstream political institutions – parties, parliaments, elections and so on; the major exception is F. G. Bailey (see for example 1969). Instead, the politics studied by anthropologists, especially over the past decade, has been on (externally-supported) state interventions in the socio-economic configurations of local communities. The core of this mode of analysis relates to development interventions and their consequences.

The politics of development is, of course, very much a politics of the state. Indeed, for many communities, the face of the state takes the form of a development project. Yet, 'development' begets a particular kind of politics, involving very specific forms of engagement. Resistance to the oppressive or arbitrary use of power within a development intervention seldom leads to effective demands for democracy. Project designs are not the product of representative bodies, nor do project staff enjoy a popular mandate. The politics of development is articulated through a vocabulary of empowerment, consultation and participation, not one of accountability or responsible leadership.

This vocabulary reflects, in Ferguson's (1991) seminal coinage, the way in which the exercise of power in development interventions has been depoliticized. The basis of this depoliticization is, as Ferguson suggests, the way that multilateral aid bureaucracies like the World Bank dictate the goals and design of interventions. Recipient states have little sovereign power over the machinations of 'development' and cannot, therefore, be held accountable for the repercussions of the interventions. An esoteric technical language ('development speak') obscures the lack of statutory political procedure in the processing of decisions about development means and ends. Over the past decade numerous inquiries have sought to deconstruct the technical discourse of development so as to reveal the empirical intrigues of power behind the depoliticized façade, for example Marglin and Marglin (1990) and Escobar (1995).

Two streams emanate from this literature. One is a normative alignment with the 'victims' of development. A sprawling sub-literature is devoted to problems of participation and empowerment in development projects. Ironically, much of this work is funded by aid agencies, either directly or via non-governmental organizations (NGOs) that themselves rely on official funding by the donors. Perhaps for this reason, the empowerment literature largely reproduces the depoliticized character of development speak.

Another strand of analysis does, in contrast, underscore democratic politics; but the focus is the need to democratize development aid, and to create mechanisms for holding transnational elites accountable for the consequences of their actions (Escobar 1995). This perspective is not guilty of wholly ignoring large-scale power structures or the specific example of the transnational financial system. Yet, here too, the state and the political configurations upon which it stands are scarcely subjected to critical scrutiny.

Why this reticence to confront the state? Nagengast (1994: 16) claims that anthropology has viewed the state as an 'unanalyzed given'. Trouillot (2001: 126) traces this oversight to anthropology's empiricist and methodological individualist legacy, exemplified by the founding ancestor A. R. Radcliffe-Brown (1881–1955), who 'conceptualize[d] the state into oblivion'. Anthropologists do indeed have a methodological predisposition toward an immediate, richly contextualized empirical engagement with social processes. Intensive, long-term, localized field-work allows ethnographers to document and analyse social experiences of power and domination, authority and leadership as recounted by groups of respondents enmeshed in dense social networks. As a result, anthropologists have had much to say about patterns in the narration of political experience and about the unarticulated or unacknowledged structures of meaning informing political action.

Reliance on first-hand evidence implies both strengths and weaknesses for the study of aggregated processes at the level of 'regime transition' and 'state formation'. The ethnographic perspective provides a rich basis for assessing the empirical substance of state–citizen relations and for detailed deconstructions of the mechanisms of rule. Yet the demands of methodological/normative context specificity can be difficult to reconcile with the summative analysis of multidimensional political transformation on a national, much less a global scale (Trouillot 2001). Can the localized assessment of political relations link up with the analysis of qualitative change in the aggregate? Naturally this will depend on the choice of theoretical framework and its origins.

The liberal conundrum

The prevailing, mainstream usage of democratization underscores its roots in liberal political theory. Applying this to a specific context subsumes a wide range of institutions and associations within a model of political action grounded on certain assumptions about the relative autonomy of politics with respect to other spheres of social activity, about individuality, freedom and the dictatorship of individual preference. This is problematic for anyone who consider liberal political theory to be a culture-specific perspective on social action (and human nature), the applicability of which cannot be assumed beyond the scope of its Euro-American origins, if indeed even there.

The relation of the individual to the social is a theoretical quandary upon which modern social science was founded. Anthropologists have not resolved this issue (nor can we even agree about the terms of the problem among ourselves). Yet one can safely say that anthropologists are on the average more sceptical than, say, many political scientists about claims concerning the universality of the 'rational-instrumental individual' as a general template for conceptualizing the Subject of social action (Englund 2002). Anthropologists insist that the motives and preferences of individual actors be situated in an empirical social context. This often draws accusations of particularism and relativism.

The fact is that anthropologists tend to eschew an aggregated, over-generalized view of moral personhood. Instead, when seeking to understand human behaviour they prefer above all to comprehend moral choice as an outcome of negotiated meaning among social actors involved in a specific historical and institutional situation. But to label the entire anthropological enterprise as relativistic is to miss the crucial methodological point. Most anthropologists would not reject the possibility of 'universal human qualities', or even the likelihood that certain 'norms and values' (a preference for justice, for example) could have quasi-universal appeal under normal circumstances. But this is a far cry from the quintessential liberal claim that predefined individual rights and freedoms will be compelling to social actors irrespective of and *prior to* a detailed empirical analysis of the circumstances within which social actors interact.

In this sense an agenda of inquiry harnessed to the normative *telos* of liberalism is anathema to the anthropological endeavour. This is not because anthropologists subscribe to the unassailable moral authority of communitarian values, but because the very idea of positing pre-empirical assumptions about the strategic parameters and ideal commitments of social actors contradicts the rationale of ethnographic inquiry.

That said, there is clearly nothing in the methodological or theoretical arsenal of the anthropological discipline that counsels hostility to democratic politics. Quite the contrary: as concerned citizens anthropologists are no doubt as agreeable as anyone to ideas of accountable and responsible leadership, government based on consensus rather than coercion, and political processes that are responsive to the preferences of those affected by a given policy, decision or legislative enactment. For example, in the writer's experience many and perhaps most Zambians (among whom he has work extensively), would also endorse such ideals. The problem is that in practice 'democratization' as discussed above does not always seem to promote these concrete democratic ends. The much heralded 'democratization' process in Zambia that brought the Movement for Multiparty Democracy (MMD) to power in 1991 with strong Western endorsement has hardly promoted democracy. A good ten years later Zambia's politico-legal system is in ferment as citizen groups and opposition politicians campaign to bring the MMD's ex-President Chiluba to trial on counts of massive embezzlement, fraud and corruption. Elsewhere, Lund (1998) recounts vividly how poorly managed processes of politico-legal liberalization in Niger produced chaos in the administration of local justice. The extent of unpredictability and confusion in the legal system was so great that it led one informant to muse plaintively, 'When will this democracy be over?' (Lund 1998: 204).

One might ask, then, if anthropology has little to contribute to the instrumental agenda of democratization, what views do anthropologists have about the factors promoting or hindering mechanisms of political accountability, equity and justice in everyday life? For insights we can turn to an emerging wave of political anthropology. Compensating for decades of indifference to state politics, these new anthropologies of the state constitute one of the most dynamic areas of intellectual activity in the discipline.

Anthropologies of the state

The impetus for a rekindled anthropological interest in state politics is above all empirical. In the 1990s the relationship between anthropologists and post-colonial state politics underwent a belated post-colonial shift. Democratization and other modes of conditionality-induced state reform played a crucial role here. Because of widespread political pluralism and liberalization of the media, the rhetoric of liberal democracy experienced an 'indigenization' in many places where anthropologists work. Somewhat unexpectedly, local political parties and social movements emerged in highly centralized polities articulating a vocabulary of liberal democratic politics, nowhere more so than in southern Africa. Of course, the indigenization of the rhetoric of democracy was not unrelated to the generous provision of 'democracy support' to pro-liberalist groups and organizations by the US and other Western governments. Nevertheless, in empirical terms, the rhetoric of democratization suddenly appeared as an indigenous cultural register lodged in popular discourse, in many instances reaching right down to the proverbial grass-roots of society.

The upshot has not been at last an anthropological discovery of liberalization and democratization as empirical givens or explanatory models for ethnographic analysis. Anthropologists vent little enthusiasm for democratization as a self-fulfilling liberal narrative of the modern state. Yet increasingly we have been obliged to accept that the social manifestations of power observed in the field are inextricably tied up with the dynamics and 'effects' of the state (see for example Mitchell 1999). Rather than a reversion to normative universalism, however, what is emerging is a growing ethnographic interest in 'liberalism' and 'democracy' as rhetorical elements and legitimizing narratives in the contestation of power between and among the various state and non-state actors.

The rising anthropological interest in empirical states has been paralleled by a growing puzzlement about how 'the state' should be theorized. The closer one looks at local configurations of power in the wake of the 'third wave', the more ephemeral 'the state' appears. On one level, as Lund

(2002) argues, actors and institutions are intensely preoccupied with the state; and yet it is increasingly difficult to locate a single source of public authority. This too must be seen in context. The privatization of state assets and social services has led to a widespread deregulation of social life. Viewed from the perspective of ordinary citizens, it is evident that state institutions can no longer claim an effective monopoly over legitimate violence or over the administration of justice (Hansen and Stepputat 2001). The progressive deregulation and arbitrary devolution of state authority has called the very *idea* of the state into question. Or more precisely, the cogency of the state idea has not so much declined as multiplied. The image of an absolute state authority that dominated generations of colonial and postcolonial actors lives on in the social imaginary, but its empirical referent has become indistinct. 'The state' of recent anthropological interest is less an efficacious regulatory force, than a quasi-mythical entity with which competing actors attempt to associate, and thus legitimize, their claims to public authority.

There are two ways in which recent anthropological engagements with the state can fertilize debates about democratic politics. First, ethnographic study reveals how local actors translate notions like democracy, liberalization or human rights within specific social contexts. Second, anthropological analysis deconstructs mechanisms of rule and hierarchy in local political relations, thus providing a litmus test of the validity of political claims promoted at more aggregated levels of society. There are several areas of empirical investigation – corresponding to various aspects of state–society relations – where recent anthropological findings provide insights into these relations. The remainder of this chapter discusses just two of them, very briefly: identity politics (registers of citizenship), and issues of public authority in local political arenas (legitimacy).

Identity politics

Political pluralization in Africa, as elsewhere, has heightened political competition and multiplied the issues around which support for parties and agendas can be mobilized. The bulk of the attention addressed to this phenomenon has accentuated the politicization of 'ethnicity'. Ethnic politics is commonly stigmatized as 'uncivil' and thus anathema to democratization, in that it promotes divisive rather than inclusive social solidarities. Karlström (1999: 110), however, argues that since ethnic-based solidarities are unlikely to weaken in the near future, 'the analytical task will be to try and understand the conditions under which they can perform [a] mediating role constructively and the circumstances under which they become divisive and destructive'. Karlström's analysis of the political trajectories of Buganda royalism in Uganda – a rather special case, granted – suggests that the Ugandan government's policy of ethnic accommodation may well have defused civil conflict. It thereby secures the political stability upon which President Museveni's National Resistance Movement is striving to consolidate its version of 'no-party democracy' – something that conventional models of liberal democracy in the West have difficulty in embracing.

Karlström's primary interest is not in ethnicity *per se* but in the conceptualization of 'civil society' in an Africa context. The broader issue at stake is the multitude of ways that different categories of citizens position themselves in relationship to the state. Clearly, membership in a group defined by language, territory or custom can be an important rallying-point for political mobilization. Werbner, however, suggests that the importance of 'ethnic' identities has been greatly exaggerated: They are in fact 'merely a small fraction of the many identities mobilised in the postcolonial politics of everyday life' (Werbner 1996: 1) Increasingly, anthropologists have been broadening their purview to interrogate other registers of political selfhood. The marker that has attracted most attention is probably that of citizenship.

Citizenship is central to most understandings of democratic politics, embodying as it does a normative standard for assessing the quality of the relationship between subject and authority. Conventionally, citizenship is discussed as an element of state–society relations. In place of the conventional, jural notion of citizenship, anthropologists tend to stress its historically contingent, dynamic and contested nature. Rather than engage with the core juridical issues of

constitutional politics, anthropologists have been more interested in the margins of political selfhood – in transnational
situations such as those involving migrants, or vigilantism,
and transborder residents, or in situations where countervail-
ing authorities compete with the state for the loyalty of
subjects. Indeed, in problematizing the very category of 'the
state' recent anthropological work on post-colonial Africa
poses a question that is particularly challenging to the discourse of democracy: Citizenship of what?

Public authority in local political arenas

Questioning the validity of the state, both as analytical
category and as real-life authority, inevitably invokes the
notion of *legitimacy*. For anthropologists the fact of legitimate authority is, once again, an empirical puzzle that can only
be solved within the context of the meanings embraced (and
contested) by the actors whose compliance (or resistance) is
at stake. This is quite different from privileging a 'culturalist'
explanation of legitimacy – one that evokes fixed custom-
ary/symbolic referents to explain certain modes of behaviour.
The debate between anthropologist Lentz (1998) and political
scientist (1993) on the essential nature of 'African power' is
illustrative.

Schatzberg claimed that the 'moral matrix of African
governance', unlike the 'transformative' nature of Western
power, is grounded in cultural parameters linked to consumption ('father, family and food'). Lentz (1998: 46) counters
that social debates about the 'morality of power and desirable modes of governance' in Africa are too complex to be
reduced to such simple terms. Thus legitimacy is not a one-
dimensional quality, to be measured in degrees, but rather
a 'conflict-ridden and open process in which "big men" and
politicians as well as their audiences intervene' (Lentz 1998:
47). In her view, then, 'big men' perform the testimony of
their legitimacy for specific audiences or 'moral communities
. . . [that] in part overlap and share similar images of legitimate power and wealth' (Lentz 1998: 47). Actors are not
free to invent and manipulate the standards by which they
are assessed; structures of 'expectation' constrain the ploys
of those with public/political ambitions. But although Lentz

differs from Schatzberg on the complexity and, by inference, the substance of the 'moral matrix' of legitimacy, she does not disagree with the basic premise that grounds legitimacy in the realm of socially constructed moral judgement.

A different, albeit not contradictory, approach to the legitimacy puzzle can be found at the juncture of legal history and anthropology. Studies of customary law in colonial Malawi and Zambia (Chanock 1985) and of the historical transformations of legal processes on Mt. Kilimanjaro (Moore 1986) highlighted the complexity of factors affecting the codification of local normative systems. Such studies investigate how a plurality of normative codes compete for legitimacy and how social actors navigate and manipulate these codes in the course of their various economic and political pursuits. For the legal anthropologist, it seems, social actors are fundamentally instrumental actors who draw on whatever normative argument supports their immediate aims. The primary fonts of continuity and change reside not so much in the transformation of moral sensibilities, as in the material forces that sculpt the politico-economic conditions with which actors must come to terms.

At the other extreme, van Binsbergen (1995) inflates the 'moral community' premise into a culturalist axiom. His account of 'grassroots political culture' in two African countries addresses the predominant sub-theme in the Africanist literature on competing modes of legitimacy: the relationship between 'traditional authorities' (chiefs) and the state. He positions himself in diametric opposition to the modernist notion – argued compellingly by Mahmood Mamdani (1996) – that central state authority is more democratic and, hence, intrinsically more legitimate than the traditional leaders' authority. For van Binsbergen, genuine grass-roots democratization presumes the incorporation of traditional – spiritually legitimized – authority. In his view:

> The continuity of a cosmologically-anchored local world-view with its own conceptions of legitimate political power and procedure; the interaction between, on the one hand, traditional leaders and, on the other, those of their subjects pursuing modern careers outside the village settings; the prominence of religious alternatives for the symbolic restructuring of society . . . these would seem to be important factors in the production of a democratic political culture in the global sense. (van Binsbergen 1995: 12–13)

This culturalist hyperbole rows vigorously against the contemporary anthropological tide. The actors populating the narratives of mainstream analyses today are far less obsessed with cosmological continuity than with the rational-instrumental ends of material security, respect and power. But what unites all the above-mentioned anthropologists is the conviction that it is vital to have a detailed empirical understanding of what is going on in grass-roots politics.

Rethinking the local state

The study of 'local politics' is a path well traversed by anthropologists. With its extensive literature and blossoming sub-fields such as ritual and performance analysis and religious studies, even a cursory overview is not possible here. Instead, the focus is on a body of work that is unique in the fragmented field of political anthropology for its theoretical and methodological coherence – the research of the 'APAD' school of rural anthropology, which has systematically surveyed transformations of local political arenas, primarily in francophone West Africa, since the early 1990s.[2]

Olivier de Sardan characterizes the work of APAD as 'development anthropology'; much of the APADian literature deals with development interventions – a theme noted earlier. Unlike most writing on development, however, APADian analyses generally proceed from an elaboration of the social context of the intervention, not from the logic of the project. Thus, while they participate in topical debates about the effects of 'development' in the countries concerned (mainly local sites in Benin, Niger and Senegal), the transcendental value lies in the analysis of fundamental social processes and institutions in these societies.

APADian researchers generally work on the 'local level', but stress the importance of comparative analysis. This is made possible by a common approach – akin to that of the legal anthropologists discussed above – that conceives of local political arenas as 'semi-autonomous fields' occupied by instrument-rational social actors (see for example Lund 1998). These arenas are characterized by a game-like logic of interaction: actors are in competition with one another for various rewards, and yet, there is no single set of rules, rewards or sanctions governing the political 'game'. Instead

> actors all develop personal and professional strategies, deployed in keeping with various criteria: for some, increasing patrimonial land, for others, obtaining a vehicle and the fuel to make it run, . . . : enhancing one's position within an institution, obtaining a better contract, increasing one's network of social contacts, becoming indispensable, earning more money, keeping an eye on a neighbour or rival, pleasing one's friends and relations, keeping a low profile and playing it safe, etc. (Olivier de Sardan 1995)[3]

Thus while actors are assumed to behave in a strategic, even instrumental way, they can be motivated by virtually any mode of utility, from predatory to altruistic.

Issues of decentralization and local power constitute a major theme running through the work of APAD. The general thrust of APAD's and similar studies is that decentralization has become part and parcel of a donor-endorsed agenda of state reform, and has a recurrent (if uneasy) status on the agendas of 'good governance' and 'democratization' promoted by the international 'development community'. Decentralization is widely recognized to be a problematic element in state reform; the successful devolution of powers and responsibilities from central government is never smooth, owing to the shortage of qualified managers and the weak institutional capacity of bottom-rung administrative structures in post-colonial states.

Decentralization remains popular with donor agencies, however, for many reasons. As an aid conditionality, demands for decentralization can be used to undermine the power monopoly of an entrenched political elite. Also, the possibility of channelling aid to an empowered local administration promises to shorten the distance that development resources have to travel from donor to ultimate recipient (and to lessen the possibilities for rent extraction by intermediaries). Furthermore, the combined effect of prolonged fiscal crisis, economic stagnation and downsizing of the public sector under structural economic adjustment have tremendously weakened the capacity of central government to regulate and administer rural areas. In any event, then, with or without an explicit programme of decentralization, most African states are undergoing a process of 'decentralization by default'.

Decentralization reforms are seldom implemented as planned, owing to capacity problems, and because of resistance among upstream politicians and within civil service bureaucracies based in the capitals. Thus it is not only the effects of the policies that need to be documented, but also the discrepancies between official intent (as expressed in policy guidelines) and real outcomes. Both the intended and the unintended aspects of a reform affect the 'rules of the game' of local politics, creating risks and opportunities for different sets of actors.

However, APAD's interest in decentralization is not primarily concerned with advancing the reform agenda, with making local administration more efficient, or with improving the mechanisms of civic participation in decentralized governance. Instead, the approach starts from the premise that any effort at radical state reform is fraught with contradictions. Particular studies then proceed to investigate the ramifications of attempts to decentralize government for the local, empirical exercise of power. APAD's empirical research demonstrates how decentralization reforms have important, if unpredictable, implications for the configuration of power in local political arenas. Whole new categories of actors can be brought to the political forefront – as when a decentralization reform creates a niche for locally based organizations and entrepreneurs to tender for the contracts to provide certain public services. Some familiar actors find their conventional roles, and options, radically changed in the new configuration. And above all, the relations between different actors – private/public, formal/informal, centre/local, political/administrative, 'modern'/'traditional' – are transformed, as mechanisms of power and political alliances are reorganized through processes of contestation, negotiation and accommodation.

Conclusion

Over time, the research agenda of anthropologists interested in the state and democratic politics has evolved, and this is quite natural. From rather simple, quasi-moral characterizations of political relationships (clientelism, corruption and so on), efforts are now emerging to formulate more rigorously non-normative conceptualizations of the professional and personal strategies of local state actors – clearly a basic precondition for understanding the limits of democratic local governance. From a rough dualistic opposition of state to non-state, the analytical framework is moving toward a more complex configuration of public authority, including a rethinking of legitimacy beyond 'the state'. Clearly this sort of examination is central to any meaningful attempt to understand both 'decentralization' (as a donor-driven programme of liberal state reform) and the possibilities of democratic politics. The question that remains is: Are localized analyses such as these adequate to grasp the full scope of the issues at stake?

One possible obstacle is a persisting fetish of 'the local'. There is much talk about the impact of globalization on local political arenas, yet the anthropological predisposition toward in-depth, localized fieldwork renders translocal factors hard to grasp. The participation of transnational actors – international private aid agencies ('INGOs'), private corporations, and public agencies – in local processes is acknowledged, but the trails of these players are not traced 'up' or 'across' all levels and processes, to garner a fuller image of their strategies, aims and means.

Anthropologists are beginning to see what critical students of international relations have known for some time: 'democratization' is a translocal phenomenon in which transnational actors such as financial institutions, public aid agencies, and private advocacy organizations are key players. Detailed empirical research of the kind carried out by anthropologists indicates that citizens at the grass-roots seem to have gained little from the 'third wave of democratization'. At the risk of appearing cynical, it is perhaps fair to ask whether the transnational actors that are most vigorously pushing the reforms are not the real beneficiaries? To answer such a question, and to understand the scope of its implications, will require marrying the anthropologist's attention to site-specific empirical detail to a sophisticated cognizance of complex aggregate tendencies at the transnational level. A related issue, deserving an essay of its own, concerns the normative (non-)alignments of such inquiry. How should anthropologists position themselves in the diffuse, dispersed and multi-sited field of transnational political forces?

Notes

1 Shils's immediate reference is to sociology, but he equates sociology with anthropology in a way that justifies the substitution here.
2 APAD is an acronym for the *Association Euro-Africaine pour l'Anthropologie du Changement Social et du Développement*. Olivier de Sardan (1995) summarizes the theoretical and methodological resources APAD scholars draw on.
3 Olivier de Sardan's (1995) book will be published in English by Zed Press in 2004.

3

Economics

TONY ADDISON

Industrialization and democratization could not be achieved at the same time. When my father became president, this country was in terrible poverty. The first thing he had to do was to save the country through industrialization and from that followed democratization. (South Korean presidential candidate, Park Geun-hye, on her father, Park Chung-hee, who took power in the 1961 military coup, quoted in *Financial Times* 12 March 2002)

The quotation that starts this chapter expresses a sentiment that was common currency in the early days of development economics, but is heard less often nowadays. From the 1940s to the 1960s it seemed to many observers that living standards could be raised irrespective of whether a country was democratic or not. Indeed, some technocrats maintained that democratic debate could only hinder the implementation of their carefully crafted development plans. And aid donors were largely amenable to single-party rule in newly independent states, especially when it seemed to meet their own strategic or commercial interests. India was the big exception – national democratic debate was vigorous following the adoption of universal adult franchise at independence – but otherwise the case for democracy in poor countries was mostly neglected.

From the 1950s to the 1980s, economic success enabled the authoritarian governments of South Korea and Taiwan to achieve a large measure of popular support despite the absence of democracy and notwithstanding serious human rights abuses. This lesson was taken to heart by the Chinese Communist Party, which began the transition to a market economy in the 1970s, the resulting economic growth thereby enabling the party to retain political control and helping it to overcome periodic unrest (notably Tiananmen Square in 1989).

But while autocracy seems to have delivered the economic goods in East Asia, it was a dismal failure in much of Latin America (during the region's periodic bouts of military dictatorship), and a complete disaster for the economies of sub-Saharan Africa (SSA). African leaders sought acquiescence to single-party rule in exchange for delivering development. However, by the late 1970s this promise was no longer credible: terms of trade shocks together with erratic policy-making combined to deepen the region's poverty and undermine many (but not all) of Africa's old dictators. And for the Middle East, the view that authoritarian rule lies at the root of the region's failure to diversify away from dependence on oil, and to create more employment for its young population, has gained converts with the debate over the causes of the terrorist attacks on the United States on 11 September 2001.

This is not to say that democracy will necessarily do any better in these regions; but it is certainly the case that autocracy has achieved very little for their economies and has, in many cases, impoverished people even further. Moreover, democratic transition in South Korea and Taiwan has now occurred, accelerated in its last phase by the Asian financial crisis of 1997–98 (which also initiated democratic transition in Indonesia). This revealed that the structures of economic management created under authoritarian rule – which were so successful in the initial phase of industrialization – were no longer suitable for managing mature and globally-integrated high-tech economies. Exposure of corruption and malpractice in state–business relations in South Korea was especially important in completing the country's democratization. Finally, the importance of good information communication technology to attracting foreign investment and to penetrating global markets makes it more difficult for national authorities to both promote rapid structural change and simultaneously suppress the flow of political information, a dilemma now facing the Chinese authorities.

In sum, discussion of the relationship between democracy and development has evolved over the years in the light of new research as well as of country experiences. This chapter identifies the main themes that have emerged in economics. The principal focus is on the developing countries, but with some references to the literatures for the developed and transition countries. The order of presentation will be: democracy as a determinant of economic growth as well as growth's contribution to democratization; the different consequences of democracy and autocracy for property and contract rights, and therefore for the incentive to invest; social polarization and its effects under democracy and autocracy; and the interaction of democracy with human development, in particular education and the formation of human capital. The conclusion argues that democratic politics can suffer from failure: elections represent 'incomplete contracts' between voters and politicians. In this regard, democratic politics is like the market economy: to work well both need considerable investment in supporting institutions to protect the public interest.

Democracy's interaction with economic growth

Does democracy increase economic growth? This has been a key question for economists. The possible ways in which democracy may raise (or lower) the growth of Gross Domestic Product (GDP) per capita include its effects on: the creation of property and contract rights (and thereby the incentive to invest); the formation of economic policy, in particular whether it increases or reduces the likelihood of growth-promoting policies; and the formation of human capital through education and other services (such as basic health care), thereby raising growth by increasing labour productivity. Empirical growth economics has been a highly active field over the last decade or so, albeit replete with methodological controversies. Economists typically investigate democracy's growth effects on cross-sections of countries by regressing growth on its possible determinants – usually physical and human capital, population growth, openness to trade, macroeconomic policy, and measures of institutional quality – including indices of democracy. The most commonly used data are the Freedom House index of political and civil rights (Freedom House 2002) and the

Polity III data (Jaggers and Gurr 1995). Political scientists have also been active in using these data in quantitative studies of democracy (see Landman 2000).

What does the empirical evidence show? Kormendi and Meguire (1985) and Scully (1988) found positive effects of democracy on growth. Similarly, Nelson and Singh (1998: 690) conclude that: 'when other factors influencing growth are controlled for, we find strong statistical evidence that developing countries with governments that provided higher levels of political and civil liberties to their citizens achieved significantly higher GDP growth rates than those with autocratic governments'. However, other studies show negative effects. Barro (1996) argues that earlier work was statistically biased owing to the omission of a number of growth's determinants – in particular, measures of the degree to which property and contract rights are respected – and that once these deficiencies are corrected for, a moderately negative effect of democracy on economic growth is found. Helliwell (1994) finds a negative but non-significant effect of democracy on economic growth. However, the negative effect in both the Barro (1996) and Helliwell (1994) studies is statistically weak. Tavares and Wacziarg (2001) specify a more detailed model of the linkages between democracy and growth, and report results that democracy's overall growth effects are negative (but again only moderately so).

In summary, the econometric evidence points both ways on democracy's growth effect: in some studies it is positive, in others it is negative. Looking at the last thirty years of development we can find growth-promoting policies both in democratic countries (like Botswana and Costa Rica) and autocratic ones (China and South Korea before 1989). Growth-reducing policies are evident in democracies (for example Argentina and Zambia in the 1990s) as well as in dictatorships such as Burma (Myanmar) and North Korea. Given this variety of outcomes, the inconclusive nature of the cross-country econometric work should not perhaps surprise us.

Before moving the analysis to property and contract rights, however, it is worth noting that economists have also had something to say about how growth affects the chances of becoming a democracy. This is an old, but nevertheless crucial, question. Barro's econometric work shows that improvements in real per capita GDP significantly increase the chances of a country democratizing, thereby confirming Lipset's (1959) classic argument that democracy tends to follow prosperity (Barro 1996). Przeworski and Limongi (1997: 165) find that democracies with per capita income of less than US$ 1,000 do not last more than 8 years on average; so economic growth is clearly important to the survival prospects of new democracies in poor countries. The omens are therefore not good for SSA: 45 countries had multi-party constitutions by 1999, compared with only 8 in 1988 (Thomson 2000: 216); but SSA's GNP per capita annual growth rate was *minus* 0.4 per cent during this time (UNDP 2000: 205). Achieving sustained growth in SSA could do much to increase the chances of democracy consolidating itself.

Democracy's effects on property and contract rights

The econometric work on democracy's effects on growth is inconclusive. We must therefore be clearer about the linkages between growth and democracy if we are to be more definitive.

The degree to which property and contract rights are respected under democracy and autocracy is an important starting-point. The existence of such rights provides a favourable incentive for investment, especially the kind of investments that involve large immediate fixed costs and a long time-horizon before profits are realized (such as planting tree crops whose yield is 4–5 years away, manufacturing plants that involve an extensive and capital-intensive phase of construction before they can begin operation, and so forth). If my property rights are insecure, and I cannot effectively get redress, then I will be less inclined to invest in production. I will be more inclined, if I invest at all, to put my money into trade, where my fixed costs are lower and my working capital is the main expense (trade therefore has much shorter time-horizons than production between the outlay of capital and the return on investment).

When property and contract rights are only weakly enforced then investment is likely to be low, and particularly low in agriculture and manufacturing – the main sources of economic growth, structural change, and employment in low-income societies. Societies in which insecurity is high and rising (the situation in many African countries today) are characterized by the withdrawal of smallholders into subsistence food production (and away from non-food cash crops, which typically have longer time-horizons), the contraction of manufacturing, and capital flight. Trading in ever-scarcer goods and the provision of personal services become the economy's mainstay as well as the livelihood for even more people (Afghanistan and Angola are examples). Respect for property and contract rights is therefore critical to investment in the production sectors that are at the core of economic development.

On the basis of his empirical work, Barro (1996 and 2000) argues that respect for property and contract rights (which he calls the 'rule of law') has a strongly positive effect on economic growth, whereas the relationship between democracy and growth is weakly negative, although he does find some evidence that the relationship is non-linear: 'more democracy enhances growth at low levels of political freedom but depresses growth when a moderate level of political freedom has already been attained' (Barro 1996: 23). He also finds that democracy has no significant effect on property and contract rights, although his data are limited (Barro 1996: 13). On the basis of his empirical evidence, Barro (2000) concludes, somewhat controversially, that: 'The problem with the US recommending democracy in a country such as Zaire (DRC) is not that democracy harms economic performance but, rather, that it has little impact. If a poor country has a limited amount of resources to accomplish institutional reform, then they are much better spent in attempting to implement the rule of law'.

Accordingly in Barro's view authoritarian states can raise living standards provided that they respect and enforce property and contract rights, thereby providing a favourable climate for private long-term investment. But before we accept this conclusion we need to go deeper, and specifically to look at the incentives and constraints facing the people who make the decisions about rights under democracies and autocracies. This is the approach taken in the work of

Mancur Olson and his associates, on which the following discussion is based (see Clague *et al.* 1996; Olson 1993, 2000b). They first consider the incentives facing a single autocrat. An autocrat with a long time-horizon (feels secure in power), and who is rational (seeks to maximize self-interest) can gain from granting protection to property and contract rights. But if his time-horizon is short then he gains more by expropriation. There are historical examples of each type of autocrat.

Now consider democracies. A long-standing democracy will have constructed institutions and laws that constrain individual behaviour: the democracy will have survived in large part because leaderships, while self-interested, have incentives to comply with electoral and constitutional law (they want to get re-elected), and others – for example the judges in constitutional courts – have incentives to ensure that politicians abide by the law. Abuses will certainly occur, but long-standing democracies also have active and independent medias, with incentives to root out miscreants (and vigorous civil societies with a similar zeal). But in *new* democracies this web of institutions may be barely evident. An active civil society may exist (local non-governmental organizations, churches, possibly a trade union movement), but the system of formal laws governing political practice will be new, often underdeveloped and, critically, untested (so that a body of statute and precedence has not been established with which to judge and punish misdemeanour). Long-standing democracies in the developed world have histories of often bitter struggle to create and maintain supporting institutions, and histories in which democratic reversal has, for periods, occurred.

In new democracies, elected leaders face fewer constraints. It may be in their self-interest to subvert property and contract rights, either because such rights cut against their personal business interests (for example, elected leaderships may attempt to shut down competitor businesses) or because they can improve their prospects for re-election (for example nationalizing without compensation an unpopular minority or foreign investor). So whether the leaders of a new democracy act to protect property and contract rights is critical to whether the democratic transition proves conducive or not to investment and growth:

in autocracies it is the time horizon of the *individual autocrat* (or occasionally the ruling clique) that is the main determinant of property and contract rights, whereas in democracies these rights depend on whether the *democratic system* is durable . . . Any autocratic society will sooner or later come to have rulers with short time horizons due to succession crises or other causes. We therefore hypothesize that democracies that have lasted for some time and expected to last much longer provide better property and contract rights than any other type of regime. (Clague *et al.* 1996: 246, emphasis in the original)

The empirical results confirm the hypothesis that long-lasting democracy provides better protection for property and contract rights, and is therefore better for economic development, than autocracy. But they also show that these benefits take time to appear: property and contract rights are often poor in new democracies, sometimes substantially poorer than when the countries concerned were autocracies (Clague *et al.* 1996: 271).

This may explain the somewhat inconclusive nature of the literature on democracy's growth effects that we discussed in the last section, since these studies generally fail to account adequately (if at all) for the *duration* of democracy. If the results of Clague *et al.* (1996) are correct, then it may no longer be the case, as Barro (1996, 2000) argues, that donors would do better to promote property and contract rights directly rather than to focus on democracy among aid recipients. For if democratic assistance can help to consolidate a new democracy then it will also eventually achieve an improvement in property and contract rights as well, which will have long-term development benefits.

Democracy and social polarization

Our discussion so far has one major drawback: it fails to take account of differences between social groups (by class, ethnicity, religion, region and so on) and differences in income, assets, and access to infrastructure and services between them. Sharp polarization between groups is usually associated with more competition than co-operation, as the weak attempt to achieve redistribution and the strong resist. High income inequality will encourage a poor majority to vote for redistributive fiscal measures, and when inequality is very high the poor may be quite willing to vote for very high taxes on the rich even though such taxes may deter investment and thereby reduce growth. This argument has come to the fore in explanations of why high initial inequality may be harmful to economic growth (for example Persson and Tabellini 1994, who also discuss the 'median voter' theorem that is at the core of these models).

Note that this line of reasoning is not exclusive to democracies; it may also apply to an authoritarian regime (a populist military leader enacts redistribution in favour of the poor) or if the poor themselves mount a successful revolution followed by a redistributional dictatorship. Moreover, the growth-reducing effect of the redistribution arises when it takes the form of distortionary (investment-reducing) taxation. But some forms of taxation may be less of a disincentive to investment, and if the higher revenues are allocated to basic pro-poor services then labour productivity and growth may rise instead of falling (human capital investment is discussed below). Despite these caveats, the inequality-democracy-growth argument retains its power, since it seems to fit many of the facts (growth in high-inequality Latin America has been much lower than in more egalitarian East Asia).

High levels of social polarization can also affect the conduct of government itself, with detrimental development effects. Democratically elected governments in polarized societies can be riven by competing factions, each attempting to influence policy and institutions for its own ends, with little consensus on economic policy (at the time of writing Madagascar has two administrations after a violent dispute over the results of the December 2001 election). Again, this problem does not just afflict democratic governments. Rather than there being a single autocrat, or a group that acts like a single autocrat (as in Olson 1993), the autocracy may instead be split by competing groups able to co-operate to defend their collective interest against outsiders but otherwise unable to co-operate on economic policy.

In summary, some economists take the view that whether a society is a democracy or not matters less for economic growth than whether it is highly polarized or not: 'The crucial distinction is not between autocracy and democracy (anyway there's no evidence that one is better for growth than the other). It is between a weak central government made up of a coalition of polarized factions and a strong central government made up of supporters in consensus' (Easterly 2001a: 260–1).

Of course, groups may not confine their competition within the framework of political institutions that set the 'rules of the game'. In highly polarized societies, groups may reject the rules of the game (including election results), and resort to violence to defend or overturn the status quo. In SSA this violent competition has a strong ethnic dimension, particularly where colonial governments exacerbated existing ethnic differences in order to 'divide and rule' (as in Burundi and Rwanda). In such societies, increasing mistrust leads people to focus more than ever on the short term: they look to redistribute the existing social pie in their favour (through violence if necessary), disregarding the longer-term benefits of co-operation. The resulting destruction and violence does of course reduce the size of the social pie; but even so one group may come out ahead. Economists have therefore increasingly looked to polarization and social conflict as one reason for development failure. Easterly and Levine (1997) conclude that ethnic divisions are a powerful explanation for Africa's 'growth tragedy'.

Such considerations imply that efforts to re-establish peace must have an economic as well as a political dimension if they are to work. Peace agreements that require free and fair elections are unlikely to yield peace or democracy if the underlying causes of social polarization remain. For instance, the peace agreement that ended 36 years of civil war in Guatemala included explicit economic measures to redress the grievances of the disadvantaged indigenous population (who formed the core of the insurrection). But it has been tough to fulfil these promises: measures to raise taxes on higher-income groups to pay for the provision of basic services to the indigenous and poor population have struggled through a legislature that is traditionally dominated by Guatemala's wealthy elite. If groups cannot reconcile their differences, then secession may occur: this can be peaceful, but is more often violent.

Traditionally, democracy has strengthened as a middle class emerges, that is, as social polarization declines, in part because economic growth raises people out of poverty and into the middle class. Such authoritarian states as South Korea and Taiwan achieved a fast and substantial rise in living standards that provided these states with considerable support in their early stages of growth. But as living standards reached developed-country levels, a broad middle-class challenge to authoritarian rule emerged, and this contributed to their democratic transition (similar pressures are now evident in China). This was accompanied by a sharp rise in wage levels. Easterly (2001b) finds that a rise in the share of income going to the middle class raises political rights (democratization).

Although pressure for democratization can come from below, it can also arise from changes in strategy within the elite. In authoritarian societies characterized by a growing disparity of income between rich and poor, the elite will have to devote more resources to suppressing the social unrest associated with rising poverty and inequality. Elites may be able to use state violence to control the poor for quite some time (apartheid South Africa is one example). But the desire to avoid violent unrest and possibly revolution by the poor (leading to expropriation of the rich) is one reason why elites may see it as in their *own interests* to facilitate democratization, even if democratization is likely to result in increased taxation of the rich as the newly enfranchised poor vote for redistribution. Why rich elites should back redistribution, and the dilution of their political power through democratization, is an issue that has recently captured economists' attention.

Acemoglu and Robinson (2000) develop a model of democratization in which the elite extends the franchise in order to avoid revolution or social unrest. This constitutes what economists call a 'commitment device'. They argue that this was the main reason why the franchise was extended in western Europe during the nineteenth century. This may also explain why income inequality began to decline after the franchise was extended, as new voters pressed for redistributive measures and why, starting at a low level, income inequality first increased with development (before the franchise was extended) and then eventually fell back (the so-called 'Kuznets curve') in the development experiences of Western societies.

Still, democratization is not a one-way process: particularly striking is the oscillation of periods of democracy with periods of autocracy in Latin America. Acemoglu and Robinson (2001) show that the level of income inequality is an important determinant of whether democracy consolidates or not. In high-inequality societies (such as those in Latin America) elites may have an incentive to renege on democratization, by supporting a military coup, if redistribution under democratization is especially onerous.

Democracy's interaction with human development

The discussion so far has focused on economic growth, and the accompanying rise in per capita income, as a development goal. But the last decade has seen an emphasis on non-income measures of human welfare as well, in particular such human development indicators as literacy, life expectancy, and infant mortality (Sen 2001; UNDP 2000). The poor not only have low incomes, they also have low human development indicators, and much can be done to raise the latter without necessarily achieving strong increases in income as well (although raising incomes does help).

Education is an important aspect of human development, and it is one of the components of UNDP's human development index (UNDP 2000). Since poor households find it difficult to borrow to pay for private education, their educational prospects largely depend on the scope and quality of public education, especially primary education. We would expect the poor to receive more education (and basic services) under a democracy because they can vote. Historically, democracy was one of the factors driving social spending's share of the economy: Lindert (forthcoming 2002) finds that, in the nineteenth century, countries where the majority of adults voted had the highest school enrolment rates. Note, however, that causation runs both ways: investment in education increases the likelihood of democratization, its sustainability, and the scope of the franchise.

The human capital created by education can be an important source of economic growth. Saint-Paul and Verdier (1993) argue that democracy leads to redistribution through greater education spending, thereby raising human capital, labour productivity, and growth. This conjecture is supported by empirical work: Tavares and Wacziarg (2001) find a positive link from democracy to growth through human capital (although in their results this positive effect of democracy is outweighed by other negative effects, so that democracy is moderately negative for growth).

Note, however, that autocracy is not necessarily inimical to basic education (or other poverty-reducing services such as basic health care). Although there are plenty of examples of autocracies that have neglected basic education and health, for example Burma, authoritarian governments have made large investments in basic education and other basic social services (notably South Korea in the 1960s). Again, income inequality is important: leaderships in South Korea and Taiwan engaged in early redistribution through land reform and higher pro-poor public spending (in part to win political support against communist insurgency).

In contrast, many societies that have long histories of high income inequality find it difficult to raise taxes to finance basic pro-poor services, and what public money is available is spent disproportionately on services of most benefit to urban elites and their supporters. Addison and Rahman (2003) find that across countries the allocation of public money to primary education – the level of education of most benefit to the poor – varies inversely with income inequality. This finding confirms the model's assumption that the already wealthy have more influence on the political process (irrespective of whether the country is a democracy or an autocracy) and favour spending on those education services of most benefit to themselves.

Hence in Latin America, where income inequality is high, democratization may not lead to the hoped-for investment in basic education (as well as other inputs into human capital such as health) that is needed to reduce poverty significantly. The majority of countries in the former Soviet Union and eastern Europe experienced rising inequality as well as a marked deterioration in mortality and morbidity indicators in the process of transition to market economies (occurring simultaneously with their democratization), an increase that was at least partly due to badly designed economic liberalization and privatization programmes. New wealthy elites may control and influence legislatures to an extent sufficient to benefit only themselves (as is very evident in Central Asia). This may suggest that 'the current level of democracy is a very imperfect proxy for the real level of democracy, namely that in order for democracy to "work" on inequality through various redistributive mechanisms, sufficient "democratic time" needs to elapse' (Gradstein and Milanovic 2000: 21). This conclusion parallels the results of Clague *et al.* (1996) for property and contract rights, which also show that democracy's benefits take some time to emerge.

Conclusions

This chapter has looked at how economists approach democracy, highlighting some of the main themes of this work. We have seen that empirical research finds both positive and negative effects of democracy on growth. Economists are still debating the overall effect – some find it strongly growth-increasing, others find it moderately growth-reducing – but the recent literature on property and contract rights seems to indicate that if a democracy can consolidate then it will generate better long-run economic performance than autocracy. We have seen that societies that are sharply polarized can experience economic problems under both democracy and autocracy; reducing inequality is therefore essential if they are successfully to democratize and develop. Finally, we have shown that democracy can have strongly positive effects on human development, but that democratic consolidation is essential for such effects to manifest themselves.

Economic theory is based on the premise that individuals seek to maximize their well-being (utility in economist's jargon) subject to their constraints (income in particular). Just as rational calculation leads me to choose one commodity over another, so it also leads me to choose one politician over another, and utility-maximizing politicians compete to offer me the best political menu at election time. But, like market economies, democratic politics can also suffer from failure: elections represent 'incomplete contracts' (politicians can fail to keep their promises once elected and may break the law). So other institutions, such as constitutional courts, electoral law, and an independent media, are needed to reduce the inherent imperfections of the electoral process. For an economist it is no surprise that the introduction of competitive elections is but one of many steps needed on the road to full democratization, just as economic liberalization is but one step on the road to a market economy: in both cases institutions must be built to protect the public interest, so ensuring that social goals are met.

Note

This chapter is an output of the UNU/WIDER research project on 'Why some countries avoid conflict while others fail'. The views expressed are the author's alone and should not be attributed to UNU/WIDER or its funding agencies.

4

Gender Studies

SHIRIN M. RAI

In order to explore feminist perspectives on democratization we need to understand both feminist frameworks and
methodologies. This chapter outlines what a feminist framework might be and then uses this perspective to analyse
feminist engagements with the theory and practice of
democratization.

Democratization can be defined as the process of 'making democratic' regimes, practices and discourses of public
power. Luckham and White (1996b: 2–8) have identified
four areas of inquiry for democratization analysts: (1) the
nature of the particular institutional form of democracy;
(2) causes and contexts of democratization; (3) prospects for
the sustainability and deepening of democracy and (4) the
relationship between democracy and socio-economic development. Rueschemeyer *et al.* (1992) highlighted three
factors that affect the actual working of democracies: (1) the
international factors – such as inter-state relations; (2) the
individual state itself and its political institutions and
leadership – the role of the military as opposed to civilian
leadership, for example; and (3) 'civil society', which reflects
the social and interest groups with a stake in society. It is,
they argued, the constellation of these three factors that
makes for the possibilities, or otherwise, of a successful
democratization process. While valuable in themselves, both
these explanatory and analytical frameworks share one fundamental characteristic – the focus is on spaces where actors,
states and individuals act in the public political sphere.

The following sections present four insights arising from
the work of feminist scholars that extend our understanding of democratization at the theoretical level. The analysis

then moves to the specific field of gender and democratization and the nature of women's participation in politics. The final section reflects upon the wider socio-economic context in which men and women are engaged in democratization struggles. The conclusion holds that democratization is an untidy and unfolding process and that feminist insights are crucial for understanding it.

Feminist engagements

Public and private spheres of political action

Perhaps one of the most enduring contributions of women's activism and feminist theorizing is the challenging of the boundaries between the public and the private as defining (out) politics. In Pateman's (1983: 283) words, 'the separation of the private and public is presented in liberal theory as if it applied to all individuals in the same way'. Feminists argued that public political life was built upon the absence of women from it; that the exclusion of the private sphere was essential for the primacy of the public. By expanding the definition of politics to encompass both the public and the private spheres, indeed, by asserting that the two were mutually constitutive, feminists have been able to challenge the dominant understandings of politics itself, and therefore of democratic practice and discourse. For example, in the democratization movements against the military dictatorship installed by the coup of 11 September 1973 Chilean women called for democracy in the home as well as in politics. However, these struggles have not always been successful. While the discourse about women's position and role within the family has been carried out in the public sphere, women's presence in the public sphere has continued to be a controversial issue.

Differences remain among feminists about the nature of the public/private divide. While radical feminists have seen the obliteration of this distinction as necessary to a democracy that is inclusive of gender-based difference, others have seen such a bridging of the public and private as a transitory phase – a phase that would allow the entry of women into the public arena as independent actors (Phillips 1991 and 1993). Some feminist scholars have argued that, while democratizing the private domain is crucial for women's participation in the public, it ought not to be confused with issues of civic participation and rights (Dietz 1992). Young, for example, has stressed the importance of maintaining the separation between the two spheres. She suggests that the private sphere should be thought of as 'that aspect of his or her life and activity that any person has the right to exclude from others. The private in this sense is not what public institutions exclude,' she argues, 'but what the individual chooses to withdraw from public view' (Young 1990: 119–20). Lister (1997: 121) quite rightly points out the problems with this articulation of the public–private divide: 'it does leave open the question as to which individuals have the power to make their choices stick'. I would also emphasize, however, the need for a simultaneous, but parallel, demo-cratization of both the public and the private spheres. Here we should insist, with Dietz, upon keeping the two domains separate. It is important to mark a conscious transition that women must make to politicize the issues that affect them within the private sphere. Rather than focusing on the issue of exclusion from the private sphere, I would emphas-ize the terms of *inclusion* into the public sphere. For it is only through making the private public that we can move forward on this issue. While not entirely answering the question of agency raised by Lister (1997), such an under-standing of the bringing together of the public and the private would do so in part through the social mobilization of women (and men) on particular issues in the public sphere. Such an analysis of the public/private divide not only allows us to focus on the importance of the private for the public, but it also provides us with a measure for assessing the pro-cesses of democratization. It is both a framework of analysis and a methodology for assessing political change.

Feminist methodologies

Building upon this debate, the second insight that feminist scholars have offered is by paying particular attention to 'experience' as an important starting-point of knowledge, which contextualizes the basis of politics itself (Scott 1992). Gender, as social construction of sex, then is reflected in the political roles that women and men are able to perform, and 'frames the very definition of politics, and by default, what does not constitute politics' (Rai 2000: 156). From an analytical framework, which challenges the public/private divide and insists upon experience as a valid form and basis of knowledge, there emerges a radical visualization of politics itself. This visualization sees the universalized language of politics, of citizenship and rights for example, as marking the erasure of structurally embedded differences between individuals. As Blacklock and Macdonald (2000: 19) argue, women's movements are 'exposing the limitations of a discourse which, in its universalism, conceals a gendered and racialised subject identity, a Western, ethnocentric conception of rights, and an ontology which denies heterogeneity and diversity'.

The importance of context has been the third intervention that feminists have made in the debate about democratization. Feminists have pointed to the diversity of women's histories, and to their differential experiences of 'the public' on account of class, race, disability and sexuality, to argue for the essentially contingent and contested nature of the debate on the distinction between the public and the private spheres (Lister 1997: 122–5). They have also quite rightly asked the question: What are the costs – social, economic and personal – of political participation for women? Who has the resources to be able to participate directly? These costs are not the same, and quite often depend upon the social and economic resources that women are able to mobilize in order to access political life, to participate in informal and formal processes and political institutions. Religion, class and caste, ethnicity and sexuality, disability and language all mediate with gender to influence the outcomes of democratic participation for women and men.

Patriarchy and democratic politics

And finally, feminists have theorized on democracy with regard to the meta-framework of patriarchy. Patriarchy has been defined as a 'system of male authority which oppresses women through its social, political and economic institutions . . . a sex-gender system and a system of economic discrimination operate simultaneously. Patriarchy has power from men's greater access to, and mediation of, the resources and rewards of authority structures inside and outside the home' (Humm 1989: 159). While there are different feminist positions on the nature of patriarchy, broadly speaking the concept does define the feminist position on social relations. So when feminists have addressed the issue of democratization, they have asked different questions and sought answers that go beyond the mainstream debates on democratization. Questions of access to and participation in the political and the socio-economic spheres, the deepening of democracy within and outside the home, are therefore, considered to be deeply gendered. The next section of this chapter builds on these discussions to assess the nature and outcomes of democratization debates and initiatives from a gendered perspective.

Gender and democratization

Waylen (1994), in her survey of the democratization literature, poses four questions about women's participation in the process of democratic transitions and consolidations: (1) Why women choose to organize or not? (2) Where they exist, what is the nature of these movements? (3) What is the interaction between women's political activities and the process of transition? and (4) What are the outcomes for women of transitions to democracy, as well as of further democratization of consolidated political systems?

Women's movements and democratization

Social movements have been defined as 'organized efforts at the grass roots to represent interests excluded from or poorly represented in formal arenas of authoritative negotiation and value allocation' (Teske and Tetreault 2000: 9). In this sense women's movements have always been part of political processes in different contexts. It is through their participation in these movements that women and women's groups have been able to stake a claim to equal representation in political life and institutions (Jayawardena 1986), on the one hand, and to focus attention on the necessity of deepening democracy within the home as they negotiate the terms upon which they participate in social and political movements in the public sphere. For example, the Hudood

Ordinances decreed in Pakistan by its military ruler Zia ul Haq (1977–88) provoked a strong response from Pakistani women. They led to the establishment of the Women's Action Forum, which has not only mobilized against the Ordinances, which were clearly discriminatory against women, but also joined and strengthened the struggle for democracy in Pakistan (Ali 2000: 46–50). The movement of the Mothers of the Plaza de Mayo in Chile against the Pinochet regime also shows how women have challenged the separation of the public and the private by building on their role as mothers within the home to challenge authoritarian regimes in public: 'Their refusal to acquiesce in the loss of their children was not an act out of character, but a coherent expression of their socialisation [as mothers] . . . True to themselves, they had no other choice but to act, even it meant confronting the junta' (Navarro 1989: 257).

An important and complex area where the overlaps between the public and private spheres create challenges for women is that of 'culture'. Feminist insights have insisted upon de-mythologizing an 'essential woman' through the study of difference – between men and women and among women – as a theoretical strategy that underpins women's struggles for empowerment (Fuss 1989). However, even movements of democracy create their ideal woman erased of all differences – authenticity of culture is inscribed on women's bodies and roles. Women have sought to democratize this discourse on two counts – first, by challenging the 'orientalist' and imperialist discourse of rescue of the women of particular (non-Christian/Western) cultures (Liddle and Rai 1998); and second by challenging the codes of silence that their own communities impose on them in the name of anti-racism. By challenging both these positions women have attempted to open up and deepen the democratic debate. This has not always been easy, and at times has sat uneasily with the mainstream public debate on democratization.

Nature of women's political participation

Participation in political movements has been a crucial element in the struggles for democratization. It has contributed to the creation and expansion of civil society as well as being critical to the claims of various marginalized groups for representation in national political institutions. Feminist scholars and activists have long been aware of the dilemmas of participation. On the one hand it is a powerful means of access and empowerment, and on the other, it places differentiated burdens and costs on participants. Issues of difference are important when discussing the nature of political participation, as is its stabilization within specific political systems. While on the whole mainstream democratization theory has been sceptical about participatory politics owing to its unpredictability and doubtful of its long-term efficacy, feminists have embraced it despite the above reservations. Lynch (1998: 162) has argued that 'theorising about social movements in the 1970s and 1980s made a double move – from a critique of capitalism to an interest in the "higher goals" of rights, peace, and democracy, and from a focus on "particularistic" movements . . . to movements motivated by "universalistic" values and objectives'. For the women's movements this double move created new opportunities and solidarities within the broad framework of democratization. An arena of public politics where women's movements have attempted to bring together the public and the private has expanded to include important issues of human rights[1] and citizenship. While rights, like the state, provoke different responses from feminists (see Rai 1996), human rights discourse has been central to the struggles for democracy in the 1980s and 1990s. In Guatemala, for example, the exposure of human rights violations was the first step towards building the movement for democratization. However, the movement also tried to conscientize the popular masses with 'the longer-term goal of preparing *pobladoras* to become citizens by organising their communities'. By raising awareness that 'all people are "entitled" to [human rights], the women's organisations are attempting to construct *pobladoras* as new "subjects of rights", new political actors, and new citizens' (Blacklock and Macdonald 2000: 22–3). It is through this linking of state-based rights and citizen-based conscientization that the women's movements are participating in the creation of a civil society that might be able to sustain the expansion of formal rights, as well as to challenge a universalized understanding of rights themselves.

Women's movements have also reflected the unfolding nature of citizenship. They have pressed for different facets of women's lives to be reflected in legal and constitutional arrangements – from the early-twentieth-century demands in many countries for universal political rights, to the current insistence upon mainstreaming a gendered perspective in political institutions. Thus, while feminists and women's movements have been wary of institutional power and discourses of universality, by opening up the issue of difference they have sought an intersection of the two. The interest in the 'third generation' of group-based human rights is evidence of this (Kymlicka 1995). In terms of democratization, this has led to some initiatives of securing women's participation in institutional politics through group-based quotas, with mixed and sometimes controversial outcomes (Rai 2002).

Women's participation in institutional politics

While mainstream democratic theory has concentrated largely on representative as opposed to participatory politics, it is only relatively recently that feminists have explored the possibilities of representative institutional politics. Debates about rights and participation in movements for democracy have led women's groups to the recognition that it is imperative that the gains made through participation are institutionalized through laws, constitutions, and political machineries and practices. Interventions of international organizations such as the United Nations also helped to emphasize the importance of working with state institutions in order to improve the living conditions of women.

Here we find significant variations depending upon the nature of political transitions and political systems, and political ideologies of leaderships, as well as different trajectories of change. Thus, during the period of transition to a democratic South Africa, the aim of the Women's National Coalition (WNC), which was the umbrella organization for 90 women's organizations representing about two million women, was to ensure that by participating in debates on the writing of the constitution they 'would be able to secure a consistent gendered perspective throughout this most important document' (Zulu 2000: 174).

While the South African case is a success story for a gender-sensitive transition politics, the experience of eastern Europe has raised important questions for women's movements as well as for democratization struggles. The democratization of eastern European states did not lead to more representative political institutions. On the contrary, there was a 'dramatic drop in levels of female political representation to 10 per cent or less in national assemblies after the first and second democratic elections in East Central Europe' (Einhorn 2000: 108). Together with the enormous economic pressures that families have had to experience and the abandonment of the earlier pattern of state-based participation in political institutions, women have largely stayed away from political institutions. Women have continued to be active in some eastern European countries at the level of informal, civil society politics, where they have channelled their input into being lobbying and advocacy groups under 'severe limitations on their ability to shift state policies grounded in a culture of exclusionary ethno-nationalism' (Einhorn 2000: 109–10).

Within specific contexts, strategies for democratizing the state as well as civil society have thus been on the agenda of feminist democratic practice. However, a crucial context within which these strategies have taken shape and have been tried out is that of economic liberalization.

Democratization and entitlements

Feminist scholars have long challenged the view that there is a positive correlation between political and economic liberalization (Elson 1989). They have argued that the increased pressures arising from economic liberalization are increasing the burden that women carry in their daily lives and therefore reducing the time and space for them to be politically active. Globalization as liberalization is putting under pressure the idea of a stable social compact between citizens and the national states (Rai 2002: 157).

Structural adjustment policies and citizenship entitlements

Reductions in state spending on health are adversely affecting women's health as families make choices about spending limited resources on men or on boy children, and is also increasing the care burden of women as they look after elders and children in the absence of state provision. Similarly, education of girls has fallen dramatically in countries where structural adjustment policies (SAPs) have meant cuts in state education budgets. According to UNCTAD (2000), girl child enrolment in sub-Saharan Africa has plummeted with the introduction of SAPs. In terms of the development of the human capabilities of poor women and particularly of the women of the South, this falling investment is resulting in the erosion of their future abilities to contribute to the family income, as well as to participate in the wider political processes important to the development of their countries. Even the expansion of women's participation in the sphere of waged work in liberalized economies is no indicator of their empowerment. It could simply 'be the result either of progress towards the homogenization and equalization of the male and female employment roles, or be caused by persistence of differences in sex roles on the labour market, with demand for female labour protected by rigid patterns of sex segregation' (Rubery 1988: ix).

It could be argued that the dislocations in gendered regimes of power at the local levels caused by the expansion of female labour in export processing zones has led to women's acquiring a higher status within the family, and the opening up of new spaces outside the home for their political mobilization. Women have participated in trade union struggles as well in the wider anti-globalization/liberalization movements. In November 1998, for example, '182 women from 22 countries representing 104 organizations met in Kuala Lumpur to Resist Globalization and Assert Our Rights'. They argued that 'privatisation of health care is a violation of women's basic human rights to total well-being' and asserted that Third World women have suffered most from globalization in Asia, where economic crisis has brought large-scale unemployment and displacement, deepening poverty, food insecurity due to increasing loss of biodiversity and the appropriation of land and water resources by large transnational corporations (TNCs) and the elite. They concluded: 'our governments, local elites and local businesses are the collaborators and implementers of this agenda'.[2]

Given the context of poverty and exclusion, such struggles are impressive. However, they also alert us to the limitations of the democratization discourse if we do not take into account the socio-economic context of political processes. Indeed, an attention to the question of citizenship entitlements of health, education and freedom from poverty is crucial if the democratization debate is to be inclusive of those on the margins of civil society. To facilitate women's active citizenship, Einhorn argues that what has been called 'exchange entitlement mapping' must be enhanced through the strengthening of the economic as well as the political rights of women.

Democratization and globalization

As is evident from the above discussion, while it may be focused on national states and political institutions and processes, democratization can no longer be discussed without attention to globalization. Thus, Held has asked: 'Whose consent is necessary, whose agreement is required, whose participation is justified in decisions concerning, for instance, the location of . . . [a] nuclear plant? What is the relevant constituency? Local? National? Regional? International?' (1991: 143). We have seen the exponential growth of financial and trade flows, helped by a revolution in communications. The result has been arguments about the deterritorialization of politics, the retreat of the nation-state, and the convergence of economic policies, and about a reflexivity about the world that we inhabit and whose citizens we are. Thus it could be argued that globalization has led to the transformation of our daily lives. However, feminist engagements with globalization theory also point out that 'it is perhaps a particularly weak version of democracy that has been institutionalized on a global scale – liberal democracy in its most elitist, least developmental form' (Eschle 2001: 151). It has been argued elsewhere that '[a]s the global reach of social and political movements increases through technological and information networks, and as the pressures of international trade and markets begin to impinge significantly on the national economies leading to a fragmentation and repositioning of nation-states, the relationship between local struggles, social movements and the national state is being constantly reshaped' (Rai 2002: 205). Indeed, increasing attention is being paid to relations between women's group across national borders, focused on networks of women straddling North and South, and on the way in which cyber-technology is changing communications among and for women. Women are participating in struggles at the local/national as well as local/global levels (Parpart, Rai and Staudt 2002). Movements of citizens' boycotts of particular transnational corporations or products, ecological struggles for the protection of bio-diversity, the indigenous peoples' movements and indeed the women's movement have all had to operate across traditional national boundaries, and therefore to negotiate in the global political space. Issues of accountability, agenda-setting and interest representation, as well as institutionalization, have become globalized. Democratization is no longer confined within national boundaries, even though states continue to be the focus of convergence of liberal democratic institutional politics. The pressures to liberalize economies as well as polities continue to be seen as markers of convergence of democratic practice even while the outcomes of these pressures sharpen differences between states and among people.

In conclusion

As Luckham and White (1996b: 1) point out, the democratization 'wave' had already begun to recede by the mid-1990s as entrenched regimes either resisted the trend, or merely went through the democratic motions, or as newly democratic regimes succumbed to various forms of authoritarian reversion. Women's groups engaged in democratization struggles have been acutely aware of a need for constant vigilance in any engagement with state-dominated processes of democratization. Global economic trends also affect the processes and stability of democratization. Feminists' interventions in struggles for democratization have alerted them to viewing democratization as a context-bound process. State formations, the contours of particular civil societies, the possibilities of women's mobilizations, the entitlements that women have (or not), and institutional arrangements that give shape to particular citizenships have profound impacts upon the possibilities for women to participate in political life. As economic downturns affect different governments, issues about entitlements to citizenship become increasingly more important.

Political practice has also clarified the fact that democratization is not a wave that comes or goes – however much its jagged nature might be emphasized; it is an unfolding and untidy process. Successes in one area are not suggestive of a completeness of the process. Issues are, and need to be, revisited, with startlingly different results. Institutions that have been stable for decades, as well as new institutions of state power, need to be opened up for scrutiny. This is important because the dominant discourses of power have begun to engage with the struggles of marginalized groups, and need to be stabilized within old institutions that had been put together in another historical context. Gains that have been made must be cemented within new institutions and old. The unfolding nature of democratization is also evident when we examine the question of entitlements. As transitions from one set of socio-economic relations to another make clear, political and social citizenships do not necessarily go hand in hand. The tension within liberal democracy – of individual rights embedded in a socio-economic context of unequal access to resources – continues to haunt throughout all the debates on entitlements. Newly democratizing nations and old democracies both are sites for the struggles for the democratization of politics.

Finally, we also need to emphasize the importance of comparative work so that women can view, analyse and perhaps use strategies for enhancing women's participation in politics across the boundaries of nation-states. The debates on citizenship – in the universalist discourse as well as those focused upon women's group rights – are particularly important in this regard (Young 1990; Lister 1997; Yuval-Davis 1997). The language of rights, of equality, of difference, and of entitlements have all been employed by women as they strategize in their pursuit of greater freedom. International fora provide meeting-places where women from different countries cross boundaries, create networks, confront constraints and explore democratic possibilities. Global frameworks, while necessarily limited, have also been utilized by women's movements to build bridges and create solidarities across national borders in their struggles to democratize politics. Feminist debates on democratization continue to contribute to such a rooted crossing of cultural, historical and political boundaries.

Notes

1 Only in 1991 did Amnesty International put the violation of women's rights on its agenda. Prior to this, feminist activity was not a recognized 'political' category except when integrated into the programme of a political party or trade union (Ashworth 1986: 11).

2 Statement of the Third Women's Conference Against APEC, 50-years@igc.org.

5

History

PETER CALVERT

The main purpose of this chapter is to show how historians have contributed to our understanding of the processes of democratization. In the course of this the main focus will be on the different views historians have taken of alternative paths to democracy and particularly its early stages – the so-called 'first wave' (see Huntington 1991). To do this, however, we have first to take into account the ways in which different historians have approached the writing of history.

Democratization here is taken to be a process by which popular participation is enhanced. It is not confined to periods of passage from authoritarian to popular government. It includes (but is not confined to):

- the establishment of the principles of representative government, accountability and the rule of law;
- the extension of participation, either by the formal widening of the franchise, or by the informal empowerment of new social groups that have not previously participated, or both; and
- the continued modification of modern systems to facilitate popular understanding of and ability to participate in government. Such modifications are, in the United States the passage of the Freedom of Information Act, in France the end of the prefectoral *tutelle*, and in the United Kingdom the devolution of powers in the late 1990s to the Scots Parliament and the Welsh Assembly.

While it is easy to say that understanding the present is helped by a knowledge of the past, in practice things are far more complicated. This is because historians do not and (more to the point) cannot agree on the past; when presenting their narratives they impose their own versions of rationality and orderly development. But, far from this implying that historical research only makes the challenge of making sense of recent democratization even more problematic, the main inference is that students of democratization in other disciplines, who constantly rely on historical works to fill out understanding, absorb the assumptions of history along with the content, and that they should therefore remain alert to this.

Different approaches to the writing of history

Perhaps the greatest contribution history can make, therefore, to the understanding of democratization is to enable us to understand better how historians' questioning of the foundations of their own discipline can have implications for our understanding of accepted 'facts'. The founder of modern historical scholarship, Leopold von Ranke, unintentionally pointed up the ambiguity between aspiration and actuality in his celebrated comment (which was meant only to apply to the specific work): 'History has had assigned to it the task of judging the past, of instructing the present for the benefit of ages to come. To such lofty functions this work does not aspire. Its aim is merely to show how things actually were (*wie es eigentlich gewesen*)'.[1]

The Rankean view that history based on original sources is definitive (fact) has long since been modified. It has, indeed, been wholly abandoned by the post-modernists; but the arguments of philosophers such as Richard Rorty and the historian Hayden White basically only amount to an assertion that nothing can ever be known for certain (see Jenkins 1995). Yet for a variety of practical reasons we need to have some agreement about what happened in the past – if only to try to plan for the future. However partial this 'knowledge' may be and however uncertain we may be that it does in fact constitute 'knowledge', the historian does not have the freedom of the poet or the novelist to dismiss certainty as impossible and leave it at that.

A more crucial objection is posed by Ankersmit (1983), who argues that there can be no general descriptions in history. Terms such as 'the Enlightenment', for Ankersmit, are simply 'names given to the "images" or "pictures" of the past proposed by historians attempting to come to grips with the past'. If this were true, then this argument that 'the past itself has no narrative pattern or structure' would be equally valid for 'democratization' (Ankersmit 1983: 99, 110). McCullagh (1998) accepts that different historians will have different views about the past, and consequently that they will have different views about all such classificatory terms and generalizations. However, as he points out, all such views do in fact have much in common. They may be unique in detail, but they can still be identified as referring to the same thing and be classified as belonging to the same family of descriptions. And, 'once it is admitted that there are criteria for the application of most general terms in history, then the possibility of them being true becomes plain. A general description of the past is true if the criteria for its application are satisfied' (see McCullagh 1998: 68).

There is therefore still a discipline termed History, and it is distinguished by its methodology. Philosophy offers us one sort of understanding about the world we live in. Science and History each offer us alternative understandings. As it did for Ranke, History still involves the interrogation of written and other material from some time before the present in order to arrive at an understanding of the past. History depends on the existence of written sources, and without sources is not recognized as such (hence we have to talk of prehistory for the times before which written sources are available).

Historians have almost unlimited freedom to dispute what meaning they should attach to their source material, and in recent years have shown a great deal of ingenuity in identifying and interrogating material that was not previously consulted. What they cannot legitimately do is either to ignore evidence to the contrary of which they are aware, or to insert material for which they have no evidence whatsoever. Speculation, up to a point, is perfectly permissible for the historian,[2] but it must be labelled as such. In the twentieth century interrogation of the sources expanded, with (a) utilization of new sources (from account books to oral history); (b) new techniques for interrogation (statistics,

scientific analysis of materials, radiocarbon dating, archae-
ological research); and (c) ability to access and to store much
larger quantities of data. Historians, however, remained
suspicious of frameworks such as the 'models' employed
by other social scientists that are specifically intended to
present a selective picture of reality.

The discipline's main contribution to understanding also
presents problems, which the post-modernists have been
quick to claim support their pessimism. To be rendered
intelligible to the reader, history has to be set out as narrative. But history as narrative imposes a sense of rationality
and orderly development that is in some sense the creation
of the historian. Take one example: the concept of a 'century'. The long-held assumption that 1914 marks the true
end of the long nineteenth century has been challenged for
many years (Seaman 1966). And it already has been argued
that the 'short twentieth century' began in 1914 and came
to an end as early as 1989, presumably consigning the history
of 'third wave' democratization to an equally elastic twenty-
first century (Hobsbawm 1994).

A more serious criticism has been made by various
writers, notably the US historian, Hayden White (1966),
that the narrative form in itself is misleading in its whole-
ness. Though there is no real history for White, what people
experience as history they do not see as a narrative – and
necessarily so, since they do not have foreknowledge of
what is to come. History cannot therefore constitute a logical progression towards the present, still less towards an
ideal future state such as is implied by the term 'democracy'
as it is currently used. In fact, in some complex situations,
such as the French Revolution, narrative cannot easily cope
with the complexity of events, and it is partly in consequence of this that successive generations of historians
have needed to reinterpret it. We shall see how this has
been done as we examine in turn the three main historical
models of democratization. As was noted above, historians
are rightly suspicious of models. Yet we can identify three
streams of historical debate corresponding to three different
models of the way in which the foundations of democracy
were laid. These are: the myth of American exceptionalism,
the Gladstonian view of British history, and the French
Revolutionary tradition.

The myth of American exceptionalism

We can begin with Gladstone's apothegm that the US Constitution was 'the most wonderful work ever struck off at a given time by the brain and purpose of man'. One could challenge this judgement on many grounds. American historians have long since come to see the American Revolution not as a form of Constitutional debate but as the consequence of a deep-seated conflict of interest between Britain and its colonies – a view, moreover, with which Thomas Jefferson would undoubtedly have agreed. The Jeffersonians correctly saw the seat of popular will as lying in the States, but for some reason it has always been difficult to persuade British observers to interest themselves in the minutiae of state government. The US Federal Constitution deliberately limited the power of the people (as for example by the creation of the Electoral College), even while creating a structure designed to preclude any notion of a return to monarchy. It was republican rather than democratic. With the election of 1828 and the arrival of the Jacksonians the system was radically changed by the growth of political parties, even while the formal structure of the Constitution remained unchanged.

By 1843 the extension of the franchise to all white males had been achieved. The way was open for George Bancroft in his 10-volume *History of the United States from the Discovery of America* (1834–87) and his followers to write a new 'democratic' history, presenting the citizens of the Republic with a flattering and patriotic self-image with which they were only too ready to identify. Far from the corruption and decadence of Europe, they had on the frontier developed the qualities of self-reliance, liberty and honesty that found their outcome in the extension of popular government. Bancroft was not a professional historian. His impact on the public stemmed from his persuasive thesis and was reinforced by the massive scale of his work – made possible by a new technique of treating the writing of history as a team enterprise. His *History of the United States* was to the late nineteenth century what the *Encyclopedia Britannica* was to the twentieth. A most unfortunate by-product was the way in which the frontier thesis effectively wrote the native American out of the mainstream of American development. Despite many detailed studies of the Revolutionary period in the twentieth century, however, the frontier thesis remains part of the founding myth of the United States of America. It contributes to the self-image that that country has a mission to spread its distinctive brand of democracy to the rest of the world.

Gladstone's eulogy of the US Constitution is the more curious because it was uttered so close in time to the Constitution's most evident failure. The American Civil War, 1861–65, marks a critical passage in the survival of the first-wave democracies. However, if books on Lincoln are legion, the era of Reconstruction has largely been left to professional historians. So too has the Progressive Era and the 1920s, while the Civil Rights movement of 1950–70 appears as if from nowhere. Meanwhile Charles Beard's *An Economic Interpretation of the Constitution*, published in 1913, challenged the idealized view of the making of the Constitution. It substituted for the older view that it was primarily concerned with civil liberties a well-argued case for seeing it as first and foremost a document designed to facilitate the transfer of economic power to a new governing class.

The rise of the US to world power status, on the other hand, gave rise to a new sub-genre of US diplomatic history. With varying degrees of subtlety it conveyed the message that the US was uniquely privileged to use its unparalleled powers for the betterment of mankind as a whole.[3] The challenge of the Cold War and the hazards posed by nuclear armament instead led to an urgent search for leadership and the rise of the Imperial Presidency (most notably Presidents Johnson and Nixon). Ironically, the rise of the Imperial Presidency coincides with historians' rejection of the 'great man' view of historical causation; while the popular view that Ronald Reagan was a great president suggests we should seriously reconsider the position traditionally ascribed to others. The regular polls of American historians on the greatness (or otherwise) of US presidents have shown interesting changes as the liberal consensus of the 1960s gave way to the New Right in the 1980s. Meanwhile the rise of the United Nations and the emphasis on the right to self-determination in Asia and Africa raise some awkward questions. What, if anything, did Woodrow Wilson mean by the right to self-determination?[4] How far has the US supported self-determination in practice as opposed to theory? How does it fit with the history of the protectorates the US established in Central America after 1911 and was to revive in the period of the Cold War? Why is US foreign policy so intolerant of Iraq and so tolerant of Israel?

The Gladstonian view of British history

A second model of democratization, which I shall call the Gladstonian view, is rooted in the so-called 'Whig view of history' as 'the story of our liberty', and continues to underlie the story of what Huntington (1991) was later to call the 'First Wave' democracies.

> According to this view, all Englishmen [sic] were beneficiaries of the centuries-long evolution of constitutional liberties, achieved for the most part by gradualist methods which respected the past. Though usually known as the 'Whig interpretation of history' it was in fact bipartisan and effectively reinforced the legitimacy of the country's political institutions. In its foremost champions it inspired an almost mystical reverence for the English [sic] way in politics. (Tosh 1991: 7)

This Whig view of history received its last and certainly its most effective popular statement in Lord Macaulay's famous 4-volume *History of England* (1848–55). Deliberately written to achieve popular literary success, it achieved this objective triumphantly, becoming required reading for the educated in both Britain and the United States. It is also, as Tosh (1991: 33) argues, 'a significant primary source' in its own right 'for anyone studying the political and social assumptions of the early Victorian elite'.

The Whig view (shared by the American colonists) that the reign of King George III posed a challenge to this orderly process of development was later to be decisively challenged by Lewis Namier (1929). Setting aside the assertions and counter-assertions of politicians, and basing his case on the immense archive of the Duke of Newcastle and the correspondence of other leading politicians of the period, he demonstrated that party structure in the nineteenth-century sense had yet to develop. Furthermore, the power of the Court to influence electoral outcomes was much less than had previously been assumed. Above all, Namier made clear that both George I and George II were much more active rulers than had long been thought, so that in taking a similar role George III was acting fully within the Constitution as it was understood at the time. Still, each generation rewrites history in the light of contemporary debates. History is distilled by education into the common knowledge of the public; but the process is slow, and it takes a long time for revisionist views to find their way into common currency.

The public were happy to accept the view of Gladstone, who contrasted the US Founders' act of creativity with the slow development of the British Constitution, which to him had had an equally successful outcome; the full quotation is indeed: 'As the British Constitution is the most subtle organism which has proceeded from the womb and long gestation of progressive history, so the American Constitution is, so far as I can see, the most wonderful work ever struck off at a given time by the brain and purpose of man.'[5] But did Britain have a Constitution then, and does it today? There are, it is true, a number of written documents that establish constitutional principles, so that today the Constitution is regarded as uncodified rather than unwritten. But the perception of the British Constitution in its modern form is largely the creation not of historians but of the lawyer Walter Bagehot, in his *The English Constitution* (1871), with a new edition containing an additional chapter published the following year. It is now commonplace that Bagehot did not so much describe the Constitution as it was, but argue how it could and should develop. It is also true that many of its main features were either challenged or modified in the last quarter of the twentieth century.

So too have been our views of earlier stages in the evolution of representative government and popular participation. In the seventeenth century the theory of the Norman Yoke held that the natural liberties of Anglo-Saxon society had been subverted by the imposition of an alien French-speaking monarchy. Stubbs's (1866) compilation of charters began to lay bare the raw material for the actual study of the period, and to show how very different were the assumptions of the period from those of later generations. With time the harsher views of the seventeenth century have been modified. Clarendon (unexpectedly) was the first to try to give a balanced view of Oliver Cromwell, in his *The History of the Rebellion and Civil Wars in England* (1702–4). Carlyle, in *Oliver Cromwell's Letters and Speeches* (1857), established Cromwell as a 'great man', if not necessarily a very congenial one, and not always on the soundest of evidence. Whatever he was, Cromwell was not a dictator; the history of the protectorate is a lesson in the limits of constitutionalism. However despite the work of historians, the traditional view dies hard. Lord Rosebery failed to convince the House of Commons that it should commemorate with a statue someone who with all his faults had been a great Parliamentarian. The statue that now actually stands and that he unveiled he paid for himself. Churchill's imaginative proposal to name a battleship after the Lord Protector was vetoed by George V (see Davis 2001: 50, 54–6, 59, 64).

Victorian histories now seem particularly dated because they associate the success of British representative government with the expansion of the Empire, and in the post-Imperial age these two objectives are seen as being incompatible. Yet for over a hundred years a belief in progress and Imperial expansion went hand in hand. J. R. Seeley, who was appointed Regius Professor of History at Cambridge in 1869, was an active politician, given a political appointment, and the effective founder of the Cambridge historical school. As author of *The Expansion of England* (1883) he was a pioneer of Imperial history; he is best known today for his remark that the British Empire had been acquired 'in a fit of absence of mind'. For Seeley the main concern of history was with politics: 'History is past politics: politics is present history' (cited in Burke 1991: 3). In fact, in his inaugural lecture he rather surprisingly called for Cambridge to teach political science – an excellent idea that was not to be heeded for nearly a century.

The multi-volume *A Short History of the English People* by J. R. Green (1893) is important because in it he turned away from what he termed derisively 'drum and trumpet history'. His early emphasis on social history was very popular, but it had the limitation that it relied almost exclusively on literary sources. It was to be left to the twentieth century to try to find other sources that would give a better idea as to what the public actually thought, an essential precondition of understanding. In Britain it was only on the eve of the Second World War that the Mass Observation project, a pioneering effort by a sociologist and an anthropologist to find out what the people in general really thought, was organized on a sufficiently large scale not only to be valid social science, but also to offer a reliable source for future historians.[6] Reasonably accurate public opinion polling only came into general use after 1945.

Long before that, Social Darwinism, which assumed that a democratic Britain had the right to rule over many millions who did not have any say in Imperial policy, was explicitly challenged by the early socialist H. G. Wells, as for instance in his novel *The War in the Air* (1908). Wells was not a trained historian, but when he came to write his history of the world he was the first to set the history of humankind in the setting of the natural world. His book was concise, clear and immensely popular. Yet the impact of his ideas came rather through asides in his many popular novels (such titles as *The History of Mr Polly* and *Tono Bungay*), and his vision of the future in *A Modern Utopia*, of a world ruled by an educated Samurai elite, is far from democratic. In the 1990s the term 'meritocracy', originally intended to be critical, was converted into a New Labour ideal.

With the post-1945 end of Empire British politicians came to assume a 'special relationship' with the US, embodied by Winston Churchill the politician in the notion of the 'three spheres' of British interests. As an author and (less probably) a Nobel prizewinner for literature Churchill (1956) spelt out his belief in the common historical heritage of the English-speaking peoples in *A History of the English-speaking Peoples* (1956). In political battles post-1953 the dominant myth is one of decline (it is not always clear whether relative or absolute). In the 1980s 'heritage', with all that that means for the simplification and popularization of history, emerges as the basis for nostalgia. The Constitution becomes a bulwark of 'little Englandism' against the 'European federal superstate'. Logically, former imperialists should have welcomed a European superstate as an alternative; in practice the myth of the Anglo-Saxon mission to be different was too strong. And the political notion of the Anglo-Saxon, whether in France or the UK, has had little or nothing to do with the scholarly research on the Anglo-Saxon period, any more than the Scots followers of Celtic Football Club are likely to know that some scholars now have doubts whether there ever really were any such people as Celts!

One thing is clear: historians did not (and do not) have a common view on what constitutes democratization. Conversely, little historical work on the micro-management of political systems finds its way into the common discourse. A striking example was the way in which the debate on devolution in the UK was dominated by the Tory argument that any compromising of the rigid formalistic structure of the UK would inevitably lead to its disintegration. Yet this argument was comprehensively refuted a century ago. In Ireland, where they might be expected to know, hardly anyone disputes that the failure to grant Home Rule in time discredited the moderate nationalists and opened the way to Sínn Féin. Similarly, George Dangerfield in 1936 dramatized *The Strange Death of Liberal England*, helping to consolidate the view that the decline of liberalism and the rise of Labour was in some sense inevitable. Yet the pattern in other Commonwealth countries was very different, and it can be argued that the Liberal Party rather than Labour was the real victim of the 1931 political coup and the so-called National Government. Until devolution rendered it inevitable, the post-1931 Labour Party as a matter of consistent policy blocked any attempt at any level to enter into coalition with other parties, helping to ensure that the UK could not develop its own distinctive form of consociational democracy.

The popular picture of the democratization of Britain, in fact, still focuses on the mid-to-late nineteenth century. It is perhaps irretrievably distorted for most of the British public by the facts (a) that the account of far-away parliamentary battles is not intrinsically very interesting and (b) that, perhaps inevitably, democratization proceeds more easily in that absence of charismatic figures. Despite (or perhaps because of) an unhealthy interest in his relationships with 'fallen women', Gladstone means little to the modern televsion audience. Disraeli has been more fortunate, for obvious reasons.

The French Revolutionary tradition

A third model, which dominated romantic thought in the nineteenth century but is currently less fashionable to democratizers, is that of the French Revolution. Here we see even more clearly the impact of the Enlightenment and of neoclassicism. The Revolution, however, is Republican rather than democratic, and it has a dual legacy: the Republic and Bonapartism. To complicate matters, French perceptions of the Revolution have inevitably been conditioned by the emergence in France of the 'New History'. French historians influenced by Fernand Braudel and Lucien Febvre regard events as only significant as key to currents underneath. Yet it should come as no surprise that despite the influence of the *Annales* school, leading French historians such as Georges Duby and Le Roy Ladurie do not in practice reject narrative. Furthermore, Soboul (1965) makes it clear in his brief introduction to the French Revolution not only that for him it is the product of struggle between social classes and groups, and that its outcome was the overthrow of the aristocracy, the rise of the bourgeoisie and the disintegration of the popular movement, but that no other interpretation is possible. Hence he himself situates his work squarely within 'the classical historiography of the French Revolution', making clear the continuity of his interpretation with that of Alexis de Tocqueville by quoting the latter's comment that the Revolution's 'real purpose was to do away everywhere with what remained of the institutions of the Middle Ages' (Soboul 1965: 1).

It may be that every strand in French politics has its own view of the Revolution. But the sources are abundant, the narrative follows established lines, and only the analysis is open to question. The French Revolution, however, is not just a major historical event (or sequence of events). For later writers, notably for Marx and Engels, it was the type example of revolution. Hence its role in opening up access to political power for new social groups and classes has not only been disputed for its own sake. It has also been caught up through the use of comparative history in the wider debate about the nature of revolution and its capacity to further democratization (see Brinton 1952). Here too disagreements are much less profound than appears at first sight. The thesis of the US historian of the French Revolution, R. R. Palmer (1959, 1964), that events in France formed only part (if a major part) of an Atlantic Revolution, a democratic revolution not only in the larger states on both sides of the Atlantic but also in the smaller ones, has long since come to be generally accepted (a similar thesis was put forward independently by Jacques Godechot at around the same time in Paris). This has obvious significance for the evolution of popular government. Yet even this is open to reinterpretation – for example, in his short study of the Revolution Roberts (1997) places his emphasis not on its ambiguous role as an opening to democracy, but on the way in which the collapse of old institutions opened the way to social and economic modernization. It is significant also, perhaps, and certainly surprising, that Huntington himself dates his 'first wave' not from 1776, but from 1828.

A serious weaknesses of method of comparative history, however, lies in the superabundance of data and the vast number of variables involved, which creates a pressure to simplify that can easily eliminate obvious contrasts. There can be no denying the impact on nineteenth-century Europe and Latin America of the Declaration of the Rights of Man and of the Citizen. They served as an inspiration for the constitutional revolutions of 1830 and 1848, and continued to exert some influence at least as late as the Mexican Revolution of 1910. Three more specific contributions were the abolition of slavery (France, the first country to decree the abolition of slavery was, however, also the first country to restore it), republicanism, and the principle of universal male suffrage (often modified). Starting with Louis de Bourrienne's *Memoirs of Napoleon* (1836) we can also see the rival effect of the Bonapartist myth of the Great Man whose liberating armies cleared the way for freedom in the Low Countries, Italy and Germany. And at the bicentenary of the French Revolution, the conservative view that the Revolution was above all messy and bloodthirsty had clearly gained ground. It was even questionable whether it had anything to do with democratization (Schama 2000 [1989]). In this Margaret Thatcher evidently concurred: reading between the lines it is clear that nothing that had happened in France appeared to her of any significance, but anything that was significant had happened in England first.

Conclusion

The Enlightenment ideals that fuelled the Revolution, though, still survive to show how far sometimes the reality fell short of the initial bright hopes, not just in France, but in the transitions from autocracy to democracy in the 'Third Wave' since 1989. It is, after all, equally true that neither Gladstonian democracy nor American exceptionalism are as convincing now as they were in their day. Yet the common ideal of democracy lives on, and perhaps the main lesson of history is not to expect too much, too soon. If, as the Chinese premier Zhou Enlai is supposed to have said, when asked what he thought of the French Revolution, it was 'too early to tell',[7] then there must be plenty of work for historians before they will reach agreement on what has happened since 1989.

Notes

1 Leopold von Ranke, *Histories of the Latin and German Nations from 1494 to 1514* (first publ. 1824), quoted in Gooch (1952: 74).

2 It is, after all, the only technique available to the philosopher.

3 Bemis (1937) and Bailey (1940) represent the East Coast and West Coast views respectively.

4 Seaman (1966: 80) sees Wilson's failure to define self-determination as 'one of the great disasters of modern history'.

5 Famous Quotes, www.constitutionfacts.com/qbody.shtml.

6 See Madge and Harisson (1939).

7 Cited in *Asiaweek*, 26, No. 46, 24 November 2000.

6

International Political Economy

PHILIP CERNY

International Political Economy, domestic politics and democracy

International Political Economy (IPE) had already achieved prominence as a field of study by the start of the 21st century, but its role has changed dramatically, with issues of democratic governance and policy-making moving to the forefront. Originally, however, the roots of IPE lay in economic aspects of relations among nation-states in the international system – foreign economic policy, trade, the spread of production systems and firms across borders, and the international monetary system, as well as a range of international economic institutions and regimes and the interaction between domestic and international policy issues – but not with domestic politics within states. In mainstream International Relations theory, states are seen as sovereign 'unit actors', independent decision-makers of last resort, whose domestic structures are hierarchical but whose bottom line is their very survival in an anarchical world of external danger and threat. Domestic politics, in contrast, has the luxury of being able to rise above considerations of survival and power, and can paradoxically pursue 'higher' values such as the common good, welfare, liberty, equality and democracy.

However, unlike most traditional analyses of foreign policy and security studies, IPE has always had the potential to cut across this levels-of-analysis distinction. As the world has become a smaller place (the idea of the 'global village'), analysts increasingly focus on issues involving the interaction, linkages and common features of both international and domestic politics at the same time. It is not merely boundaries between the international and the domestic that are crossed, moreover, but also those between politics on the one hand and other dimensions of globalization as well – economic, social, geographical, environmental and cultural. Observers have thus come to focus on more complex processes, primarily globalization.

Most analyses of globalization today see the international political economy as relatively unregulated and increasingly integrated across borders, mixing the anarchical and the hierarchical in new ways. The political conclusion drawn from this is that existing domestic structures, including democratic policy-making, must be adapted to deal with the imperatives of such a world. Broadly speaking, when nation-states could still be insulated to some extent from international and transnational economic trends during the period of the Long Boom after the Second World War through to the late 1960s, liberal democratic national governments could trade off a certain amount of economic inefficiency for a bit more social justice. Social policy, in particular, was seen as a relatively autonomous, inherently domestic issue area that could be debated and dealt with through a combination of ethics and voter choices. The domestic left–right spectrum, rooted in the late 19th and early 20th centuries and focused on the redistribution of resources among social groups, constituted the fundamental parameters of democratic policy choice.

Globalization has undermined these economic conditions. As international trade has increased and tariffs have been drastically reduced, much of manufacturing industry and even small businesses have had to become more import-sensitive, export-oriented, multinational and dependent on global financial markets for investment. Multinational capital looks increasingly to trade off capital-intensive, high-value-added processes in the advanced industrial (or post-industrial) countries for cheap-labour production in labour-intensive industries located in China and less developed countries. Meanwhile technological change – especially information and communications technology, the lowering of transport costs and the increasing flexibility of production methods – and the growth of service industries undermine trade unions' ability to pressurize employers and governments to protect their members. The result is fragmentation of traditional class identities and political loyalties too. The globalization of financial markets and firms has caused interest rates to converge across borders, rewarded the purveyors of 'hot money', and made anti-inflationary policies and a new embedded financial orthodoxy the touchstones of governments' monetary policy.

In addition to these more direct effects – imposing a new embedded financial orthodoxy on the state and emulating business models of organization – globalization has two indirect political effects. In the first place, it fosters a wider ideology of the *marketization* of public policy and of the state apparatus itself. This is supplanting what social historians call 'status' by 'contract' as the dominant mode of social relations – the replacement of customary entitlement to goods and services, based on a priori social position, class or standing, with contracts negotiated on the basis of price and/or reciprocal rights and obligations. In the second place, globalization has led political actors across the party spectrum to alter their policy prescriptions to adapt to what they see as the 'realities' of a more open and globalizing world. That means not only making policy more economically 'efficient' but also reshaping their underlying political coalitions as various social groups fragment, shrink or expand in response to new global constraints and opportunities.

These changes alter some of the most fundamental elements of the way democracy works in the contemporary world. At one level, liberal democracy as we know it did not become a major mode of governance in modern times simply because of the abstract progression of ideas about the best way to achieve a better society or polity. On the contrary, its origins and dynamics sprang from the process of consolidating the nation-state and, indirectly, the international system of states. Those groups, whether elite or more popularly-based, that came to see themselves as having a stake in the emerging nation-state order consequently wished to stabilize and control the manifest and latent conflicts inherent in that order, especially with the coming of industrialization and mass politicization. They increasingly found it useful to do so through the uneven but widening inclusion into the system of individuals and groups who might otherwise threaten that stability and control rather than continuing with the increasingly knotty and counter-productive strategy of bypassing and repressing them (Laslett 1970). Thus modern liberal democracy has from the start been inextricably intertwined with the development of the modern nation-state.

Today, however, cross-cutting and overlapping governance structures and processes increasingly take quasi-private, oligarchic forms. At the same time many of the more inter-ventionist and redistributive instruments of public and social policy that had developed over decades in response to democratic demands are being undermined in a world of marketization and commodification. The result is the emergence of a range of often *ad hoc* public and private governance structures that constrain the democratic state from above and below, leaving an untidy jumble of overlapping and competing institutions, often only semi-formed, and increasingly lacking in democratic accountability. This uneven dispersal of authority and 'governmentality' – the effective capacity to exercise power – goes hand in hand with a fragmentation of identities, the alienation of a grow-ing number of individuals and groups from democratic political processes and an erosion of commitment to ideas of the public interest.

Thus globalization constrains both the state's capacity to act upon traditional collectivist – interventionist and redistributive – demands and actors' ability to build coali-tions around those demands. Increased structural complexity is altering the range of public goods the state can effectively supply, moving away from those that take activities out of the marketplace to those that actually reinforce and promote marketization. The former include such policies as nationalization of industry or the provision of monopoly public and social services, the latter being exemplified by privatization and regulatory reforms that include both deregulation and pro-market re-regulation. Another example is the agenda of so-called 'new public management' or 'rein-venting government' (including the welfare state) along busi-ness lines.

Furthermore, however, globalization is also generating new and more complex forms of social, economic and political pluralism – not merely the benign pluralism of

mid-twentieth-century democratic theory, but rather the
more unequal and disequilibrating kind called 'neo-
pluralism' (Lindblom 1977). In neo-pluralism, those social,
economic and political actors with the greatest access to
material and social resources predominate, but are not necessarily in control. And even powerful actors are unlikely to
agree with each other on every issue, even where they may
have common priorities, such as the promotion of some
particular version of capitalism. Moreover, there may be
other distinct groups that have resources they can mobilize,
and rules to appeal to, especially in liberal democratic
political systems; they are able to exert leverage and punch
above their weight in crucial situations. So outcomes tend
to be determined not simply by coercion and/or structural
power but by how coalitions and networks are built among
a plurality of actors in real-time circumstances. In a globalizing world, the changing distribution of resources and
balance of power between old and new actors are producing
new inequalities and disparities of power and the fragmentation of traditional social classes (Murphy 2002).

Therefore individuals and groups are less drawn to promote their causes or make their demands through the
formally institutionalized democratic processes. Instead,
they seek out specialized niches for exercising influence,
in what has become a more heterogeneous but unequal
or asymmetrical transnational opportunity structure (for
elaboration see Cerny 2000a) – what Hülsemeyer (2003)
characterizes rather grandly as a kind of quasi-corporatism
at meso and micro levels. Nevertheless globalization,
although fostering this uneven pluralization of politics,
does not provide effective systemic outlets, regulated by
democratic processes equivalent to those found within
nation-states, for those groups' demands and goals. On the
contrary, it creates a world of special interests, domestic
and transnational quangos (quasi non-governmental organizations), private regimes and inter- (and intra-) institutional
conflict and competition, thereby frustrating any aspirations to develop a genuinely transnational or cosmopolitan
democracy. It is too late to insulate and recreate the kind
of nation-state that characterized Polanyi's 'Great Transformation' (Polanyi 1944). But the world order has yet to
see a coherent successor structure; instead, there is more a

quasi-medieval combination of competing and overlapping institutions, authorities, jurisdictions, interests, pressures and demands.

Democracy, globalization and the nation-state

Both democracy and globalization are deeply contested concepts. Democracy has several theoretical fault lines, but there are two sets of intertwined questions that dominate traditional debates about democratic theory. The first concerns the concept of 'rule by the people' (the etymological meaning of the word 'democracy'). What or who are 'the people'? And what institutional form might (can? should?) a democratic superstructure take in pursuing what the people want, whether holistic or fragmented, centralized or decentralized? The second concerns the generic functions of states or governments. The potential range is vast, from a minimalist concern with the rule of law to the larger ambition to pursue a revolutionary restructuring of society. Possibilities for direct or indirect participation, popular sovereignty, sense of common purpose, freedom, equality and the like have all faced quite different sets of real-world opportunities and constraints, depending on whether they were applied in small groups, city-states, feudal societies, empires, nation-states, or international (inter-state) institutions or whatever.

In the last analysis, however, some form of effective centripetal sovereign authority rooted in distinct territories was arrived at by historical trial and error as being necessary (if not sufficient) for the democratic resolution of deep-seated conflicts among competing interests and values. Some minimal overall level of endogenous structural coherence and exogenous structural autonomy has been required for stability and effective governmentality. Thus what we instinctively think of as 'modern democracy' has been built on the presumption that the underlying 'society' that is to be democratically governed is a coherent *national* society, and that the democratic state by its very nature is (or should be) an expression of that society if it is to be stable, effective and legitimate.

Furthermore, the state in a globalizing context, while increasingly constrained in pursuing certain kinds of collective goods (macroeconomic management, social welfare, fiscal policy, control of the money supply and exchange rate policy, trade and industrial policy are just some possible examples) also possesses a range of roles that contribute to globalization's growth. This is partly a matter of trading new functions for old, as states search for different ways of securing national economic and political advantage. Indeed, in their search for global competitiveness states may adopt practices that actually undermine their own autonomy and policy capacity, and irretrievably so (see Cerny 2000b), especially when promoting market sectors characterized by relatively non-specific asset-based structures (Cerny 1995). And paradoxically the state may even expand certain of its roles and functions, such as that of monitoring and enforcing market-based regulatory structures – for example, strengthened policing of insider trading rules, accounting standards, corporate governance and the like – as an inherent part of the globalization process. Indeed, formal sovereignty and the rule of law at the level of the state are increasingly taking on this global 'enforcement function' (Streeck 1996).

If democracy is seen as primarily about pluralism and individual or group autonomy, then of course the complexities of globalization are such that it may foster increased diversity and possibilities for autonomy. This is the argument for 'cosmopolitan democracy' as developed most notably by Held (1995), and it may be appealing to some social movements like the feminist movement, or for transnational interest and cause associations, or for certain ethnic groups. However, the more democracy is seen to involve some collective values such as social justice achieved through redistribution, and to require the provision of those collective goods the market will not provide, then the greater the challenge that globalization with all its diversification and differentiation poses. Put differently, democratic governance must possess a significant element of collective accountability and authoritative (but not merely repressive) policy capacity (governmentality) if it is to be genuinely democratic. Globalization threatens this democratic chain of accountability.

Western nation-states only managed to achieve genuine structural cohesion after several centuries of uneven consolidation, trial-and-error and solidarizing international conflict/competition. This was done by adopting systems of election and representation and the transformation of hierarchical repressive structures into quasi-'rational' public bureaucracies subordinated to political officials and agreed rules of the game. Despite being 'sub-optimal' structures in all sorts of ways, modern states resembling Max Weber's bureaucratic model emerged as being the least relatively inefficient institutional framework for long-term contracting domestically and entering into credible commitments externally in a world of rapid and uneven economic, social and political change (Spruyt 1994). In an increasingly stalemated power balance in post-feudal Europe, proto-nation-states took on an ever-wider set of tasks, roles and activities. Standing armies, taxation systems, the promotion of economic development where it was necessary for war or brought more wealth into the coffers of the state, the search for financial backing from holders of private or quasi-private capital, and the administrative (bureaucratic and regulatory) structures necessary for overseeing and coordinating such activities all increasingly became part of the state apparatus. The apparatus may have revolved around a revered monarchy; but it became a growing imperative for states to survive the threat and often the reality of international war. The feudal system of entrenched privileges, status-based castes, fluid territorial frontiers, entailed property, competing institutions, overlapping jurisdictions and multiple loyalties was eroded, overwhelmed and co-opted into nation-state political structures and allegiances.

Such centripetal state structures also reached deeper and deeper into society, and fostered economic developments that uprooted sections of society, ranging from noble to serf, from their status-bound situations and pushed and pulled them into contractual relations with each other as well as with other individuals and groups. In contrast to feudal society, overlapping webs of negotiated (and renegotiated) contractual relationships were drawn into the orbit of the state and its legal, regulatory and developmental framework. The state claimed overall authority and responsibility for the well-being of the 'whole', while that whole became increasingly pluralistic. Indeed, as more mass groups became uprooted from their subsumed, generally rural status and were involved in more contractual labour processes and given the promise of political citizenship, they had to be included too. Because of the international expansion of the modern capitalist world-system, expectations of growing inclusion became entrenched in both popular and elite culture (Anderson 1991). If monarchs (or their ministers) claimed to be pursuing the common good of the people and wanted the people to pay taxes and even to follow the Crown to their deaths in its name, then they faced a growing need to elicit some sort of quasi-voluntary acquiescence or consent. People had to be both inspired and bought off. To grant some sort of symbolic participatory privileges in the state itself, along with meeting growing claims for civil rights and welfare – paid for by taxes levied on capitalist economic growth – became an increasingly efficient means of controlling free-riding. Liberal democracy is thus profoundly 'locked-in' to the development of the nation-state – and the states system.

Globalization and corrosive pressures on the nation-state

Several factors and trends are usually seen to characterize the globalization process. First, there is the internationalization of markets. There are, of course, as many different kinds of market structures as there are industrial sectors, and some markets are more globalized than others (McMillan 2002; Fligstein 2001). Globalized markets are markets where, broadly speaking, products are substitutable and widely traded across borders. Capital is increasingly mobile, not particularly site-specific, and will move to different locations if profits there are higher (and secure). Consumption patterns in different countries are not mutually exclusive, or at least can be catered to by extending the product range; and prices are sensitive across borders and predominantly set in world (cross-border) markets. Economic globalization is also driven by new flexible, 'post-Fordist' production techniques, superseding the workplace organizational innovations pioneered by the Ford Motor Company in the 1920s

(Amin 1994). Recent electronics-based developments in information and communications technology are also crucial for co-ordinating these changes, transforming industrial sectors from within, shifting the balance of economic activities from manufacturing to services, and multiplying the productivity of capital. Financial services, finally, form the backbone of any international market economy by setting the price of capital and by establishing the framework within which prices for other products are determined; they too increasingly involve pure information products and processes.

In public policy terms, whereas a Keynesian approach to macroeconomic management was once the norm, any attempt to revive or return to its essentials would be extremely difficult, because of increasing vulnerability to the mobility of capital, both at home and across borders. Mesoeconomic and microeconomic interventions by governments are increasingly shaped by the perceived need to maintain or regain international competitiveness, not by objectives of domestic welfare goals. The regulatory power and effectiveness of the state in a range of sectors is seen as eroding through 'regulatory arbitrage' – firms choosing to locate where regulation is most favourable and/or using such a possibility to pressure governments to deregulate. And the growing complex cross-border linkages between firms, domestic socio-economic groups (and indeed between individuals as both producers and consumers) and transnational and transgovernmental interest groups and policy networks are widely seen to undermine the sense of overarching national identity and loyalty cherished by political thinkers, leaders and movements of various ideological complexions in the modern era.

Social and cultural changes are also challenging the discourse and social reality of the nation-state. The pace of information flows and the attention to image-building that characterize the modern media, along with the fragmentation of post-modern culture and the growing salience of multicultural identity-formation, create a disorienting disarticulation of previously embedded cultures both from above (the 'global village' combined with the 'clash of civilizations') and below (such as ethnic sub-and-cross-nationalism and alienation of ghettoized minorities). These interacting forms of social and cultural fragmentation are undermining over-arching national identities based on the reconciliation of conflict and competition among contending groups that have underpinned the widespread acceptance of the democratic rules of the game.

Finally, states themselves are deeply involved in the glob-alization process. State actors, in seeking to placate those domestic constituencies that can eject governments in democratically organized elections, are finding that sources of side-payments can only be expanded (or their shrinkage avoided) by promoting international competitiveness. Policy instruments are dismantled and disarmed, strategic compet-ences broken up through liberalization and privatization, state agencies either hived off or made more independent of central control, transgovernmental policy networks ex-panded, and institutional gatekeepers (such as central banks) set to enforce international market discipline on their own state apparatuses. These developments are pluralizing, unbundling and disarticulating state tasks, roles and activ-ities. The confluence of these variables creates splintered states and fragmented authority. It blurs the boundaries between both state and private sector responsibilities and capacities, on the one hand, and domestic and international decision-making networks, on the other. And it is not just the effectiveness of democratic governance that it under-mines. It erodes the very confidence and trust – legitimacy or 'system affect' (Almond and Verba 1965) – essential for democratic systems to convince people of the value and utility of democracy, engage them in participatory processes like elections, and make them feel secure in the belief that their voices are being heard.

The impact of globalization on democratic governance

This process has knock-on effects at several levels. The first has been the 'fiscal crisis of the state' (O'Connor 1973), or what has recently been termed 'fiscal degradation'. The costs not only of expanding but even of just maintaining state functions and structures began to outstrip sources of taxation and other income after only two decades of the

Long Boom itself. On both left and right, growing social and economic functions of the state were blamed. The Phillips Curve (which posits an inverse relationship between rates of inflation and of unemployment) was replaced in the public (or at least the elite) imagination by the Laffer Curve (which states a close relationship between tax rates, revenue and productivity). The second effect was that the Long Boom involved an expansion of international trade and financial flows. That at first reinforced domestic economic management and the social democratic functions of the industrial and welfare state (through 'embedded liberalism': Ruggie 1983). But it also quickly built up both political and market pressures for financial liberalization, which rendered states increasingly vulnerable to international capital mobility. In this context, the question of allotting specific rights and obligations to particular individuals (and legal 'persons' such as firms) becomes more complicated. The explicit association of democratic rights with a specific geographical entity is greatly weakened, as those rights cannot be so easily located in spatial terms. Some individuals and groups (but not others) can 'arbitrage' rights between different locations, searching out the best conditions for their own requirements, while avoiding obligations. The ability of governments equitably to provide welfare and public goods in general becomes less geographically controllable.

At another level, whereas at the beginning of the 1960s private international capital markets were highly restricted and the great majority of international capital flows were public flows, by the mid-1970s, following the breakdown of Bretton Woods, such private capital markets mushroomed. They overwhelmed both public reserves and publicly-sanctioned international capital flows. In the money and finance issue-area, for example, for governments to have both monetary policy autonomy and effective exchange rate control, capital controls must be introduced and enforced (B. J. Cohen 1996; Goodman and Pauly 1993). With the collapse of the Bretton Woods system, states abandoned continuous control of exchange rates in the name of domestic monetarism. Indeed, it increasingly seems that without capital controls neither exchange rate control *nor* autonomous monetary policy can be maintained, leading to increased emphasis on anti-inflationary policy in general, attempting where possible to balance budgets at lower levels of taxation and expenditure. In this context the last few years have witnessed growing instability in global financial markets, creating a vicious circle. Given the increased weight and autonomy of private international financial markets, future decisions on monetary as well as fiscal policy are likely to lie beyond the effective scope of national democratic control. At the same time, international financial markets possess few autonomous enforcement mechanisms with which to punish or deter free-riders. The liberalization of market rules (often misleadingly called 'deregulation') creates knock-on effects beyond borders and impacts on not merely short-term international capital flows but longer-term investment patterns too. Consequently, a process of regulatory arbitrage has developed in which market actors pressure governments to open their markets and liberalize their regulatory systems.

Even state legal systems – the core framework of national sovereignty – are increasingly being bypassed, especially by the most internationally-linked firms and market actors. The changing nature of public–private relationships, accelerated and deepened by the crystallization of private sector interconnections across borders, is leading to the development of new legal approaches and procedures that are replacing what Held (1995) has called 'democratic public law' with negotiated private law. At the level of the nation-state, this is leading to the emergence of a 'new administrative law' embodying and embedding transnational and global dynamics at the heart of the state (Aman 1999). And at the transnational level, private arbitration procedures involving multinational corporations and other private market actors are not simply shoring up but often substituting for national-level dispute resolution and, indirectly, regulatory rulemaking processes (Cutler, forthcoming 2003).

A further impact of globalization on states involves a host of *ad hoc* international and transnational institutions and regimes that have been appearing for some time now. While these regimes have traditionally been set up and/or backed by the authority of states, analysts in recent years have noticed a trend towards the emergence of an increasing number of private regimes, or regimes where the balance of authority and decision-making influence is shifting towards private actors. These developments are sometimes presented as a quasi-democratization of the international system, by international and transnational co-operative mechanisms that are supposedly replacing realist anarchy with multi-lateral co-operation. However, they can also be seen as the extension at international level of a kind of oligarchic societal corporatism. Although in the past 'private interest governments' have usually been seen to derive their effect-iveness and authority from direct or indirect delegation of state authority (Streeck and Schmitter 1985), now there is an increasingly dense web of transnational private interest governments crystallizing.

Finally, globalization erodes the capacity of the state to provide physical security. The end of the Cold War, far from ushering in a more stable peaceful world, has instead seen an increase in new theatres and forms of violent conflict. Violence today is less and less the province of national governments and more and more the domain of ethnic groups, drugs cartels and mafias, mercenaries and paramil-itaries linked to firms and other sub-state or cross-national organizations. This is true not only in the Second and Third Worlds, but in the First World too, as private security firms increasingly supplement or replace public police forces, prisons, and so on. Anarchy in the international system is no longer confined to conflicts between states, and at home the state no longer holds an effective monopoly of legitim-ate violence. There are strong grounds for arguing that the fundamental bond of physical security and protection, which has legitimated nation-state structures in general and provided a bottom line for democratic legitimacy too, is continually eroding (Cerny 2000c).

Concluding thoughts: what next for democratic governance?

States today are increasingly bad at certain key tasks that are important for democratic responsiveness, accountability and effectiveness. These underperformed tasks include re-distribution, regulation and the delivery of public services. Social neoliberals, for example the 'reinventing government' school, try to make a virtue out of this: 'Governments should steer but not row', say Osborne and Gaebler (1992). However, the power and capacity of the state is being eroded most rapidly and most thoroughly where more mobile factors of capital can most easily 'exit' state jurisdiction in one way or another.

Nevertheless, states still remain relatively good at certain tasks, and some of those tasks may indeed be expanded and reinforced. Governmentality remains strongest or is being most effectively reconstituted where more immobile factors of capital are concerned. Labour, particularly low skilled labour, is one of these; such people have fewer of the resources necessary for exercising the 'exit' option. Minimal welfare states will therefore have to be maintained and restructured (Clayton and Pontusson 1998), unless societies are prepared to risk the unrest and political destabilization that could arise where there is no public safety net. Furthermore, the state is still relatively good at prudential regulation and *ex post facto* enforcement of contracts, as well as the promotion of certain forms of competitive advantage in a more open world through limited industrial and trade policy measures.

In fact, however, what the state is best at – indeed, some would say, what the state has always been best at – is enforcing the norms generated and decisions made at the international and transnational levels. As long as market outcomes, the transformation of production processes, technological innovation, socio-cultural globalization, and the marketization of the competition state combine to transform nation-state structures and processes, state capacity in terms of enforcement will continue to grow and state functions expand along pro-market lines. This of course presumes the continuing absence of effective direct international 'police powers' and judicial/legal systems. However, the processes of enforcement will increasingly involve norms, rules and decisions that will *not* in the first place have been arrived at by democratic procedures. Indeed, in structural terms the world may come to look somewhat more like the Middle Ages again. The relevant characteristics can be summarized as: (a) competing institutions with overlapping jurisdictions (states, regimes, transgovernmental networks, private interest governments); (b) more fluid territorial boundaries, both within and across states; (c) contested property rights and legal boundaries; (d) a growing alienation between global innovation, communication and resource nodes (global cities) and disfavoured, fragmented hinterlands; (e) increased inequalities and isolation of permanent sub-castes (the underclass); (f) multiple and/or fragmented loyalties (ethnic conflict and multiculturalism); and (g) the spread of what Alain Minc (1993) has called 'zones grises', or geographical areas and social contexts where the rule of law does not run (both localized ghettoes and international criminal activities) (Cerny 1998).

We now live in an era of increasing expectations, events that assume global dimensions, and extremely rapid diffusion of information, together with relentless technological innovation. Against this background further changes may either accentuate post-modernistic fragmentation, producing the breakdown of nations and states, or alternatively lead towards the imposition of increasingly hierarchical 'global governance'. Contemporary debates on democracy and democratization in International Political Economy tend to pit the kind of neomedievalist, fragmentation-of-governance thesis presented above against what is often seen to be the more idealist 'cosmopolitan democracy' thesis (Archibugi and Held 1995). There is also a third position – that the ability of states to reconstruct governmentality is still strong and that social democracy can be reconstituted along more familiar statist lines by incorporating some neoliberal features (Hirst and Thompson 1999; Giddens 1998). Nevertheless, the task of globalizing the democratic chain – recreating effective governmentality and establishing the capacity of authoritative international agents to make the kind of side-payments and engage in the kind of monitoring necessary to control free-riding and assimilate a huge range of alienated groups into such a society – is daunting. 'Really existing democracy' as we have known it during the evolution of the nation-state and the states system is likely to function much less effectively in this emerging world of fragmented globalization.

7
Law

JOHN MCELDOWNEY

This chapter offers a legal perspective on democratization by focusing on a tightly linked set of issues straddling the border between political and judicial power as they have arisen in, first, the United Kingdom, second, Britain's relationship with the European Union, and third, the wider international system. The discussion illustrates the claim that no analysis of democratization can be complete without taking into account the dimension of judicial power and its implications for democratic accountability even, perhaps especially, in countries considered as exemplars for new and emerging democracies. The development of strategies under the umbrella of legal technical assistance that seek to enhance the standing of political decision-makers while remaining compatible with the principle of judicial oversight poses perhaps one of the most important challenges for democratization in the present century.

Countries in the process of devising new institutions for a democratic political regime aiming to give enhanced legitimacy to the exercise of power have much to learn from the experience of their mentors in those Western democracies that have already undergone a significant incremental growth in judicial power (Sweet 2000). How far is judicial power compatible with democratic government? That key question will be addressed in the following way. First, the source and growth of judicial power in the Anglo-American tradition of jurisprudence will be outlined. Second, the United Kingdom's experience of adopting the Human Rights Act 1998 is discussed as an example of a potential shift from political decision-making to judge-made decisions, and this potential is assessed.[1] Third, the growth of judicial decision-making within the European Union is considered as a further example of how judicial power is incrementally increasing. Fourth, the development of the international criminal court is noted as an example of how judicial power is increasingly seen as the means to ensure global standards for justice and the rule of law. Finally, following Loughlin (2001: 41), it is argued that over-reliance on the judicial element at the expense of democratic institutions sets a dangerous precedent as to who legitimates the legal order in society, and may undermine political and economic sovereignty. The lessons of Western democracies should not be lost on developing countries undergoing institutional reform.

The judicial power in the Anglo-American tradition

There is an active debate in the United States between those who consider that the role of the judges is to act as independent principals and those who see the judges as faithful agents interpreting the law according to the plain words in front of them (Eskridge 1994). The former adopt a purposive approach in which the courts are expected to carry forward into practice the aims and objectives of statutes and the interpretation of parliamentary intent. Judges are free to exercise an independent role in their decision-making. The latter see the judges as having a more restricted role defined by textual analysis, requiring judges to be dutifully bound to act within the limits of the statute. Judges are expected to undertake the task prescribed by law and within the narrow confines of decision-making to take account of the limits on judicial power and the constitution. There appears to be common ground between these perspectives: the role of the judicial power and how it is interpreted is called into question. In reviewing some of the historical evidence it is clear that judges from the earliest beginnings were prepared to go beyond the plain meaning of words and take account of extraneous material. In many instances this was a practical response to the problems of interpretation, and rarely did it seem to challenge the interests of the state. In the English common law this may have been because of the absence of any formal doctrine of the separation of powers; but it is more likely to have reflected a period before the development of a strong tradition of parliamentary sovereignty.

The history of the English common law is instructive as to how judicial power emerged through the centuries of royal power. Judges possessed widely drawn powers. The early commentators noted how the rules of statutory interpretation were developed on an eclectic basis. A common approach was to consider the canons of statutory construction around principles of 'equitable' construction. Textual analysis was accompanied by various techniques and methods of statutory construction. In the eighteenth century Blackstone's monumental *Commentaries on the Laws of England* demonstrated the wide range and diversity inherent in judicial discretion. The pragmatic qualities of the common law allowed the creativity of the judges to develop its own methodology of statutory construction. Various approaches to statutory interpretation developed in order to give effect to 'the natural' meaning of the words, and the 'will and intention of the legislator'. The fiction of the 'reasonable man' was frequently employed to set standards and direct outcomes. And in some instances the courts attempted to discover 'the mischief' that was behind the legislative enactment in order that the common law should provide a remedy. The early case law is rich in the adoption of modes of interpretation to fit the circumstances of the case. The revolution culminating in Parliament's victory over the Crown in the 'Glorious Revolution' (1688) came as the courts recognized the authority of parliament and its ultimate law-making authority. This provided the judges with the dominant paradigm of interpretation, which for centuries has been used to expound and explain Parliament's will and by so doing to give effect to judicial discretion. On the boundaries of law-making and judicial interpretation rests the key distinction between parliamentary and judicial power. The paradox was that, while the judges recognized Parliament's ultimate law-making authority, it was on their own authority that they articulated the nature of the parliamentary sovereignty that they recognized. In truth it was finely balanced as to whether ultimate judicial or Parliamentary authority might prevail. In the famous *Dr Bonham's case* (1609) Sir Edward Coke somewhat ambiguously suggested that the common law might 'controul Acts of Parliament and some times adjudge them to be utterly void: for when an Act of Parliament is against common right and reason or repugnant, or impossible to be performed, the common law will controul it, and adjudge such Act to be void'.[2]

The idea of judges being capable of testing statutes to destruction if they were found to be against a fundamental principle of law raises the possibility for judicial power rather than parliamentary to sit at the apex of the constitution. However plausible this interpretation might appear, a more realistic assumption is that Sir Edward Coke believed that as far as it is practical it is necessary for the courts to try to give effect to the meaning of the statute that is consistent with parliamentary intention. This is the meaning accorded to Coke's verdict by Blackstone. Some observers might think that the ascendancy of Parliamentary authority is commensurate with a demise in judges closing loopholes and developing their own equitable solution beyond the true intention of Parliament. But this is barely plausible once the scale of judicial creativity is recognized. Keeping in mind that judges developed legal tests for the purposes of instructing and controlling the jury, it is by no means clear that the judiciary adopted a more limited role for their own authority. A far more compelling preoccupation for the judiciary throughout the eighteenth and nineteenth centuries was to develop contract law, through the insistence of the doctrine of freedom of contract and settling land disputes through the development of land law and equity.

The judges have continued to think of the common law as equivalent to a fundamental law capable of wide-scale judicial interpretation. Instances where the courts settled fundamental constitutional issues include the *Case of Proclamations* (1611), which claimed the common law as providing the courts with overarching powers of review. In 1839 the privileges of Parliament were settled in *Stockdale v. Hansard* (1839) where the courts articulated the jurisdiction of the courts to define parliamentary immunities and privileges.

The tradition of judicial innovation and creativity survives today. Scattered throughout the law reports are some glimpses of how proactive judges have become in an era of increasing judicial self-confidence. All the law relating to administrative law is judicially created and self-executed in terms of legal tests and criteria for the grounds for judicial review, the rules of standing and the remedies available to the claimant, culminating for the first time in the creation of an administrative court. The articulation of common law fundamentals may take a number of forms. The rule of law, a rhetorical term (much cited in political discussions of recent attempts at democratization around the world) has in the hands of the senior judiciary become a principle of legality. In the case of *Entick v. Carrington* (1765) it was held that the Secretary of State had no powers to issue a general warrant on the basis of state necessity. The absence of legal authority provided the opportunity for the courts to consider whether there had been a trespass that was a violation of property rights. More recently, Lord Nolan referred to the rule of law in *M v. Home Office* (1992) – a case involving deportation – as 'the submission of the executive to orders of the court'.[3] The courts have traditionally sought to uphold the rule of law and due process. Lord Bridge explained the importance of the rule of law in the context of the constitution as a whole: 'The maintenance of the rule of law is in every way as important in a free society as the democratic principle. In our society the rule of law rests upon twin functions: the sovereignty of the Queen in Parliament in making the law and the sovereignty of the Queen's courts in interpreting and applying the law.'[4]

The creation of an enlarged administrative jurisdiction of the courts has been largely undertaken by the judges on their own as an attempt to keep pace with the desire of successive governments to change and modernize. Past practices and older legal interpretations are frequently revisited and re-interpreted in the light of modern experience. The rule of crown immunity, drawn from the idea that the 'king can do no wrong', has been replaced by the courts claiming inherent jurisdiction over government powers, including the use of the prerogative. The rule that no injunction may lie against the Crown has also been reconsidered in the light of current practice.

In terms of judicial powers and their relationship to the democratic principle, then, there is a dialogue between the courts, the legislature and the government of the day. In practical terms this has set the boundaries between judges and politicians. There is a similar dialogue in the United States as to how far judicial power should be self-executing and how far it is confined to textual analysis. In the United States in the landmark decision of *Marbury v. Madison* (1803) Chief Justice John Marshall applied a pragmatic approach by re-interpreting the statute, re-wrote the text and gave a new meaning to the law that departed from what was included by the original draftsman. Many of the early decisions of the United States Supreme Court follow the pattern of thinking evidenced in the development of the English common law. It is clear that rules or canons of statutory interpretation leave judges considerably empowered with the discretion as to how to develop and extend legal principles to do justice in the case in question. Many commentators see this as resting on liberal foundations that declare the courts independent from the state as guardians against oppression. Yet there appears to be little consistency or predictability. At times the US courts adopt a strict interpretation and appear highly restrictive. At other times the courts become more libertarian, and appear to fulfil the role of protecting the individual. In adopting either interpretation the courts have seen their authority continue with the boundaries between judicial and political power often ragged and unclear.

The Human Rights Act 1998: a case study

The Human Rights Act 1998 came into force in Britain on 2 October 2000. The Act provides a useful case study of how incorporation of the European Convention on Human Rights into domestic law of the United Kingdom may provide judges with greater discretion than hitherto. This has the obvious danger of shifting political decision-making to come within judicial power. The Act has provided opportunities for litigation and greater legal complexity in decision-making. There are ongoing lessons to be gained from this experience, and it is instructive for countries developing reforms through legal technical assistance from countries like Britain.

The Human Rights Act 1998 significantly changed how rights are enjoyed in England and Wales, by incorporating for the first time into domestic law the main substance of the European Convention on Human Rights (ECHR) signed in 1950. This Convention provides rights such as freedom of expression and association; rights to privacy and information; and procedural protections for the individual in the areas of criminal, civil and administrative law. Under the ECHR, the European Court of Human Rights was set up to hear cases alleging breaches of Convention obligations. Owing to the high reputation of this court, the Convention is well known internationally for guaranteeing the citizen positive rights.

Uniquely amongst countries that ratified the ECHR in 1950, the United Kingdom failed to incorporate it into domestic law – even though the United Kingdom was the first country to sign it and British lawyers carried out most of the drafting. As the United Kingdom is a dualist state, it needed to incorporate the ECHR into domestic law to allow British citizens direct access to enforceable rights under the Convention in the British courts. From 1966 to the end of 1995 the United Kingdom found itself before the European Court of Human Rights on no less than sixty occasions (Gearty 1997: 84). In at least half the cases, the Court found some form of breach of the ECHR. United Kingdom legislation was found wanting, and in many cases the citizen was left with no redress. The political demand for incorporation of the Convention grew steadily, at first through pressure groups, and then, in the 1980s, through prominent lawyers, notably Lord Scarman, a serving Law Lord at the time, who argued for incorporation of the ECHR in a modern Bill of Rights. In the past five years, senior serving members of the judiciary have added their voices in approval.

The resulting Human Rights Act for the first time allows British citizens to use domestic courts to enforce Convention rights. British law is entering a period of considerable uncertainty as the transition to a rights-based culture is undertaken through cases decided by the judges. Intensive preparations were made for the Act's coming into force in England and Wales and an extra £60 million allocated for legal aid and court costs. The judiciary at all levels, from magistrates' courts to the appeals courts, were given intensive education and training programmes. A central issue is the extent of the application of Convention rights and the implications of a rights-based culture in English law. The courts have the difficult task of interpreting the proper procedures and merits of administrative decisions. So now is an opportune moment to take stock of the direction a more rights-orientated public law will lead to. There are some words of caution. While conceding, as everyone must, that human rights are intrinsic to a democratic system, there is room for consideration of the boundaries of judicial power as a custodian of rights. What degree of self-regulation should be exercised by judges when they are granted such overarching powers? How should decision-makers be advised to achieve good decisions when individual rights may serve to inhibit risk-taking and the development of sound long-term strategies?

The substance of the rights under the Convention is narrowly confined to legal rights written in the broad language of negative liberty or 'freedom from unjustified interference'. Rights included are to liberty and security (Article 5), to a fair trial (Article 6) and to no punishment without law (Article 7). There is a right to life (Article 2) and to freedom from torture (Article 3), and a prohibition against slavery and forced labour (Article 4). There are also freedoms associated with the individual in terms of religion, the right to privacy and the freedom of assembly (Articles 8–12). Such rights have been narrowly interpreted without any formal consideration of their potential impact on issues of economic, social or political significance. The 1998 Act came about through sustained pressure from the judiciary and academic writers. Despite the existence of many draft Bills of Rights (most notably those of Lord Lester), the Government delegated the drafting of the Human Rights bill to the official parliamentary draftsman. Its form was influenced by the requirements of drafting an official government bill rather than a Private Member's Bill. The latter might have resulted in a different formulation from the one favoured by the Government.

The Act is seen as a model of its kind, but distinctive in the approach taken in the incorporation of Treaty obligations when compared to the European Communities Act 1972.

Primacy is given to the sovereignty of Parliament, as the 1998 Act falls short of allowing the courts to hold that an Act of Parliament is unconstitutional or illegal. The most the courts may do is rule on incompatibility between the 1998 Act and the legislation under review. Since the Act came into force there have been three declarations of incompatibility. It is then for Parliament, not the courts, to resolve any incompatibility. The courts are not *bound* by the jurisprudence of the Strasbourg Court of Human Rights, but may give effect to those decisions.

However, it is important to recognize that legal rights developed under the Human Rights Act have the potential to shift Britain's constitutional arrangements in a new direction. In October 2001 the Court of Appeal in a series of significant judgments outlined the significance of the Human Rights Act in terms of the powers of the courts to issue injunctions in matters of planning disputes. Issues of proportionality must be considered by the courts before an injunction may be exercised under the discretionary powers of the courts to issue injunctions for threatened breaches of the law. This is but one example of the importance of the rights culture's becoming an integral part of the judicial process. It makes Ewing's remark on the danger of the unelected (judges) making important decisions over the elected (ministers) the more pertinent, even if the danger he alludes to has been addressed, in part, by the self-limitations on judicial powers that the House of Lords set out in its ruling on *Alconbury* (2001):[5] 'We now have a constitutional system in which the output of the democratic process can avoid successful challenge and possible censure only if it can pass a test of democracy developed by a group of public officials who have escaped all forms of democratic scrutiny and accountability' (Ewing 2001: 116–17).

Finally, it is clear that there is an important extra-judicial role facilitated by judges. Judges are called upon to provide the means of independently assessing facts or inquiring into accidents, government mistakes or maladministration. In Northern Ireland at the time of writing the inquiry into the events in Londonderry in 1972 ('Bloody Sunday'), under Lord Saville, a serving Law Lord, is concerned with re-examining the work of a previous inquiry held by Lord Widgery. In total it is estimated that at least a fifth of judicial time in the United Kingdom is involved in carrying out an inquiry function. Valuable though this may be, it brings judges into the front line of major political controversies and, in many instances, the full glare of publicity. This may be unearthing facts and attributing fault at the expense of eroding judicial independence. Society might or might not regard this as a risk worth taking if it provides an independent review of government decisions (Loughlin 2001: 41).

The European dimension

The development of the European Union (EU) is another example of how judges now appear to be at the apex of power. The European Court of Justice provides member states with a valuable means of resolving disputes resting on the ultimate decision-maker, the courts. The Court of Justice has had a considerable influence over the development of judicial thinking in the United Kingdom and also over the authority of Parliament. Parliamentary sovereignty, long held by the courts to be the bedrock of constitutional principles, appears considerably weakened in the context of what is now the EU. More significant is the realization that the English common law is now part of a shared inheritance with the civil law tradition. The two traditions have long been contrasted as 'codified' and 'uncodified', but their differences are more profound and far-reaching in terms of the cultural adjustment needed to understand both of them.

Membership of the EU creates a possible challenge to the doctrine of the sovereignty of Parliament. Traditionalists insist that the doctrine asserting that an Act of Parliament is free from being struck down by the courts would prevail in spite of Britain's membership of the EU. The traditionalist view is compelling when it is remembered that Parliament is led by the wishes of the majority of the electorate, through a government that endeavours to carry out its election manifesto. In this way parliamentary sovereignty translates into the wishes of the people, as opposed to the decisions of unelected judges. However, the issue that arises is whether the traditional view can be reconciled with EU membership. Tensions between UK and EU law inevitably lead to the question of which might prevail in the event of a conflict that is not resolved by Parliament or the political system, but is left to the courts to decide. One example of the need for judicial decision-making arose from a series of cases beginning in 1991 that centred around a dispute involving Spanish fishing boats operating within the United Kingdom's fishing quota. The Spanish boats formed companies and registered in the United Kingdom. The UK Merchant Shipping Act 1988 introduced various requirements such as nationality and domicile in an attempt to restrict the use of UK fishing quotas to the UK-based fishing fleet alone. The Spanish fishermen went to court in the United Kingdom and sought interim relief from the English courts restraining the application of the 1988 Act as a first step in challenging its compatibility with Community law. The supremacy of Community law, long acknowledged in the case law of the Community, appeared at odds with the doctrine of the supremacy of United Kingdom legislation. The House of Lords in a number of key decisions arising out of the dispute resolved that:

- the United Kingdom courts must give way to European Community law even if this means acknowledging that part of an Act of Parliament is incompatible with community law;
- in general the United Kingdom courts must not apply United Kingdom statutes whenever there is a potential conflict with Community law;
- the courts are required to ensure that United Kingdom law is consistent with Community law; and
- national courts are required to ensure that the government complies with the requirements of Community law, and may provide compensation in the event of any failure to do so.

It is possible to see these rulings as evolutionary as well as revolutionary. In terms of evolving principles it is clear that United Kingdom law must be held to be compatible with Community law. More revolutionary is the idea that integrating common law and civil law approaches requires the courts of the United Kingdom to be seen as part of a single unified court system. The European Court of Justice stands at the apex of judicial powers, while the House of Lords, as part of the domestic judiciary, is there to implement changes. There is much food for thought in the idea that, in developing the jurisprudence of the EU, the Court of Justice has taken on powers to constrain member states, and the member states are being led by the court rather than taking the lead. On that analysis, the United Kingdom has unwittingly developed a Supreme Court system, composed of the House of Lords and the European Court of Justice, with inherent jurisdiction over community law in the United Kingdom. In a pragmatic and case-by-case approach it is possible to see the beginnings of a common law shared throughout the Community (Craig 2000: 211). The impact of the Court of Justice is currently difficult to calculate in full. But it is clear that the scope of the jurisdiction of the court is sufficient to provide a coherent convergence of common law and civil law systems. This is a trend that is likely to continue and intensify as the appropriate balance between the Court of Justice and the other Community institutions is worked out as the EU evolves while it continues to expand.

The wider international dimension

At the global level the development of *ad hoc* international tribunals and the International Criminal Court (ICC) is part of the ongoing expansion in judicial power. The beginnings of the trend to confront war criminals through a judicial process began with the international military tribunal at Nuremberg and the Tokyo tribunal at the end of the Second World War. More recently, there has been the establishment of the international criminal tribunal for the former Yugoslavia and for Rwanda. In July 1998 the UN conference adopted the Rome Statute of the International Criminal Court and agreed to found a permanent International Criminal Court. The creation of a war crimes jurisdiction has some way to go before it is universally accepted by all countries in the world; but it is indicative of a developing role for judges.

In developing a criminal law jurisdiction the judicial approach draws on the crimes of genocide, crimes against humanity and the crime of aggression. Article 23 of part 3 of the Statute covering the ICC incorporates the basic fundamental principles of the criminal law. A person is not criminally liable unless his conduct constitutes a crime under an existing law. This principle builds on the general principles to be found in international criminal law, which in turn reflects the Anglo-common law approach in defining judge-made law. The developing jurisprudence of the international court will undoubtedly draw on the contribution of the Anglo-American tradition, with its pragmatic and eclectic qualities of judge-made law. The extent of its jurisprudence may impact on national sovereignty and autonomy. The *Pinochet* case is illustrative of the problem. In the *Pinochet* case (2000), the panel in the House of Lords included Lord Hoffman, in a case involving the claim for sovereign immunity against extradition made by Senator Pinochet, a former Head of State (Chile). In reaching its decision, the House of Lords allowed a variety of human rights interest groups to give evidence, including Amnesty International. Lord Hoffman was chair of a Trust set up to administer funds in connection with Amnesty International. This link was sufficient to establish that Lord Hoffman fell within the category of having an interest in the case. As a result it was considered that Lord Hoffman should have been automatically disqualified from membership of the panel. The earlier decision of the House of Lords had to be set aside and a second hearing had to take place. The case is illustrative of the potential for judges to become automatically disqualified from hearing cases in which they may have an interest. There is thus a real possibility that alongside the accumulation of judicial power questions will increasingly be raised about judges and their politics (Griffith 2000: 159).

Conclusions

The foregoing analysis provides an explanation of how judicial powers have become central in many instances to the resolution of disputes involving the implementation of legal reforms in Western countries. In many instances judges command a powerful influence, offering independence, public acceptance and legitimacy to the decision-making process. In countries such as the United Kingdom the incremental increase in the powers of the judiciary has brought attention to the mode of judicial appointment. The increase in judicial powers has not always been commensurate with an increase in the status or protections afforded to judges. In fact judges are easily susceptible to accusations of political bias or prejudice when asked to confront policy matters or resolve the merits of a dispute involving the government of the day and the courts. The central question is how to provide the most appropriate balance between judicial and political power, especially when in many instance the judges are appointed while politicians are elected.

The judicialization of government decision-making in an attempt to 'judge-proof' decisions may have important effects on the way the legal system works. Access to legal advice is not uniformly or universally available. The more impoverished sectors of society may become excluded. Lawyers and legal solutions are often expensive, and provide greater degrees of complexity than informal systems of decision-making. The hierarchical nature of judicial power, with a focus at the senior levels of the judiciary, often distracts attention from the lower courts, which are often underfunded, poorly resourced and susceptible to problems of inefficiency or at worst corruption. This is especially the case in a number of the newer democracies and in poor countries. But great care should be taken in considering the role of judges when legal technical assistance to such countries is being formulated. Much of the politics literature on democratization views the judiciary as an essential check on executive power and crucial to the rule of law that is central to the workings of liberal democracy. However, there are alternatives to judicial decision-making: informal mechanisms for dispute resolution, the use of administrative tribunals, and the ombudsman can all provide contributions that should be specifically tailored to the needs of individual countries. As Sweet (2000: 204) so rightly concluded, 'in the end, governing with judges also means governing the judges'. The advance of judicial power is probably unprecedented, and it becomes more essential than ever to reflect closely on where the *actualité* of the boundaries of political and judicial power might be set.

Notes

1 For a recent example see the *Guardian*, 16 October 2002, p. 1 report, 'Woolf [Lord Woolf, Lord Chief Justice] warns government on human rights'.
2 Dr Bonham's case 77 Eng. Rep. 646 (CP 1609).
3 M v. Home Office (1992) 1 QB 270 at 314H–315A.
4 X Ltd v. Morgan-Grampian Ltd (1991) 1 AC 1.
5 R (on the application of Alconbury Developments Ltd) v. Secretary of State for the Environment, Transport and the Regions (2001) 2 All ER 929.

8

Sociology

GEOFFREY WOOD

In his classic work on *The Sociological Imagination*, C. Wright Mills argued that it 'enables the possessor to understand the historical scene in terms of its meaning for the inner life and external career of individuals' (Mills 1959: 5). In other words, sociology seeks to explain the experience and life chances of the individual in terms of the wider historical and institutional context. Sociological accounts of the nature of democracy and democratization are thus less concerned with the formal constitution of governmental structures than with the effect they might have on the individuals that constitute society in terms of promoting or inhibiting social equality and better life chances, and vice versa. In this chapter, classic and contemporary sociological approaches to understanding democracy and democratization are highlighted, with particular attention being accorded to the post-1989 period.

Classical sociological perspectives on democratization

Given the central concerns of the sociologist towards democratization, it is inevitable that key practical issues that have concerned sociologists include questions of social stratification, progress and development. The development of classical social theories of democracy can be broadly summarized as in Table 8.1. These categories are not totally watertight; some theorists straddle more than one tradition. All three traditions are centrally rooted in the Enlightenment, with its emphasis on rationality and social progress.

Table 8.1 Classical (pre-1940) sociological perspectives on democratization

Political science/ rational actor perspective	Political Economy tradition	Interactionist and consensus sociological theories
Key Theorists North American economics/ political science	Marx, Engels, Lenin, Frankfurt School	Durkheim, Weber
Perspective on the state Theories of polyarchy	Marxist theories of the state: state is an instrument of class dominance	Democratic state represents the outcome of the increased rationalization of society and/or the development of the collective consciousness/ social organization to a specific level

However, what distinguishes the classical interactionist and consensus social theories is their close focus on the process of rationalization and the consequences for modes of social organization; the former would, however, place greater importance on the role of human actions, and the latter on objective social structures.

While what is sometimes referred to as the 'political science tradition' emerged from outside sociology, it has had a strong influence on a range of sociologists from North America, most notably in articles published in leading journals such as the *American Sociological Review*. In recent years, this perspective has become increasingly theoretically sterile, amounting to little more than a commitment to certain methodological assumptions that are central to neoclassical economics, namely that society is made up rational profit-seeking individuals whose behavioural patterns can be readily quantified.

The classic political science explanation for democratization is that, in many respects, it represents 'an accident of history that leaves a balance of power or a stalemate – a dispersion of forces and resources that makes it impossible for any one leader or group to overpower all the others' (Olson 2000a: 134). In other words, if the division of society into small autocracies between rival groups and individuals contending for resources is not possible or feasible, then the alternative is to 'work out a framework for mutual toleration' (Olson 2000a: 134). While a fair number of democracies have not resulted from such spontaneous and autonomous transitions, that is because democratization has been imposed from the outside (for example, the democratization of Italy and Germany after the Second World War), and/or because of the influence of an already-democratic state.

In contrast, Marxist theories of the state centred on the view that political life under capitalism is inherently repressive, 'crushing the everyday life, economic life, the real life of individuals' (Lefebvre 1966: 130). In other words, under capitalism, the state is simply there to ensure that favourable conditions for capital accumulation are created. Democratization is not something that is achieved, but an ongoing struggle that can be carried forwards or forced into retreat. The struggle is about going beyond a democratic state to building a society without state power, Marx's communist utopia. Working for democratization is about finding out the truth of politics under capitalism, and seeking to eliminate formal politics altogether (Lefebvre 1966: 138). Thus, while Marx saw the modern capitalist state as more advanced than any previous form of state, it remained imperfect and must be done away with. To Marx, as long as the fundamentals of capitalism remained in place, any apparent element of pluralism in the capitalist state was of little worth.

Finally, classical social theorists such as Max Weber and Emile Durkheim locate democratization in terms of the gradual rationalization of society, and the consequences of this for economic organization. Two main strands can be distinguished here: interactionist and consensus theories. Interactionism is a broad school of thought that is deeply influenced by the writings of Weber. He explored the manner in which individuals interact, and the relationship between changes in belief systems and social behaviour. Weber believed the rise of Protestantism created the conditions for the emergence of rational capitalism. In turn, capitalism could not survive without the rational legal administration of the modern bureaucratic state (Giddens 1971: 179). Democratization is closely related to the rise of the latter; there can be no demands for equality before the law, unless the law is a rational and formal code governing behaviour. Yet there is a central tension between democratization and the bureaucratization process; for democratic rights to be exercised, additional bureaucratic regulations are needed. Democracy requires the impersonal selection of individuals in key government posts, a process that will necessarily result in reduced accountability. Yet for Weber, unlike Marx, democratization along multi-party lines was no sham. Democratic societies were characterized by higher levels of equity than those encountered under any other state form. Direct democracy is not possible in mass societies; representational democracy is thus the only option. Under universal suffrage, leaders must have a degree of charisma, encouraging 'Caesarist' tendencies in political leaders. However, that can be checked through vigorous parliamentarianism, which provides the means by which leaders who overstep the mark can be brought to book (Giddens 1971: 181).

Sociologists in the consensus tradition accord somewhat more attention to the evolution of social structures, and the role they play in moulding social behaviour, in building a broad consensus. In many respects, the father of consensus sociology was Emile Durkheim. Durkheim believed that 'as societies become more complex, a major trend is to the emancipation of the individual from the collective conscience', that is from the accumulated bodies of attitudes, norms and values that govern human behaviour (Giddens 1971: 101). In other words, individuals become freer from the straitjacket of tradition and its associated social taboos. Durkheim (1933) maintained that the increase in the division of labour as societies evolve necessarily involves an increase in government. However, associated with the process of development is the emergence of moral ideas that stress the rights and dignities of individuals. These pressures result in the state in most modern societies becoming more democratic, an institution 'primarily responsible for the provision and protection of these individual rights' (Giddens 1971: 101). However, the process of democratization is not inevitable or irreversible. It is possible that the activities of the state will expand to a level where they become a repressive agency, a situation that will emerge if the 'secondary groupings' (civil society actors) that intervene between individual and the state, and that serve to counter-balance state power, are not fully developed. Thus, for democratization to be secured, it is necessary that active attention be accorded to developing civil society.

To Durkheim, a society is more or less democratic if there is effective two-way communication between state and society; in mature democracies accepted norms for the conduct of social life take on a conscious or directed character through the actions of the state. In other words, the democratic state can be seen as the 'ego' of society; it is creative and both leads and is led by society (Giddens 1971: 102). Again, civil society groupings have a vital mediating role to play to ensure that the state is not constantly buffeted by day-to-day changes in the popular mood (Giddens 1971: 102).

Democratization secured?

In the early years of the century, formal democracy in many of the advanced societies was extremely shaky, or even non-existent. The rise of fascism in the 1920s and 1930s led many to conclude that democracy might be little more than a historical anomaly in visible decay, a perspective epitomized in the works of German novelist and social thinker, Erich Junger (1970). However, this was followed by fascism's equally rapid demise (outside the relatively peripheral Iberian peninsula), the redemocratization of much of Western and Central Europe, and the triumph of Keynesian forms of economic management. Not only did predictions of the death of democracy seem equally premature, but also the seemingly unbridgeable social divisions that had led to the crises of the 1930s had apparently been resolved; the bulk of citizens in the advanced societies now enjoyed a standard of living unprecedented in history.

By the late 1960s, evidence of mass discontent, epitomized by escalations in industrial action and student protests, and the glaringly apparent deficiencies of neo-Stalinism led to a renewed debate among sociologists as to the most desirable way forward. Among neo-liberal thinkers – a group generally in the minority among sociologists, though not so much so among economists – Nozick (1984) suggested that the only viable way forward was the minimalist 'night watchman state'. However, while conservative politicians were quick to endorse this viewpoint when it came to regulating economic activity, they tended to match this with calls for a greater regulation of social life.

The always richly diverse radical tradition became further fragmented with the rise of a new school of sociological thought, post-modernism. The similarly diverse 'neo-enlightenment approach', drawing on the works of a range of classical social thinkers, focused on issues such as the most appropriate means of realizing the goals of the Enlightenment – namely, the rationalization of social life – and the value of classical constructs for social analysis. Some of the principal theoretical strands and developments are summarized in Table 8.2.

Table 8.2 Social theories of democracy, 1968–89

	Classical Political Economy approach	Post-modernism	Neo-Enlightenment-based approaches	Economic/political science tradition
Conception of the democratic state	The state represents the apex of the superstructure of the capitalist mode of production	The state represents a particular concentration of power networks and domination – an 'apparatus of capture'	The state represents the product of the rationalization of society	Minimalist state is desirable to allow free reign to economic activity and innovation
Way forward	Socialism	Localized action; 'micro-tribalism'	'Realization of Enlightenment goals'; local democracy	Minimal government
Principal theorists (1968–89)	Althusser, Poulantzas	Foucault, Deleuze, Guattari	Giddens, Habermas	Nozick

As Crouch (1979) notes, social theory in the 1970s accorded increasing attention to the role of the state. Within Europe, much of this centred on the Marxist tradition (Table 8.2, column 1). However, within the United States, while political science accorded little attention to developing a systematic social theory of the state, a few scholars such as Robert Dahl explored the issue of community power. Other leading political scientists argued that democratic pressures from below could overload government with excess demands. Huntington (1968), for example, argued this in respect of interest groups and governments. These arguments were followed on by neo-liberal 'political science' writers in the 1980s, who suggested that the easiest way to disarm the insatiable demands of the masses was, quite simply, to do away with the state as a site of patronage.

The relative strength of Marxist contributions in the 1970s reflected Marxism's capacity to draw clear links between political and economic happenings. At the same time, it was seriously weakened by a reluctance to admit any element of pluralism within the capitalist democracies; 'real' democratization was still to happen. The traditional Marxist view was that capitalism was characterized by the domination of a minority, the capitalist ruling class; any democratic participation by the mass of society must thus be little more than a fraud (Callinicos 1997). This insistence seemed increasingly untenable, given that the 1950s and 1960s had seen material gains in the conditions of the working class within the advanced societies, and in the 1970s the crisis of Keynesianism seemed to result in a genuine policy contestation. Despite Marx's claims of historical progress, developments provided little in the way of signposts towards a socialist future that would transcend multi-party democracy (Crouch 1979). Moreover, the ostensibly Marxist states of Eastern Europe presented a most unappealing alternative to Western democracy, and were increasingly running out of economic momentum. To Giddens, the experience of the post-war years revealed capitalism's inherent capacity to reform itself and the space created by the general franchise for a wide range of social issues to be placed on the table, debated, and partially resolved.

To some writers in the Althusserian/French structuralist Marxist tradition, the matter could best be explained by highlighting the relative autonomy of the capitalist state. Capitalism is characterized by competition between different fractions or segments, whose interests may conflict, accounting for the significant policy shifts and social compromises (Strinati 1982). However, this perspective provides little room for short-term mass action aimed at expediting social redress and broadening the base of democracy (Crouch 1979), a perspective that would prove politically debilitating to its proponents.

More pragmatically, the British social theorist Ralph Miliband (1972) drew a clear distinction between authoritarianism and liberal democracy – a distinction that was dismissed by most orthodox Marxists at the time. To Miliband, a liberal democratic state is a relatively autonomous actor. The stability of capitalism can best be explained by its flexibility. The system does indeed impart significant power to the working class, enabling real gains to be made, even if the overall capitalist framework remains in place. The apparent weakness and pliability of the capitalist state underscores the need to break with structuralist Marxism, and develop a more dynamic state theory that reflects the realities of liberal democracy. Multi-party democracy thus represents an area of contestation, whose boundaries need to be advanced; democratization is an ongoing and contested process.

Other writers in the radical tradition began moving away from Marxism to alternative Enlightenment approaches, most notably Jürgen Habermas (1989, 1990) of the Frankfurt school. Many aspects of Habermas's work had much in common with earlier thinkers, such as Weber, with his emphasis on the relationship between rational discourse and social progress. Provided there is room for the former, social progress is possible on incremental lines, a good example being the growth of the welfare state in Europe in the 1950s and 1960s. Formal democracies generally provide the space for continuous improvement in the way they operate, and enable progress towards a more equitable and inclusive future; again, democratization is an ongoing project, not a process that has been completed.

Limitations with the Marxist model also stimulated a different breakaway, as a number of French writers in the broad Althusserian/structuralist Marxist tradition began to experiment with a range of theoretical alternatives. The brief flirtation of many with café Maoism soon gave way to an increasingly influential theoretical paradigm, post-modernism. In contrast to the Marxist preoccupation with class inequality, early post-modernists such as Michel Foucault focused on the workings of power and domination within contemporary society. To Foucault complex power/knowledge networks underpinned social order, a long-term historical tendency being towards more subtle methods of social control, but social control nonetheless. This would, for example, explain why the formal democratization of Western societies was permitted (Poster 1984). Real democracy – free from hidden control and domination – is only possible through localized activism, creating space for the most marginalized in society 'to speak for themselves'. What makes post-modernist views of democracy so different from the bulk of social thought is that democratization on liberal-pluralist lines is seen as neither inevitable nor desirable. Classical social theorists such as Marx, Weber and Durkheim all saw the democratization of political institutions as the inevitable outcome of social and technological progress (although for Marx this would entail their destruction). This viewpoint is shared by most modernist sociologists. In contrast, for post-modernists formal democratization is a process devoid of meaning, given the persistence of power networks and imbalances. Similarly, there is no reason why societies will necessarily be democratic once they have evolved to a certain stage.

The triumph and decay of democratization

The resurgence of neo-liberalism in the 1980s, followed by the collapse of Soviet rule in eastern Europe (and of the Soviet Union itself), and the reinstitution of democratic rule in many parts of the 'Third World' sparked renewed debate amongst sociologists as to the relationship between the state and society and the inevitability of democratization. Writing outside the mainstream sociological tradition, Francis Fukuyama (2000: 319), in an influential essay first published in 1989, argued that there was a 'remarkable consensus concerning liberal democracy as a system of government', conquering rival ideologies ranging from fascism to communism. Deploying Hegelian theory, Fukuyama argued that, while there may be temporary setbacks, liberal democracy was an idea that 'could not be improved on'; in this sense, history had ended, with the triumph of the most effective and just state form. Fukuyama's arguments were soon seized upon by a range of conservative thinkers, who argued that it was desirable to practice liberal democracy in its purest form – a democratically accountable state that would leave citizens as much room as possible to get on with their lives unimpeded (Table 8.3).

Table 8.3 After 1989 – democracy and current social theory

Minimalism	Institutionalist approaches	Ultra-leftism	Post-modernism	Local democracy/ theories of community action
Tradition(s)				
Political science/Neo-liberalism	Political Economy	Political Economy	Post-modernism	Classical Enlightenment/ Political Economy/ Theories of social movements
Conception of desirable state				
Ultra-minimalist state	Institutional mediation between individuals and corporations	Realize goals of Marx and Lenin/ Vanguardist party	Dissolution of state; power in the hands of localized groupings	Local democracy and participation; 'Third Way'; mediation between local and global
Principal theorists				
Nozick, Friedman	Regulation theorists (Boyer, Lipietz); theorists of neo-corporatism (Streeck)	Callinicos, Cliff	Deleuze	Giddens, Habermas, Castells

The adoption of neo-liberal macro-economic policies (and, in the US, the distorted 'war Keynesianism' that followed it) in the 1980s led to rising social inequality, primarily due to a widening of the wage gap, rather than increasing unemployment. In other words, while mass political enfranchisement was (at least on the surface) secure, it seemed that the economic disenfranchisement of a significant component of society had returned. Similarly, in many of the emerging 'Third World' democracies, mass participation in the electoral process appeared to do little to correct massive increases in social inequality. In any event it could be argued that the growing political clout of large corporations was increasingly divesting the formal political processes of any real meaning.

Such arguments were bolstered by evidence of a decline in the number of citizens who bothered to vote in most of the mature democracies, the triumph of the 'politics of spin' in the 1990s, and an exponential increase in political campaign spending funded by corporations seeking political access and influence. It can be argued that given the powers of large firms – some with turnovers greater than that of entire nations – some form of institutional mediation is necessary to offset the imbalance *vis-à-vis* the mass of society. To Matzner and Streeck (1991), a partial solution comprises a series of social accords (a situation sometimes referred to as 'neo-corporatism') entailing centralized bargaining between governments, unions and firms on matters relating to macro-economic policy, successful examples being in countries like Denmark and the Netherlands.

Regulation theory

A leading paradigm in the revival of institutional approaches has been regulation theory. Regulationists like Jessop see nothing automatic about the periods of stability in capitalist development; rather, this is a product of social agency (Jessop 2001a: ix). Given this, it is possible for institutions to ameliorate the worst excesses of capitalism, and to provide the basis for emancipatory alternatives, inspired by the socialist, ecological, feminist and other social movements. Although originally in the Marxist tradition, regulationism's links with classical Marxism have become increasingly tenuous; nonetheless, regulationism does provide steps to resolving the shortfalls of Marxist theory in explaining both the implications of social embeddedness and why Western capitalist states *are* formally democratic. It should be noted that, to regulationists, stability is not simply underpinned by a series of compromises between capital and labour; the relationship between state and society is also one of contestation and struggle between competing groupings in society.

But what would a regulationist political programme look like? On the one hand, there is the cautious approach. The need to develop a 'post-liberal' – and post-Stalinist – democratic strand fuelled debates within the British theoretical journal, *Marxism Today*. To writers associated with this journal, such as Martin Jacques, changes in the nature of capitalism (and most notably the shift away from traditional forms of mass production) required 'new politics'. This was a critique that 'contributed powerfully to New Labour and Blairism', with its emphasis on a third way (Jessop 2001b: xxii). Others, more within orthodox regulation theory, argued that more vigorous forms of institutional mediation are necessary.

Other writers associated with the regulationist school of thought, such as Lipietz, have argued for a new 'ecological politics', stressing the importance of sustaining the biosphere as a whole. Lipietz places great emphasis on grass-roots alliances between broad social movements as the basis for the cultivation of civic virtues, given the seeming lack of responsiveness of formal democratic institutions (Jessop 2001b: xxii). What both these strands have in common is the recognition that a large component of traditional left politics incorporated an authoritarian streak (Lipietz 2001: 502). Many progressive writers during 1920–1989 forfeited the moral high ground by acting as apologists for Soviet repression, and, in some cases, for the lunacies of Maoism as well. Lipietz (2001: 502) argues that the modern citizen is confronted with 'two leviathans', the market, which is dominated by the wealthiest, and the state, which is exterior to the community and can easily be appropriated by a minority, formal democratization notwithstanding. So again, politics and democratic participation are not simply about the state but involve contestation and compromise between interest groupings at local and national levels.

Neo-enlightenmentism and post-modernism

The focus on the rediscovery of civic virtues and the revival of local democracy has been taken even further by a diverse collection of writers from theoretical traditions ranging from neo-enlightenmentism to post-modernism. To Habermas, democratization is about securing social and political progress through rational discourse. Habermas argues that class struggle has only one aim – to create situations where the other side is forced to listen. Human beings are inherently rational, and within the advanced societies there is little alternative to rationality and its inevitably beneficial social outcomes. In his later works, Habermas argued that a particularly fertile ground for rational discourse between different interest groupings is at local level, highlighting the importance of a devolution of powers (Habermas 1990). A contrast is provided by such writers on social movements as Manuel Castells (1998), who writes:

> So there is democracy, which is a very important thing, but once we elect our representatives, they have very little capacity to really influence the events along the lines of what they promised to do. The relationship between whom I vote for and what he or she is able to do for me becomes very indirect . . . we are seeing a growing voiding of representative democracy in the sense of the ability to make a difference in our lives. It's not that democracy is finished, it's only that relationship between political representation and what happens in my life is more and more remote and indirect.

Castells argues that the inevitable response to this is the rise of new social movements, grass-roots organizations uniting people around issues of common concern when formal structures of democratic participation are seen as unresponsive. Whilst arguing that movements have a vital role to play in society, Castells cautions that they might degenerate into narrow and intolerant sectionalist organizations.

A very much more extreme version of this vision is provided by certain post-modern writers, most notably Giles Deleuze. To Deleuze, all states, even formal democracies, are inherently repressive; real progress would involve a deformalization of social relationships, with interactions being purpose-orientated, and not regulated or bound by the complexities of social norms, routines, and underlying power networks (see Deleuze and Guattari 1988: 380). Once

minorities break free from the 'plane of capital', from seeing themselves in terms of other groupings in society, it
is possible to escape existing power networks completely.
The reality, however, is that petty nationalist movements
have proliferated, in Europe and the developing areas. On
the one hand, these movements do constitute attempts to
break away from domination by what is perceived to be an
alien majority. On the other hand, few of these movements
have demonstrated greater tolerance or accountability even
towards the minority rights of other groups. Fragmentation
of multi-ethnic states has often gone hand-in-hand with
ethnic cleansing.

A very different way forward is proposed by the proponents of the 'third way', most closely associated with Giddens.
Again, the 'third way' stresses the importance of local participation. However, for Giddens, this should be on very
much more formal lines, with the positive feature of central
government being retained, and, in some cases, strengthened.

'Third Way'

Giddens (2000: 4) argues that, in first half of the twentieth
century, the major social questions revolved around the
consequences of industrialization and accommodating the
rise of unions. This led to the rise of tripartism and social
accords, solutions that are no longer workable. Instead, given
that big institutions can no longer deliver, there is a need
to move away from 'bureaucratic top down approaches'
favoured by the left. Individuals have to take responsibility
for their own fate: this underscores the need to create a
favourable climate for wealth *creation*, not simply emphasizing distribution. To Giddens, this points the way to a
'third way' distinct from statist social democracy and neo-
liberalism, a new path most closely associated with the
Democratic Party in the US and Britain's New Labour. He
argues that the 'third way' is not just about a concern with
economic development, but also with community issues,
and stresses the vital importance of social solidarity and
basic social institutions like the family. Right-wing critics
of the third way claim it is purely amorphous and avoids
hard choices that are necessary if the market is to function
with minimal interference. Writers on the left claim that
it acquiesces in the failure of governments to stand up to

the excesses of the market and is silent on rising social inequality.

However, despite the influence of 'third way' thinking neither the Clinton administration in America nor New Labour succeeded in redressing the large-scale social inequality that had re-emerged under previous governments. Moreover, in the desire to attract and retain corporate support there seems little taste for restraining the market (or even for limiting an expansion of its role), even in areas where its failings have become glaringly obvious. Thus, while democratic institutions remain in place, the range of areas where voter preferences can have a significant impact has narrowed.

Varieties of Marxism

Finally, although their ranks are greatly depleted, there persists a grouping of scholars who remain committed to their interpretation of traditional Marxism, most notably those within the Trotskyist or ultra-left camp. To Callinicos (1997: 206), the Western pluralist state

> is not a neutral institution which somehow rises above and regulates society. Ultimately it represents the concentrated and organised force of the capitalist class. This class uses many devices to ensure that the state acts in its interests . . . and at the core of the state apparatus are the repressive agencies – army, police, and intelligence services – which again and again have shown their loyalty to the status quo.

Trotskyists were always outspoken in their condemnation of Stalinism, and so escaped the crisis of confidence that beset other many other strands of Marxism following the collapse of the Soviet Union. To ultra-leftists, full democracy is only possible under socialism. To expedite socialism, it is necessary to have a vanguard party on Leninist lines; the status quo is likely to respond to any challenges in a 'centralized' manner, necessitating clear, coherent and unified strategic responses (Harman 1998). 'Democratic centralism' provides the unity and discipline needed to pursue a democratic struggle, absolute unity and order being necessary to implement decisions that have been democratically discussed – a viewpoint based on a rosy interpretation of the internal life of the Bolshevik party in the pre-Stalin era. Ultra-leftists remain unable or unwilling to accord any worth to the formal democratization of political institutions in the advanced societies, despite multi-partyism's superior track record to any other system of government to date. They remain mired in the controversies of the past. To Trotskyists, a vital problem remains to identify the reasons why the Russian revolution degenerated into Stalinism, and how revolutions elsewhere can be more successful, despite the fact that very few revolutions to their liking have taken place since.

A rather different account of the nature and consequences of elite domination is provided in the recent work of Charles Tilly, influenced by both the Marxist tradition and consensus-derived elite theories. Persistent or 'durable' inequality reflects clear social divisions, themselves generated through the operation of social organizations, exploitation being the 'pivotal mechanism' through which inequality is generated (Wright 1999: 7). The deep social embeddedness of social inequality and its constant reconstitution by established organizations will result in the continued marginalization of key segments of society, the mass franchise notwithstanding.

The de-democratization of society?

In a recent popular volume Noreena Hertz (2001) argues that the power of large corporations has led to the 'death of democracy'; the democratic process has become meaningless, given the unwillingness and inability of governments to restrain the worst excesses of the market. This development has become increasingly apparent to ordinary voters, many of whom seem inclined to withdraw from normal political processes.

Hertz's account is problematic in many ways, not least because it lacks a certain scholarly rigour. It is also problematic in that the experience of democracies continues to be diverse. Electoral participation in many emerging democracies is very high, even where the governments palpably lack the power to regulate adverse market forces. Moreover, despite the crisis of neo-corporatism, countries such as Ireland and the Netherlands continue to operate social accords in defiance of neo-liberal conventional wisdom, in opposition to the antipathy of the International Monetary Fund, for instance.

At the same time, Hertz's account does point to a very real crisis in the advanced democracies. Politics in many cases has been divested of meaning. Even where there seems to be overwhelming popular support for non-market solutions – for example in Britain, for the provision of mass transport and health care – governments have been extraordinarily reluctant to embrace them. Political parties appear reluctant to entrust voters with the right to choose between coherent policy proposals, seeking refuge instead in the politics of slogans and soundbites. At the same time the decline of participation in formal politics is matched by the rise of new social movements, most notably the anti-globalization movement and associated campaigns.

The 'compartamentalized' and essentially neo-liberal economic system that the US and Britain exemplify has been foisted on many newly democratized countries in the 'Third World'. And more regulated systems such as those in continental Europe and Japan have come under great pressure to be more 'flexible', curtailing the market's accountability to political institutions. At one time proponents of the Anglo-American model could point to the apparently more robust performance of the US in comparison to more regulated alternatives. This illusion was shattered with the bursting of the internet stocks bubble and global economic slowdown in the early years of the new millennium. That revealed some of the central contradictions of the compartamentalized economy, with the boom of the late 1990s being driven by consumer spending, itself funded by unprecedented levels of household borrowing, at a time of stagnant real wages for all but those in the highest salary bands. This stands in sharp contrast to the Keynesian era, where consumer spending was made possible through redistributive policies. Again, this underscores the nature of the relationship between politics, economy and society in the early 2000s, and the increasing divorce of economic and political elites from the bulk of society. Thus the democratic project remains incomplete. MacEwan, in the aptly titled *Neoliberalism or Democracy?* (1999: 16) agrees, and furthermore repeats the claim that in the advanced societies democracy is contested.

To bridge the gap between political elites and society-at-large, democratic initiatives must make a real difference in people's lives. Existing relations of power and authority must be challenged; greater accountability is essential. More democratic economic development would revitalize political democracy and vice versa.

MacEwan's contribution is a good place to bring this review to a close, for he highlights a central question that has run throughout the chapter: does multi-partyism and the associated institutions familiar in the West constitute a mature or completed process of democratization? Is democratization a journey with a final destination that all societies can eventually reach, or an ongoing process that is unlikely ever to be fully completed? To conservative exponents of politics formal democracy is a completed project in the West – perhaps a manifestation of the 'end of history' – so long as the existence of free markets continues. To most current sociologists (post-modernists being the exception) the democratization of the West helped provide and at the same time reflected an unprecedented improvement in the human condition, an improvement that should be emulated worldwide. *However*, they would hasten to add that democratization is not a one-off 'historical accident'; rather it is an ongoing process. The boundaries of democracy are contested, and need to be further advanced to ensure that a range of social and economic questions of immediate concern to the bulk of society are debated and addressed satisfactorily.

The contested nature of democratization is particularly apparent in those nations where it is a relatively recent phenomenon. To developing states and in large parts of eastern Europe the introduction of political pluralism has coincided with a requirement to implement structural adjustment policies and privatize state assets. Hence voters have very little say as to the manner in which the economy is managed, and the sale of state assets has invariably strengthened the hands of existing elites. This coincidence of formal political empowerment and economic disempowerment leads Perry Anderson (2000) to an ambivalent conclusion. A real process of democratization is taking place on a global scale, even in hitherto unexpected locales such as South Africa and East Timor. But at the same time democracy has been 'hollowed out at its core' – in the advanced societies – where debate is 'asphyxiated' by the interests of the political and economic status quo, a trend heightened after the terrorist events of 11 September 2001.

There is little doubt that contemporary sociological theory continues to devote much attention to the nature of democratization and the extent to which political institutions can ever represent the interests of all society. However, not only has there been a tendency for suggested remedies to become more timid and reformist, but also for social theory to become somehow less theoretical. While regulationism and social movement theories continue to locate current debates within a broad political-economy theoretical framework, the latter has become increasingly over-stretched, given the continual modifications to cope with the actual course of events. Much current writing tends to be very issue-orientated, eschewing grand theoretical questions that could become mired in the controversies of the past, even in the case of writers such as Giddens, whose earlier works embodied explicit metaphysical pretensions. Finally, although there has traditionally been considerable cross-fertilization between sociology and the disciplines of politics and economics, in recent years this has diminished owing to the growing hegemony of rational choice models within both economics and politics. Rather, sociological perspectives regarding democratization have had greater influence in the emerging trans-disciplines of socio-economics and political economy, which have attempted to break free from the rational choice straitjacket.

Conclusion

What all these sociological theories have in common is that they seek to understand the nature and desirability of linkages between formal political institutions and the make-up of wider society. In the early years of the twenty-first century there is little doubt that democracy in the advanced societies is at a crossroads. This reflects the re-emergence of the central social question – are current levels of social inequality and uneven political accountability desirable, and what is the most acceptable way forward? These questions are posed even more starkly in the newer democracies of Africa, Latin America and eastern Europe. Can democratization be considered to be complete, given that ordinary people have little effective say on a range of central issues concerning economy and society? For the time being, however, there is insufficient pressure for such issues to be fully addressed, unless confidence in the status quo comes to be shaken severely by economic downturn and greater popular pressure emerges within and without the formal political processes.

Part II
Areas

9
Africa

ROGER SOUTHALL

It remains fashionable to refer to the contemporary impetus for democracy in Africa as the 'second wave of independence' or as a major aspect of 'African renaissance'. Such terms embody two major meanings: the disastrous failure of democratization efforts following political independence in the 1960s; and the umbilical relationship between social and economic development and democratization, if the latter is ever to take root in an Africa that is mired in poverty. The view that Africa is 'trying again' points not only to how a paradigm of democratization has assumed primacy in analysis of the continent's condition since the early 1990s, but how that paradigm has become inextricably entangled with political and intellectual activism. Indeed, the urgency of democratization debates flows both from the desperate condition of the mass of Africa's people and from the fact that, while on the one hand 'democratization' has in essence replaced Marxism as both explanatory device and panacea, it has on the other been appropriated as goal and tool by Western policy agendas.

Democratization in Africa: the first wave

Early approaches to democratization in Africa were largely subsumed under the closely interrelated perspectives of modernization and nationalism. The study of democratization arrived in the 1950s and 1960s as an accompaniment of decolonization, and in its most systematic and coherent form drew heavily on American political science. The study of politics in Africa was discouraged during the colonial era. African peoples were regarded as backward, if not barbaric, and hence unsuited to the pursuit of 'politics' – conceived in terms of a civilized liberal ideal. Moreover 'politics' was presumed to entail the prior existence of 'the state', which at most, was taken to exist only in potential terms under colonial tutelage. When, belatedly political science did arrive, in response to the decolonizing formation of 'new states', it did so largely with all the baggage of American liberal commitment, with its diverse mix of idealism, universalism and (paradoxically) blinkered ethnocentrism (Omoruyi 1983).

Africa's 'new states' were assumed to be in the throes of a process of political modernization, whose end-state had an uncanny resemblance to political life in the industrialized West. In part, modernization theory was a response to the failures of orthodox economics, which was criticized as failing to comprehend the complex interactions between social change and economic development. Modernization was viewed as taking place via the diffusion of 'modern values', through education and technology transfer, amongst the new African elites who were at the head of the struggle against colonialism. A central preoccupation of political scientists consisted of the difficulties of 'political institutional transfer', which ran up against the embeddedness of traditional authority, especially as represented by the chiefs, who symbolized local particularities and the communal values of tribal life. Indeed, modernization was viewed by political scientists and nationalists alike as above all Africa's transition away from an inhibiting tribalism towards a modern nationhood which, buoyed up by rapid economic development, would represent sovereign if not actual equality with the former imperial powers.

If the process of 'nation-building' or 'national integration' was the primary responsibility of Africa's modernizing elites, the principal instrument was the political party, whose function was not only to 'articulate' and 'aggregate' public opinion but to engage in the promethean task of 'political mobilization', of forging links between tribe and nation. It was in the study of parties that the supposed 'value-freedom' of Western political science most easily cohabited with political idealism. Their formation and development represented not only the most explicit embodiment of political modernization but also the condensation of heroic nationalist struggles for the achievement of the classic liberal goals of liberty, equality and fraternity. The very classification of parties symbolized the implacable advance of progress. For whereas cadre or elite parties were customarily formed as defensive reactions by traditional elites to the threats posed by modernization, mass nationalist parties were the creations of the forward-looking elites, who had appropriated the language of liberalism imported by colonialism, exposed colonial tutelage as self-serving, and honed the demand for African self-determination, sovereignty and racial equality. Significantly, however, whereas Western liberal-democratic thought was founded principally upon rational individualism as found in the political theories of Thomas Hobbes (1588–1679) and John Locke (1632–1704), African nationalism, emphasizing the putative solidarity of rapidly-forming, self-conscious, African national collectivities, had much greater affinity to the romanticism of Jean-Jacques Rousseau (1712–78). Consequently 'African democracy' soon came to resemble more the 'people's democracies' of the communist world than Western liberal-democracies. This was to have grave consequences in later decades, when the hollowness of Africa's first attempt at democracy was to be laid bare by appalling widespread violations of human rights by regimes claiming to possess popular legitimacy.

The fairly rapid political atrophy of the first wave of nationalist democracy in Africa, as first one-party regimes and then military rule took hold in an increasing number of states, was greeted in two ways. First, authoritarian trends were often conceived as a not irrational response by the modernizing elites to 'the dramatic danger of disorder and perhaps even of regression' (Zolberg 1966: 6). Thus Africa appeared to have too little, not too much, authority, although the most astute observers recognized that the conditions for authoritarian rule to bring about modernization were not yet present, and that the costs could be very great. The alternative therefore lay in the pursuit of a more limited version of democracy, one that would deal with societal stresses and strains by the sort of machine politics that characterized Western countries before they became fully industrialized and modernized. Developing institutions like the civil service and military that could contain the urban masses would also help, for rising expectations were reckoned to constitute a serious threat to the political stability upon which industrialization and modernization (and hence democratization) ultimately depended (Huntington 1968). However, in contrast to such conservative responses, the second major response to the rising tide of authoritarianism was a reaction against modernization theory and an embrace of radical or Marxist political economy.

Part of the problem for modernization theory was that its intellectual armoury was closely aligned with American foreign policy, preoccupied as it was with containing communism. There was, as Leys (1996: 11) claims, a silence about the social side of development that was cloaked by the doctrine of 'value-freedom'. The capitalist character of the development that modernization anticipated was not openly acknowledged. Yet by the late 1960s and early 1970s, the outlines of an emerging African crisis were already manifest in the form of economic stagnation, political instability, authoritarian rule, militarism and not least, the rapid and highly visible formation of African privileged classes whose typically kleptocratic behaviour challenged their characterization as a 'modernizing elite'. Not surprisingly, African scholars were increasingly drawn to the theories of the (metropolitan) 'new left' (which was simultaneously engaged in a critique of mainstream political science) and more particularly to a tradition of 'expository radicalism' in African studies – building on early works by such writers as W. E. B. Dubois and George Padmore, who argued how European colonialism had destroyed African civilizations and social and economic formations.

Rodney (1972), for instance, drew not only upon 'expository radicalism' but also Frantz Fanon's (1970) thesis that colonialism *underdeveloped* the personality of the colonized. He owed even more to Andre Gunder Frank and theorists of Latin American dependency, whose analyses and insights were now systematically applied to Africa. They built upon *Neo-Colonialism: The Last Stage of Imperialism* (1965), where Ghana's first president, Kwame Nkrumah, argued that the fruits of African political independence had been denied by continuing economic dependence on the former colonial powers. Dependency writers stressed not only the external orientation of African economies, which constrained the prospects for internal growth, but also how such 'under-development' underlay the political power of the emergent African bourgeoisies – the principal beneficiaries of 'neo-colonialism'. Even where, as in Nyerere's Tanzania, there were attempts to 'de-link' from metropolitan capitalism by pursuit of socialist strategies, state control of the economy translated into the development of a 'bureaucratic bour-geoisie' whose interests contradicted those of workers and peasants, who were accordingly exhorted to engage in class struggle (Shivji 1976). Elsewhere, the lack of an indigenous entrepreneurial class with access to investment capital still required that development be directed by the state, as in Kenya for example.

While dependency theory and Marxism contributed much to the understanding of the patterns of African development and 'periphery capitalism', they posed as many questions as they solved, not least because of their inability to delineate realistic alternative paths to development. Although there was an implied socialist alternative, it was difficult to demonstrate the existence in Africa of the indigenous social and economic forces that would carry such a revolution through. Instead, throughout the 1970s and 1980s, African countries were more typically dominated by ruling classes whose material interests were determined primarily by pre-ferential access to the state. By the mid-1980s the population of sub-Saharan Africa was, on average, considerably poorer than it had been a decade earlier. Twenty-five of the world's severely indebted low-income countries were in Africa, the continent was unable to feed itself, and AIDs was spreading rapidly, possibly affecting up to a third of the population in middle Africa. The bane of African national development was, then, not the emergence of a dominant class as such, but its parasitic character, supported by a 'swollen state'. This swollen (or 'overdeveloped') state was also, by its nature, inherently authoritarian. On the one hand, colonial experience and post-colonial contestations had left African countries bereft of institutions (effective political opposi-tions, a free media, functioning constitutions) capable of countering abuse of power and ensuring administrative accountability. On the other, the centrality of the state to resource allocation had encouraged a concentration of political power that typically saw personalized regimes ruling by a mix of coercion and clientelism – the granting of rewards and favours to particular supporters irrespective of the laws and regulations concerning public conduct.

Democratization in Africa: the second wave

The early 1990s witnessed a dramatic return of multi-party democracy to Africa. Whereas 'in 1989 29 African countries were governed under some kind of single-party constitution, and one-party rule seemed entrenched as the modal form of governance', by 1994 'not a single de jure one-party rule remained' (Bratton and de Walle 1997: 8). This was widely perceived as the local manifestation of Huntington's (1991) third wave of democracy globally. Many authors have stressed the increasing importance of political conditionality attached to foreign assistance and the emergence of Western demands for 'good governance' in contributing (with more or less effect) towards this democratic momentum. Yet although the surge of popular power in eastern Europe probably did much to undermine the legitimacy of one-party and authoritarian African regimes, there is a consensus of radical and mainstream opinion that internal forces in the form of the rise of pro-democracy movements, not external pressures, were most fundamental.

Study of 'watershed elections' demonstrates how protest movements incorporated key segments of African populations (students, trade unionists, professionals, intellectuals, some business interests, the media, women, the urban poor, small farmers and the churches) and how their demands for democracy were resisted by the ruling group, their business associates and often, their external allies (on France see, for example, Renou 2002). In apartheid South Africa especially, the combination of mass protest, declining regime legitimacy, and economic failure was widely seen as creating divisions between so-called 'hard-liner' and 'soft-liner' elites, propelling them towards multi-partyism and democratic transition. Yet political transformation in Africa at this time was both widespread and extremely uneven. A residual group of states were largely untouched by the process, either because multi-partyism was well-established (Botswana) or because demands for reform were too weak (Zimbabwe and Swaziland). In a third group of states armed rebellions engineered the overthrow of repressive regimes with the hope of representative government to come (Uganda, Eritrea and Ethiopia). And in a fourth group, state collapse saw central institutions disintegrate under the weight of looting, communal violence and civil war (Liberia, Sierra Leone, Zaire/ Democratic Republic of Congo, Congo-Brazzaville) or fall victim to the predations of rival warlords (Chad, Somalia).

Despite this unevenness, democratization was rapidly to become the central preoccupation of academic observers and engaged activists during the 1990s, spanning the ideological divide between mainstream liberal and radical/ Marxist analyses, because for both it offered significant hope of a better future for Africa. Yet there were, inevitably, important differences of interpretation and emphasis with regard to, in particular: first, elections, electoral systems and constitutionalism; and second, the relationship between democratization and development.

Elections, electoral systems and constitutionalism

Very considerable attention has been devoted to the study of elections, and not least in the period 1950–65 when electoral procedures were used to determine, or at least to legitimate, 'the form, rate and direction of the decolonization process' (Cohen 1983: 73). Later, as Cohen (1983) notes, the tendency for military regimes to *create* ruling parties and then to stage *façade elections* (Zaire, Togo, Benin, Sudan) testifies to rulers' recognition of the legitimation function of elections. And the re-establishment of constitutions providing for elections in post-military Ghana (1969 and 1979), Nigeria (1979), Uganda (1980), Upper Volta (1978–80) and the Central African Republic (1980–81), as well as multi-partyisms's re-introduction in Senegal (1976) indicated the continuing faith of some elites in the utility of elections. But the unevenness of Africa's electoral experience created a valuable distinction between categories of elections (competitive, semi-competitive and non-competitive) (Chazan 1979). Even so, overall, the shift to one-partyism and militarism led to a declining academic emphasis upon electoralism;

most scholars transferred their attentions to the state, class, imperialism and underdevelopment.

Africa's second wave of democracy re-ignited enthusiasm for the study of individual elections (see for example Daniel, Southall and Szeftel 1999). Cohen (1983) illustrated how, during Africa's first wave, analysts' theoretical concerns dealt principally with voter choice (overwhelmingly, the extent to which choice was based upon ethnicity), voter turnout (notably whether regime restrictions on political competition increased voter dissatisfaction or political alienation), and political participation (the role of elections in legitimating regimes and/or entrenching their domestic political control). These issues still retained some prominence, but in the 1990s analysts became more concerned to locate elections in the context of contemporary 'transition theory' – in turn heavily influenced by O'Donnell, Schmitter and Whitehead (1986). Apart from seeking to understand the causes of transitions and the variable rates of progress, major emphasis was also now placed upon the conditions for making successful transitions sustainable. Akin to the 'new institutionalism' interest in similar issues elsewhere, this resulted in renewed interest in both electoral systems and constitutionalism.

Africa's electoral systems were in large measure inherited from the colonial powers. Traditionally, Francophone countries have elected their rulers by systems of proportional representation (PR), Anglophone countries by plurality systems. Whereas for Francophone countries this usually involved parallel elections for parliaments and presidents, most Anglophone countries started with borrowed Westminster-style parliamentary systems before subsequently (in moves that reflected a growing centralization of power and a weakening of legislative checks upon executives) introducing separate presidential elections. This historical divide remains largely intact. Even so, significant debate has taken place concerning the qualities of different electoral systems, for two reasons. The first is that scholars, democratic activists and international agencies are seriously interested in how to prevent the abuse of elections by politicians, by means such as electoral monitoring (see Daniel and Southall 1999). A second spur has been the specific electoral requirements of South Africa's transition from apartheid to democracy.

On South Africa, a seminal contribution concerning an appropriate electoral system to best overcome the legacy of apartheid in an ideologically and ethnically divided society was Horowitz (1991), which argued for the adoption of an Alternative Vote (AV) system. A plurality system would lead to overrepresentation of a winning party, and national list PR would disconnect individual representatives from voters and effectively exclude ethnic groups not represented in a putative majority coalition (Horowitz 1991: 200). In contrast, AV would produce majority rather than coalition governments, by encouraging vote pooling and ethnic accommodation – parties would be forced to attract the second or third (party) preferences of voters. 'AV does not stand in the way of majoritarianism, but makes majorities responsive to the interests of others as well. This is an important conciliatory feature – and one that builds legitimacy – in a divided society' (Horowitz 1991: 202). In the event, South Africa opted for national list PR on the grounds of simplicity, inclusivity and the fact that no votes would be 'wasted'. (The adoption of PR as a way of easing the transition to democracy in Namibia in 1989 was also influential here.) This was of major significance, in that it represented a move away from Westminster-style, 'winner–takes–all' majoritarianism in favour of an electoral system that provides for the inclusion of minorities, which in South Africa's case are based primarily on ethnicity and race. Furthermore, it fuelled important comparative work by Reynolds (1999), who, after studying elections under plurality and PR systems in Malawi, Zambia, and Zimbabwe, and in Namibia and South Africa respectively came out strongly for PR as more likely to foster power-sharing and inter-ethnic accommodation. In contrast, plurality systems were more likely to foster majoritarianism and ethnic polarization. The drawbacks of the plurality system were to be demonstrated in Lesotho's elections of 1993 and 1998, which led to the exclusion of opposition parties from the parliament despite their gaining a sizeable share of the vote. Lesotho moved to adopt a mixed member proportional system in consequence. And South Africa is now considering the merits of the re-introduction of constituency elections for at least a number of its MPs, so as to establish a firmer connection between voters and their representatives.

As much as the debate about electoral systems has transcended academe to become an increasingly significant issue in contemporary African politics, there is widespread recognition of the need to locate any electoral system in a wider historical and institutional context. For instance, both theoretical and empirical work has concluded that the combination of a PR electoral system with a parliamentary, rather than a presidential, form of government is most likely to enhance the prospects for democracy in Africa (Southall 1999). Meanwhile Darnolf (1997) ascribes the presence of a democratic culture in Botswana and its absence in Zimbabwe to the sharply contrasting nature of their decolonization experiences – Botswana's peaceful negotiations with the departing colonial authority providing a basis for acceptance of diversity and opposition, versus Zimbabwe's bloody liberation struggle, which fostered political intolerance and distrust of opposition.

Such an appreciation of the historical legacies characterizes the revived interest in constitutions, central to the shaping and study of Africa's multiple transitions. These transitions have varied considerably, but one of the most influential models was the national conference, pioneered in Benin in 1990 and later adopted in Cameroon, Togo, and Niger, where reluctant rulers were forced to concede the re-drawing of constitutions and the formulation of new rules for multi-party elections (Joseph 1991). Although equivalent processes have been variously waylaid or avoided by authoritarian leaders elsewhere, the idea that rulers should forge a contract with the ruled and craft a new beginning has become widespread. Indeed, because prominent African political scientists and other intellectuals have been intimately engaged in democratization struggles they have had to confront the democratic potential offered by different institutional arrangements and consider if there is a sound basis for rendering constitutions viable. For many, this has been difficult, for the previously predominant Marxian perspective saw Africa's constitutions having fallen foul of what Okoth-Ogendo (1991) terms 'the power map' (whereby state elites appropriated themselves unfettered discretion over public affairs). In contrast, the new constitution-making tended to be dominated by a liberal paradigm that rested upon the twin pillars of limited government and individual rights and freedoms. As Shivji (1991: 258) wryly observed, that paradigm required Marxists and Leninists to direct their analytical skills to upholding the positions of the liberal thinkers Montesquieu and Locke! An important outcome of the resulting debate has been a critique of liberalism and 'good governance' discourse as legitimating the right of Western powers to intervene in Africa whilst shielding the 'democratic' West from scrutiny. In turn, that has been linked to an insistence that for constitutionalism to take root in Africa it must recognize not only socio-economic rights but also collective rights, notably those of internally oppressed peoples (Shivji 1991: 256). This provides something of a linkage to the important debate, in the South African context, of the potential of consociationalism.

Democratization and development

The concern to render constitutionalism viable has been closely linked to debates around the complex interrelationships between democratization and development.

Demands for democratization arrived later in Africa than the implementation of Structural Adjustment Programmes (SAPs), introduced by the Bretton Woods institutions in the 1980s in a bid to restructure economies, by reducing the 'swollen state'. By the early 1990s SAPs had been joined by a democratization agenda that called for the replacement of one-party and military regimes by multipartyism and freely elected governments. This linkage between externally-induced economic and political reform was explicit, the core of the argument being that democracy was not, in practice, to be found in the absence of capitalism. Such a position has proved immensely troubling for radical Africanists, many of whom are still having to come to terms with the collapse of the socialist model internationally.

The standard response has been twofold. First, the orthodox western-institutional position has been regularly taken to task for defining democracy in minimalist terms, that is, in terms of the existence of free elections and multi-partyism. This is routinely condemned as an extremely impoverished version of democracy. The importance of fundamental liberal freedoms cannot be denied; but they are not likely to mean much to the mass of African populations who live in dire poverty. This critique has been greatly strengthened by examples such as Moi's Kenya, where multi-partyism failed to curb rampant corruption and the continued gross abuse of human rights, and Musuveni's Uganda, where a ban on political parties is tolerated by Western 'donors' because of the proclaimed successful implementation of structural adjustment. Such cases merely indicate what many observers are convinced has become more obvious – the severe limitations of liberal democracy 'in crisis-ridden, dislocated, marginalized, and impoverished economies' (Ihonvbere 2000: 187). The solution, regularly proposed, is for African societies to become yet more democratic, for pro-democracy movements to base themselves more thoroughly upon civil society, trade unions, and human rights groups and so on to force through a more thorough-going reformulation of the state. 'This will include a restructuring of the military, a transformation of the bureaucracy, a revitalization of the judiciary, constitutional engineering, the guarantee of basic rights and liberties, and the protection of minority rights' (Ihonvbere 2000: 188).

Romantically, perhaps, 'democratization' has come to replace 'revolution' as the radical panacea. However, analytically the debate may be said to have bifurcated into a struggle between the two poles of 'liberal democracy' and 'popular democracy' (Saul 1997). On the one hand, the 'political science of democratization', typified by the work of American political scientists like Larry Diamond and Samuel Huntington, is based ultimately upon the political elitism of Joseph Schumpeter and the American theorists of 'polyarchy' such as Robert Dahl. Market economies develop, while state-socialist economies fall behind. For democratic reforms to proceed without provoking crisis, the costs to privileged economic interests must not exceed the benefits. Competing elites therefore have a formative role to play in crafting 'pacts', whilst disruptive popular pressures need to be contained. In contrast, the 'political economy of democratization' argues that such a focus on 'low-intensity democracy' abandons the pursuit of public purpose and fetishizes the market. In Africa, market reforms have undermined the capacity of states to manage economies in accordance with social, ethical and political priorities. By destroying indigenous industries and domestic employment they have accentuated social tensions. Ironically, therefore, globalization and structural adjustment undermine rather than develop a basis for democratic peace and state-building.

Saul's (1997) very influential article argues that the proponents of the 'political science of democratization', along with the World Bank and fellow donors, have increasingly come to appreciate this paradox, and have accordingly resorted to a 'political science of development' which stresses 'good governance'. This recognizes the need for viable state-like structures to maintain a minimum of order and legitimacy, and in effect to balance the contradictory pressures of political opening and economic reform, of managing dual transitions. Yet such approaches tend to downplay the socio-economic policy content that such models are designed to ensure: 'governance' is presented as 'performance-oriented', akin to business management, designed in effect to contain disruptive popular pressures that might inhibit economic 'progress'. The emphasis that such an approach places on holding the state to account and constructing democratic institutions capable of containing communal differences ('statecraft') are clearly vital (as is demonstrated by the collapse of social cohesion in countries like Rwanda and Somalia). But they can only go so far in humanizing Africa's contradictions, so long as the economic landscape remains so 'fertile' for throwing up 'pathological deformations'. In these circumstances it remains impossible to disentangle the twin issues of 'capitalism and socialism' and 'liberty and dictatorship'. While the possibility of realizing socialism looks remote, demands for democracy and equality whose realization will require progressive social and economic reorganization are rising in country after country, and in the long term have to hold out hope for Africa.

Africanists are understandably less concerned with exploring the general relationships between economic development and democratization that attract much interest in contemporary comparative politics and, even, among some economists (see Chapter 3 of this book, by Addison). As the literature tends to associate democracy with national wealth (albeit with important qualifications), it makes depressing reading for anyone concerned with the poorest continent and invites pessimistic long-term prognoses of individual cases like South Africa, widely touted as Africa's best hope for progress (see Lane and Ersson 1997). Saul's visionary perspective therefore articulates a radical optimism that for many engaged scholars constitutes an intellectual and political *necessity*. The broader consensus, however, argues that, given limited prospects for successful developmental states in Africa, liberal democracy currently constitutes the only attractive option, notwithstanding its obvious limitations.

Conclusion: the way forward

Wiseman (1999) advances the grounds for 'demo-optimism' in Africa. Obstacles to democracy in Africa remain legion, and democratic progress is highly uneven, yet the continent's political systems are, overall, more pluralistic and more open than they were before 1990. And democracy remains on the agenda because there is no plausible alternative. The debates outlined above will carry on. But alongside that, 'demo-optimism' might be reinforced by taking the analysis further forward in the following three directions.

First, there is need for more extensive concern with democratic accountability. At one level, this will require greater attention to the concept and practice of political opposition, a dimension of democratization that has been largely subsumed under studies of political transition. However, establishment of the idea of opposition as legitimate, of *oppositions* as alternative governments, and of opposition as a vehicle for movement away from a politics of communalism towards a politics of ideas is central to continued momentum towards democracy in Africa (Southall 2001). At another level, there is growing urgency for the quality of democracy, and how it can be measured, to be investigated. Baker (2000) has argued for the expansion of conventional notions of accountability (revolving around popular judgements of politicians at the poll) to embrace rendering all those who make significant societal decisions (private or public) accountable to their relevant communities. All public power-wielding bodies, legal authorities and security forces, private power-wielding bodies (from corporations to churches), individual citizens (such as large investors), international legal and political bodies like the Organization of African Unity, and international financial institutions should be scrutinized more closely. Measures for assessing the accountability of all such bodies are either available or can be developed, even though they will have to be supplemented by qualitative judgements. Their results will both allow for systematic cross-country comparison and more importantly can be utilized to strengthen and reinforce the accountability of power-holders who affect the lives of ordinary citizens.

A second, related effort should be upon expansion of the study of participatory democracy in Africa. Both the cross-national study of political transitions and individual case-studies have often been divorced from examination of grass-roots level political participation. Focus upon democratization at national level has neglected the implications for local government, even though in many countries this is where 'delivery', whether by national government, 'donors' or non-governmental organizations, has to be implemented. In contrast to voluminous writing and theorizing about 'civil society' and its centrality to democratization, there have been relatively few systematic studies of what ordinary, poor, African people understand by 'democracy' and how they view their rulers. In this regard, Cherry's work on African political participation in Kwazakele township in Port Elizabeth (1999), carried out over nearly ten years and spanning the transition from the apartheid struggle to the present day remains seminal. Significantly, she demonstrates the co-existence within popular consciousness of a joyous embrace of liberal democracy and confusion when it comes to people's experience of the institutions of direct democracy (both party and municipal). Unrealized hopes of participatory democracy have led to growing cynicism and political demobilization, posing long-term dangers to the rooting of democracy in South Africa.

Finally, there is greater need for elucidation of the interconnection between democratization and globalization in Africa. Far too often the response of African intellectuals to the impact of globalization has simply been one of rage. Hyslop (1999) protests that this is a product of a simplistic (and fashionable) notion of globalization as merely the latest stage of the expansion of capitalist production. Yet the expansion of communications and information systems, changing experiences of time and space, and massive cultural changes towards new social forms that collapse any distinction between 'modernity' and 'tradition' compete as contenders with the economic for the title of being the driving forces of globalization. African rhetoric, looking back to the autarkic logic of dependency theory, only intensifies the continent's marginalization. Instead, the way forward must be for African struggles against external economic domination, militarism, state repression and cultural imperialisms to link up with similar struggles elsewhere. Cheru (1996) admits that in the African context there is much hard work to be undertaken by social movements in developing a counter-project to current oppressions, yet this is vital if Africa is to participate in international moves towards shaping 'a just, democratic and sustainable new world order'.

Africa's internal politics clearly need to be democratized, yet there is a growing consensus that this goal goes hand in hand with growing demands for the transformation of a global distribution of power and wealth that is fundamentally undemocratic.

10

Central and eastern Europe

PAUL G. LEWIS

The passage of over ten years since the first fully competitive elections should have succeeded in putting the progress of democratization in post-communist Europe into clear perspective. By now we might expect to have a reasonably firm comprehension of how far democratization has proceeded, why – if its achievements are differentiated – it has gone further in some countries than others, and which events and processes have driven democratic change. The looking-glass of democratization studies should in this sense have been ground sufficiently finely to develop a clear image of developments in the area and uncover their main dynamics. One might also expect some theoretical insight to have been distilled from the copious information that has already been garnered, if not the formulation of a fully-fledged theory of post-communist democratization. By and large, however, the prevalent view is that achievement in these areas has been limited. Although comparative politics was largely dominated throughout the 1990s by issues of democracy and the study of democratization, to date it has issued in extensive empirical accounts and rather disjointed conceptual discussion more than a comprehensive body of theory that contributes to a deeper understanding of democratization in general. How well the studies of central and eastern Europe (CEE) compare with other regions is debatable, but the perspectives developed so far tend to identify loose associations and broad problem areas rather than more precise relations of dependence and causality. The looking-glass in this sense offers rather a blurred image – although some part of this weakness may also lie in the eye of the observer.

Taking CEE[1] as a whole the progress of democratization can be outlined in basic terms fairly precisely. Competitive elections on a universal suffrage have been held, and their conduct and results broadly validated by international observers in the majority of the nineteen countries, although they have not proceeded without reservation in Russia, Ukraine and Albania (see Karatnycky 2001). Only Belarus is generally deemed to have remained authoritarian and generally unfree as a whole – it is one of the few countries to have seen such a steady decline in its freedom ratings that it has clearly moved out of the democratic, free category altogether. On this basis, employing Freedom House ratings in 2001, eleven states have clearly democratized successfully, while seven remain in the intermediate area of partial democracy. Virtually all have also passed Huntington's (1991: 266–7) 'two-turnover test', whereby not only do authoritarian rulers have to lose power for democracy to be installed, but so have their potentially democratic successors on at least one occasion too (Milošević's loss of power in the rump Yugoslavia being too recent for the test to apply there yet).

But in other respects the area of study remains little more than 'a conceptual mess': the issues of democratic transition and consolidation have been confused and the precise line between democracy and non-democracy not drawn with sufficient clarity (Kopecký and Mudde 2000). Bunce (2000a:) is somewhat less negative, identifying five broad conclusions about democratization and three further 'bounded generalizations', in the light of specific regional experience. Pacting between authoritarian elites and leaders of opposition forces was found to be more effective as a path to democratization in Latin America and southern Europe than it was in CEE, where a 'thoroughgoing political rejection of the Socialist past and Socialist elite' was found to provide a more solid basis for democratic governance. Whereas economic reform in the Third World is a hazardous project that could undermine democracy, the opposite was true in CEE, where the progress of reform and democratization were strongly interdependent. However, Bunce also concurs with Kopecký and Mudde about the conceptual and methodological weaknesses, and directs attention in particular to problems of concepts, case selection and causality.

Kubicek's (2000) overview suggests that post-communist studies have so far contributed rather little to the field of comparative politics, and perhaps – with the exception of studies in political economy – may not generally be expected to do so in the future. The importance of social context for processes of 'transitology' (as democratization is termed here) is such that comparative study within the post-communist world is likely to be more fruitful than comparison across regions. Taken all together then, the substantial attention given to the CEE and abundant publications can only be seen as producing a disappointing outcome – but not one that differs greatly from democratization studies in other areas (Geddes 1999). Of course academic appraisals are rarely very approbatory anyway; moreover, the status of democracy in CEE (and, indeed, in regions with more established regimes) is itself still rather confused.

This chapter reviews how far democratization has progressed in CEE in concrete terms, discusses some major points of contention that have arisen, and identifies the main conclusions from the debate so far. It will show how democratization has been viewed in the CEE context and the nature of the conceptual lens (or lenses) that have been deployed to chart developments in this area. Little attention will be given to the early stages of democratization and the question of why the movement towards democracy began in the first place. Instead, the focus is on contemporary aspects of democratization and the most salient features of the regional pattern as it has developed over the past ten years.

The progress of democratization

An approximate guide to the level of democracy achieved in the region can be gained from the annual Survey of Freedom Country Scores compiled by Freedom House. The passage of time since the fall of the communist regimes gives us the opportunity to trace distinctive patterns of democratic development across the region. The country scores combine ratings for political liberties and civil freedoms that, if not an uncontentious index of democratic development, at least provide a reasonable guide. The scores have been criticized for being partial and too highly aggregated, but they do not diverge greatly from other prominent measures of democratic performance. Table 10.1 ranks CEE countries according to their Freedom Country Scores (FCS: low scores are more free) and, for those that share the same rating, by Gross Domestic Product (GDP) per capita. All 'free' countries on this basis count as 'electoral democracies', as do some of the 'partly free' countries (italicized figures) (Karatnycky 2001: 649). In 2000 Moldova, Macedonia, Yugoslavia, Albania, Ukraine and Russia all qualified as 'electoral democracies' in this category, but not Bosnia. The states with a score higher than 5.5 are categorized 'not free' (only Belarus in 2000) and are not defined as democratic.

Several features stand out. Eleven of the countries in CEE, rather more than half, were rated free in 2000 (scoring ratings of 2.5 or less), seven were partially free (from 3 to 5.5, the cut-off point between partially free and not free countries running through the 5.5 score), and just Belarus was rated not free. This was better than 1991, when only nine countries (more accurately, eight before the dissolution of the Czechoslovak republic) were judged free. All of those categorized as democratic in 1992, moreover, had maintained or improved on their score by 2000 – suggesting a general extension or deepening of the democratization process. This democratization tendency, however, did not exclude temporary backsliding in some cases. Slovakia was ranked as partly free for three years under Prime Minister Mečiar, when civil liberties were less fully observed. Estonia and Latvia also fell into this category soon after independence owing to problems in extending full democratic rights to the sizeable Russian minorities. Some observers defined the two Baltic states as authoritarian at the outset.

Of the eight partially free states in 1991, then, three had improved on their score by 2000 and five either stayed the same or regressed – three of these being the major post-Soviet republics of Russia, Ukraine and Belarus. The two countries rated not free in 1991–92 were the rump Yugoslavia and Bosnia, both involved in bitter conflict for the first half of the 1990s. The score of both improved when the hostilities ceased and the Milošević leadership in Yugoslavia was finally removed. Only Belarus remained on a resolutely 'unfree' course, as President Lukashenka consolidated his increasingly authoritarian rule. The picture overall, then, is of a certain progress in democratization through the decade accompanied, nevertheless, by a quite striking stability between the different groups of countries. Those already more democratically advanced in 1991 stayed that way and generally improved on their position. Those less favoured at the beginning of the decade often stayed at roughly the same level or actually regressed. Only Romania and Croatia moved out of the partially free into the free category. Belarus steadily moved towards the not free and fully authoritarian category. CEE developments seem to show a less uniform regional pattern of democratization than Latin America or southern Europe (Table 10.1).

However some significant associations at least can be identified, in addition to the failure of the major post-Soviet republics to improve on their limited initial standing, as shown by the comparison with trends in Gross Domestic Product. The more democratic CEE states are both physically located to the west of the CEE region *and* closer to the West in political and economic terms as well. The four richest countries (Hungary, Poland, Slovenia and the Czech Republic) were amongst the five initially targeted for early accession by the European Union (EU) in 1997, while by 2000 ten of the eleven countries rated free were engaged in accession negotiations. Most were considerably wealthier than countries rated partly free or not free. Only one partly free country, Macedonia, was as rich as any of the 'free' countries – and it was wealthier than just two of the 'free' countries. The correlation of political and economic factors raises a number of questions about the origins and pattern of democratization, both in general and in the context of post-communist CEE. It points to the possible existence of common underlying factors shaping the process and relates directly to modernization theory – one of the major paradigms claimed to provide an explanation for democratization.

Table 10.1 Freedom Country Scores in central and eastern Europe, 1991–2000

	$GDP per cap., 1992	1991	1992	1993	1994	1995	1996	1997	1998	1999	2000	$GDP per cap., 2000
Slovenia	6,280	2.5	2.0	1.5	1.5	1.5	1.5	1.5	1.5	1.5	1.5	9,320
Czech Republic	2,892	(2.0)	(2.0)	1.5	1.5	1.5	1.5	1.5	1.5	1.5	1.5	4,797
Hungary	3,613	2.0	2.0	1.5	1.5	1.5	1.5	1.5	1.5	1.5	1.5	4,734
Poland	2,197	2.0	2.0	2.0	2.0	1.5	1.5	1.5	1.5	1.5	1.5	4,108
Slovakia	2,213	(2.0)	(2.0)	3.5	2.5	2.5	3.0	3.0	2.0	1.5	1.5	3,742
Estonia	707	2.5	3.0	2.5	2.5	2.0	1.5	1.5	1.5	1.5	1.5	3,409
Lithuania	374[a]	2.5	2.5	2.0	2.0	1.5	1.5	1.5	1.5	1.5	1.5	3,045
Latvia	848[a]	2.5	3.0	3.0	2.5	2.0	2.0	2.0	1.5	1.5	1.5	3,019
Romania	859	5.0	4.0	4.0	3.5	3.5	2.5	2.0	2.0	2.0	2.0	1,596
Croatia	2,291	3.5	4.0	4.0	4.0	4.0	4.0	4.0	4.0	4.0	2.5	4,211
Bulgaria	1,014	2.5	2.5	2.0	2.0	2.0	2.5	2.5	2.5	2.5	2.5	1,484
Moldova	293	4.5	5.0	5.0	4.0	4.0	3.5	3.5	3.0	3.0	3.0	326[b]
Macedonia	1,053	–	3.5	3.0	3.5	3.5	3.5	3.5	3.0	3.0	3.5	1,685[b]
Yugoslavia	–	5.5	5.5	6.0	6.0	6.0	6.0	6.0	5.0	5.0	4.0	990[b]
Albania	195	4.0	3.5	3.0	3.5	3.5	4.0	4.5	4.5	4.5	4.5	1,195
Bosnia	325	–	6.0	6.0	6.0	6.0	5.0	5.0	5.0	5.0	4.5	972
Ukraine	397	3.0	3.0	4.0	3.5	3.5	3.5	3.5	3.5	3.5	4.5	640
Russia	565	3.0	3.5	3.5	3.5	3.5	3.5	3.5	4.0	4.5	5.0	1,697
Belarus	520	4.0	3.5	4.5	4.0	5.0	6.0	6.0	6.0	6.0	6.0	1,104

Notes: Gross Domestic Product (GDP) at current prices. Figures in brackets are for Czechoslovakia. Figures in italic represent Freedom House's Country rating of either 'partly free' (3–5.5) or 'not free' (5.5–7).
[a] 1993 figure. [b] Estimate.

Source: Survey of Freedom Country Scores (Freedom House 2002); European Bank of Reconstruction and Development, *Transition Report Update* (London, 2001).

Democratization and modernization

The association of democracy with wealth in CEE during the early years of post-communism is hardly surprising in itself and echoes a well-known association between democracy and modernization that has been widely mooted since the 1950s. The precise nature of the association has, however, always been obscure, and there has been widespread doubt about whether modernization – generally understood to be based on economic growth and adequately reflected in GDP indices – actually explains much about democratization or democracy in any precise sense. Democratization in CEE has rekindled interest in this question; possibly, this recent experience sheds new light on a rather well-worn debate. Probably the most comprehensive statistical examination of the relationship concludes quite emphatically the 'emergence of democracy is not a by-product of economic development'. But it simultaneously endorses the obvious association of the two phenomena, affirming that 'while democracy is terribly fragile in poor countries, it is impregnable in the rich ones' (Przeworski and Limongi 1997: 166, 177). In short, modernization cannot be understood to produce democracy, but once a reasonably wealthy country has become democratic it is likely to remain so.

These global findings are hardly exhaustive; indeed the relationship between modernization and democratization becomes more complex once historical and geographical differences are taken into account. Dictatorship in countries that became independent after 1950 was, for example, just as stable in rich as in poor countries (Przeworski and Limongi 1997: 176).[2] Also, it is argued that a high level of economic development has had stronger democratizing effects in European countries than elsewhere, an observation that was particularly rooted in the relatively recent south European cases. Both internal and external factors were involved here, the latter primarily based on the powerful role of wealthy close trading partners and the strong political influence they exerted through the promise of EU membership. Economic development has been claimed to increase the chance of a peaceful evolution towards democracy. Political and economic outcomes have also been closely linked in studies of post-communist development. Economic reform seems to have promoted democratization in post-communist countries more consistently than elsewhere, and this may reflect some unique features of the CEE context (Fish 1998: 238). A careful analysis of the conditions for successful economic reform in the post-communist states traces its immediate roots to the character and outcome of the initial, 'founding' elections of 1990–91 that marked the political break with communism. The more thoroughgoing and clear-cut the break, the more likely that economic reform would be successful.

This, of course, does not tell us much about democratization itself, but some of the second-order effects of the main correlation exercise do bear more closely on issues of democratic change. Greater political openness, as shown by the data presented in Table 10.1, was closely correlated with the outcome of the initial elections and produced better conditions for economic reform, while macro-economic performance was also strongly reform-dependent. While hardly surprising, such linkages provide some basis for identifying a 'virtuous circle' of economic reform and democratic change in CEE, as well as directing attention to the conditions that give rise to a 'vicious' one like that in Belarus. Lukashenka's personal dominance and growing authoritarianism were based on the rejection of anything like price liberalization that might threaten short-term economic pain. This particular analysis is interesting, too, for having prompted further examination not just of the links between political and economic variables but also of the geographical differences within the CEE region that seem to reflect and amplify them. Why precisely should the more democratic CEE states be both wealthier and more western? A recalculation of Fish's data thus includes an extra variable for the average reform score of each state's contiguous neighbours, which turns out to be significantly correlated with the original economic reform measure. That is, the more western CEE countries were more effective reformers – and probably wealthier – precisely because they were more western (Kopstein and Reilly 1999). In both an echo and advance on earlier disagreements about how far existing models of transition are able to 'travel' and furnish fruitful comparison, Bunce (2000b: 86) continued to stress the importance of regional characteristics – but with, *nota bene*, the proviso that 'it is precisely in the strategic realm – in needs, resources, possibilities, and outcomes – that regional context plays a powerful role in democratic transitions'.

The spatial diffusion of culture, power and economic variables may well, therefore, be an additional influence on the success of economic reform and the extent of democratization during this phase of the 'third wave'. Alongside a focus on political economy, democratization studies in CEE have placed considerable emphasis on the role of political culture and the nature of civil society. That is something that directs attention once more to the role in the European context of regional interconnectedness and the likelihood that, just as EU influence played a prominent role in south European democratization, so it would play an equivalent or even greater role in CEE developments. Thus 'modernization', for all its apparent links with democratization, may have little direct explanatory power in itself and offers limited value to theory-construction. But within a more closely defined historical and spatial context, its covariance with democratization indicators points to hitherto neglected ways in which regional factors and international influence can be factored into the analysis of democratic change. The implications of the analysis of CEE democratization and post-communist change more generally for the modernization perspective may thus be one part of the looking-glass where the view has indeed been sharpened and theoretically refined.

Democratization concepts – transition, consolidation and stasis

The concept of democratization as applied to central and eastern Europe has been unclear; moreover the subject has often been introduced as if the question of definition did not really arise: the process has become synonymous with a broader category of post-communist political change. This was signalled at the very outset, as the end of communist rule was unthinkingly (but almost universally) identified with initiation of the phase of democratic transition. Apart from its unhelpful teleological connotations, the 'transition' assumption embodied additional drawbacks in serving to smuggle in by these means a *'unifying* and *homogenizing* effect vis-à-vis the multiple processes designated by the notion' (Dobry 2000: 5). There has generally been a failure to distinguish between the interlocking processes of democratic transition and consolidation; no stringent line between democratic and non-democratic regimes has been established; and the definition of democracy itself has not been properly separated from identification of the process or processes that produce it (Kopecký and Mudde 2000).

For example, transition can be understood to refer to a process of change that starts with the progressive collapse of an authoritarian regime, as the adoption of a new constitution, as routinization of new democratic structures, or as the adjustment by political elites of their behaviour according to liberal democratic norms. Consolidation on the other hand involves removal of the uncertainties that surround transition and the institutionalization of the new democracy, the internalization of its rules and procedures, and the dissemination of democratic values. The extensive remit of these definitions and the evident problems of operationalizing the different variables they denote aptly illustrate the problems involved and help explain why many analysts have fought shy of confronting them. Precisely when transition has ended and democracy is fully installed raises a number of questions for which clear answers are difficult to find: how routinized do democratic structures have to be, and which are the critical ones? Precisely which dimensions of their behaviour do political elites have to adjust, and which particular democratic norms are most important? How can we tell that lip-service to democratic principles does not mask the persistence of less acceptable patterns of behaviour that are not open to public scrutiny? A further layer of questions emerges at the consolidation phase that relate yet more closely to values and questions of subjective commitment, which are equally difficult to determine accurately.

In practice, making the distinction between democracies and non-democracies has not been such a challenge, at least in terms of identifying electoral or minimal democracies; and Freedom House data offer a reasonably convincing basis for drawing such a line. The fact that ten of the eleven countries identified as free in 2000 had been so for five or more years also suggests that their transition period had ended and they are now embarked on a subsequent phase of democratic development. Of the six partially free states classed as electoral democracies in 2000 just two had improved on the Freedom Scores assigned to them in 1991/2 (one being Yugoslavia shortly after Milošević). Far from being completed, transition in this group hardly seemed to be under way at all in most cases, and the process was largely stalled. Not all countries have been moving in a democratic direction, and the barrier between states that were free and democratic from the outset and those that have hovered in a partially free, semi-democratic state has barely shifted at all.

So, while transition and consolidation have been the main concepts around which the discussion of democratization has revolved, there is a further category – for countries that have moved only very slowly towards installing a reasonably convincing form of liberal democracy or, even, its most minimal electoral form. Kitschelt (2001) noted that post-communist diversity as a whole emerged during a short period – from 1990 to 1993; since then, 'new regime structures have more or less "locked in" in almost all polities'. From this point of view, in CEE they were in fact more or less 'locked in' from the outset in 1991 and little change (in terms of broad free/non-free categories) was evident by 1994. A fuller pattern for the second half of the decade was actually apparent in 1996, after which only the former warring countries of Yugoslavia and Croatia (Slovakia is a partial exception) changed categories.

There has been in this sense an underlying condition of stasis or arrested development that characterizes much of CEE democratization. This is yet one further aspect of political change – or the lack of it – that needs to be accounted for. To do so raises further major problems and directs attention to the underlying question of whether it is just the quality of the post-communist democracy itself that is partial and/or defective, or, instead, it is the concepts that are applied to characterize it that are faulty. This is not necessarily an issue that concerns all CEE countries equally; and as an issue for post-communist democratization it does not figure strongly in studies of the subject. Rather, much of the debate has moved on to issues of consolidation, although difficulties have been encountered even there in identifying what it means and how it might be empirically assessed – and in many cases the problem has just not been fully confronted at all. Both Bunce (2000a) and Kopecký and Mudde (2000) emphasize the critical failure to distinguish between the sustainability of democracy and its quality in any particular case.

One of the earliest major studies argued that democracies needed five 'interacting arenas' in place which had to be mutually reinforcing for consolidation to exist (Linz and Stepan 1996: 7). But whether the requirements in terms of civil society, the rule of law, a usable state bureaucracy, a relatively autonomous political society and an institutionalized economic society were prerequisites or elements of consolidation itself was not clear. Most analysts in fact direct their attention to aspects of political culture and lay great store on attitude surveys in providing evidence of consolidation. One of the most wide-ranging analytical studies concludes that the countries of east-central Europe (Hungary, Poland, Slovakia and the Czech Republic) have made considerable progress towards consolidation in the light of trend patterns that 'clearly indicate a rooting of democratic convictions' (Plasser et al. 1998: 188). These countries plus Slovenia, Bulgaria and Romania were also described as heading toward democratic consolidation 'albeit with some caveats and concerns', by Diamond (1999: 184–5), largely on the basis of attitude clusters that showed citizens endorsing the present regime over the previous one, rejecting authoritarian alternatives, and broadly favouring the activities of representative democrats. Other analysts are more sceptical. To return to the point from which this discussion began, then, the looking-glass through which CEE democratization is viewed does not just help shape the image that can be perceived but may also play a part in creating the political reality that it reflects.

Conclusions: Europeanization and the quality of post-communist democracy

Different reasons have been identified to explain the deficiencies of the post-communist democracies. One dwells on the weak development of the rule of law and a consequent failure to build an adequate constitutional order (Merkel and Croissant 2000: 31–47). Another claims that basic institutions are absent: the new regimes have been installed in contexts that lack the framework of the modern state, the precondition of most 'first-wave' democracies and a necessary political basis that merits far greater attention. Thus, according to Rose and Shin (2001), many post-communist democracies (like others in the third wave) have 'started democratization backwards'; thereby failing to go much beyond 'electoral democracy'. The view that institutions often determine, rather than are determined by, the events of history is supported by a wide-ranging survey of CEE democratization processes: 'It is remarkable how the choice of this or that institution . . . makes an important change in the way that otherwise similar societies can develop at a point of major transformation' (Sadurski 2001: 455). What is not always appreciated is that many post-communist states face not just the double transition of political and economic transformation, nor even a triple change that adds state formation, but a yet more complex challenge of quadruple transition involving distinct processes of nation-building and state construction.

It is, therefore, increasingly realized that the process of post-communist democratization (though perhaps not that much less than any other) is a multifaceted and highly complex one, where several critical factors are highly interdependent. Constitutionalism is thus of great importance for the development of post-communist democracy, not just because of its association with the development of a *Rechtsstaat*, accountable democratic processes and a legal basis for the conduct of democratic politics, but also because of the less directly instrumental functions it performs in literally serving to constitute the body politic and form an inclusive political identity (Sadurski 2001: 462–3). This dimension is not far removed from the much discussed (but often loosely defined) issues of political culture that are thought to be central to the process of post-communist democratization. The character of this democratic culture is often associated with the beliefs and practices already well established in western Europe. Democratic development is often identified with Europeanization in this sense – the assumption of a consciously (west) European identity – and is in practice intimately associated with both structures and processes that are designed to lead to formal EU membership. A major problem here is that any contemporary European identity is remarkably difficult to define. The supra-national principles promoted by the EU's founders have lost much of their meaning and force, after a half-century of peace and material wealth. 'Europe' has come to represent values that are largely instrumental and has lost the capacity to strengthen or provide the democratic culture and democratic identity needed by the post-communist countries. The close link between material wealth and democratic achievement thus confirms a self-reinforcing dynamic of European integration and general westernization, but also a view of politics that is essentially technocratic.

The democratic deficit much deplored in EU institutions and processes is thus also reflected in the ambiguities of CEE democratization and the sharp division drawn between the more wealthy democratic countries close to EU membership and the second (or third) division of those slower or even stalled in the democratization process. Democratization has not always been advanced nor the cause of democracy necessarily well served by the strengthening of west European links. The top-down approaches often adopted have not been particularly effective in strengthening processes of democratic consolidation or tackling the weaknesses of civil society so often identified as major limitations. Democratic conditionality has been a blunt instrument that is disproportionately harsh on the states slowest to embark on economic and political development. Zielonka (2001) confirms that CEE democracy has been to a significant extent 'foreign made' and that democratization has been externally facilitated and supported from outside. The major question that concerns us in this context, though, is how far the actual image of democratization has also been affected by the

Western looking-glass and the interpretation of political practice in contemporary CEE perhaps distorted by requirements of conditionality or the demands of EU accession procedures. International pressures more generally have imposed strict restraints on the exercise of self-rule by CEE 'democratic' government.

Globalization clearly limits the sovereignty of the region's new democracies. It encourages unpopular policies and prompts governments to renege on election campaign promises, presses (sometimes forces) leaders to act against the preferences of the electorate, restructures the political space in ways likely to endanger democratic stability, and promotes state reorganization on more repressive lines (Zielonka 2001: 519–20). These mark out major areas of conflict between the dominant conceptions of economic and political change. Processes of democratization and capitalist development are closely linked – after all, modernization theory implies that political and economic change are in some way part of the same package. And close analysis of post-communist change indeed suggests that the economic components of the package take precedence over the political. Yet stronger arguments can also be made that the political effects of economic liberalization and market growth are often identified with democratization even though there is little empirical or theoretical support for such a conclusion.

It is the latter view that would support the case for the looking-glass of democratization studies creating its own image of post-communist political processes distinct from a more 'objective' reality. There are certainly some grounds for coming to such a conclusion, given that the idea of democracy has been stretched globally to cover a wide variety of politically unresponsive and relatively unaccountable regimes where the quality of democracy also often appears to be remarkably thin. Analysis of CEE democratization processes is also, as we have seen, highly inconclusive in the light of widespread conceptual confusion and failure to distinguish between different levels of analysis. What is more clear is that those countries that are attractive candidates for European integration and have the resources needed to participate in the process are regarded as more viable partners and acceptable democratic models of post-communist development. If the criteria for democratization themselves remain vague, there is, paradoxically, far more stability and clarity about which of the CEE states are deemed to meet them.

Notes

1 Nineteen post-communist states including Russia (also a major Asian power), but excluding the transcaucasian states and the former Soviet territories in Asia.

2 Przeworski and Limongi (1997) nevertheless restore some explanatory power to modernization by suggesting that socio-economic development at least worked in the right direction in long-standing dictatorships like those in CEE that did eventually fall. However, much of this can be attributed to the removal of the Soviet veto; and it was precisely in Poland, the leader and major catalyst of CEE democratization, that GDP began to fall in 1979 and did not regain its former level until the 1990s.

11
East Asia

SHAUN BRESLIN

The task of writing about democratization in East Asia as a whole is a hugely problematic one. It is a region that contains massive diversity in political and economic systems and one that remains in a state of considerable flux and transition. A key element in this transition is the end of the Cold War, and the resulting reduction in US tolerance of authoritarianism so long as that authoritarianism was overtly anti-communist. It is also a region where, as in East and Central Europe, communist party states are struggling with the transition from centrally planned socialist economies – though, by contrast with the European examples, and with the exception of Outer Mongolia, this is a transition that has not been accompanied by the end of communist party rule and a parallel process of democratic transition. And it is also a region where financial crises and economic recession have dominated political activity and discourse for half a decade. Perhaps more than in any other region considered in this volume, the overarching framework for political activity here is shaped by the transition from Cold War strategic structures to globalized economic structures.

A cursory analysis of the Freedom House ratings for states in the region gives some indication of the problems of considering the region as a whole (see Table 11.1). At one extreme we have the established democracy of Japan – though even here, the transition from managed factionalism within the structure of rule by the Liberal Democratic Party (LDP) to conflictual factionalism and political fragmentation in the post-LDP coalition governments has created new challenges to democratic politics. There is then a second set of states that have seen considerable moves towards

Table 11.1 Freedom House ratings for East Asian countries, 2001–2

Country	Political rights	Civil liberties	Rating	Per capita GNP (PPP US$)
Burma	7	7	NF	1,500
Cambodia	6	5	NF	1,500
China (PRC)	7	6	NF	4,300
Indonesia	3	4	PF	3,000
Japan	1	2	F	27,200
Korea (North)	7	7	NF	1,000
Korea (South)	2	2	F	18,000
Laos	7	6	NF	1,630
Malaysia	5	5	PF	9,000
Mongolia	2	3	F	1,770
Philippines	2	3	F	4,000
Singapore	5	5	PF	24,700
Taiwan	1	2	F	17,200
Thailand	2	3	F	6,600
Vietnam	7	6	NF	2,100

Notes: F = Free; PF = Partly Free; NF = Not Free. GNP = Gross National Product; PPP = purchasing power parity. While PPP figures provide a base for comparative analysis, they considerably inflate the exchange rate GNP of non-market economies – the figure for China here is nearly 4 times the official Chinese figure.

Source: A. Karatnycky, 'The 2001 Freedom House Survey', *Journal of Democracy* (2002), 13:1, 108–9; GNP estimates from CIA, *The World Factbook 2002*, at www.cia.gov/cia/publications/factbook/index.html.

democratization – in South Korea, where military rule has given way to transfers of power via the ballot box as an accepted feature of political life; in Outer Mongolia, which has moved from authoritarian to 'free' as a result of the end of communist party rule and the election of the Democratic Union Coalition in 1996; in Indonesia, which while still only partially free and retaining considerable authoritarianism has nevertheless moved to partially free; and in the Philippines and Thailand, which have moved from partially free to free; and perhaps most notably in Taiwan, which saw the end of martial law and a transition from Guomindang single-party rule to the presidency of the Democratic Progressive Party's Chen Shui-bian in little over a decade.

But before we proclaim the end of history and applaud the transition to democracy, we should consider at least three other sets of states in the region. At the other extreme from Japan, the rigidly authoritarian states of Burma and North Korea remain, perhaps more than any other states in the world, as impervious to the international system as can be today. A second set of authoritarian states is found in the residual communist party states of Laos, Vietnam and China, where political and social freedom remained strictly restrained despite increased economic freedom as a result of marketization and the retreat from socialism. A third set, on its own, is Singapore, where the electoral system should not be allowed to disguise a limited franchise, and strict state controls over social freedom. Finally, there is a set of regional states that have moved away from freedom and democratization. For example, Cambodia, which has tightened authoritarian rule despite partial freedom status in the mid-1990s; and Malaysia, which has moved from free in 1972 to partially free today. We should perhaps also include here Hong Kong, which while never having had a full and free franchise, has seen even limited democratization circumscribed by the reversion to Chinese sovereignty in 1997.

There has been no single wave of democratization in Asia, then. Though it is possible to draw comparisons from the similar processes in the transition from military rule in South Korea and Taiwan (Wu 1998; Potter 1996) – which have both occurred in the context of relations with the US and relations with rival regimes to the north – discerning region-wide patterns is not so much problematic as impossible. It is possible, of course, to provide in a chapter of this sort a short potted tour of democratization (and the lack of it) in each state – but that would be unsatisfactory. Instead, the chapter seeks to draw out conceptual and methodological issues in considering democratization in Asia – issues that will vary in importance and relevance in each regional state. At its heart is a concern with avoiding concept stretching – with avoiding the pitfall of seeing something that is familiar in the context of democratization and assuming that it functions in the same way in Asia (and indeed in other areas of the world) as it does in the West.

Asian values and the politics of rejection: what Asia isn't

A clear notion of what East Asia means in terms of studies of democratization in large part emerges from the 'Asian values' debate, which in itself has been spurred by Huntington's (1996) notion of a 'clash of civilizations'. The idea that there are a set of Asian values that are effectively different from Western traditions has some attraction – attraction in the West, as it makes Asia easier to bracket as 'different', and attraction in some parts of Asia at least, as it provides a partial justification for the authoritarian nature of many Asian regimes, and for infringements on human rights in several of them.

The argument for a concept of Asian values can be simplified in a very straightforward way. Asian societies, it is argued, have developed on a very different trajectory from those in the West, and have different philosophical and/or historical cultural roots. In the West, the emergence of democracy and notions of rights were largely devised to provide a bulwark for the individual from the state. And democracy, as practised in the West, now takes place in the context of post-industrialized societies with well-established procedures and norms for the conduct of political life.

In Asia, by contrast, the roots of the contemporary system are very different. For example, the traditional Confucian concept of society (which predominated in China, Korea and, to a lesser extent, Japan) was one based on harmony and unity between state and people – the idea of creating a bulwark against the state was anathema, as state and society should be one. Where a discourse on rights existed, it was largely conducted in terms of collective rights, where the interests of the collective – be that collective the family, the state, or even socialism – were far more important than those of any individual (Weatherley 1999).

In considering a truly comparative study of democratization, there should be sympathy for the understanding that democracy and democratization are culturally, historically and politically embedded. But the idea that there is a single set of 'Asian values' that provides a lens through which we study democracy in East Asia should be treated with considerable scepticism. In some respects, the concept helps our understanding by establishing a notion of the 'other' in which Asian debates over democracy take place. The concept of Asia that the Asian values debate promotes is a rejectionist one – what is shared is a rejection of the imposition of what is considered to be a 'Western' concept of politics and polity that has developed and emerged in specific Western contexts that are not applicable to Asia. This understanding is also reflected in other realms of politics – for example, a rejection of the neo-liberal 'Western' economic policies as embodied in the policies of the International Monetary Fund (IMF) and the Word Trade Organization (WTO), and a rejection by some of the post-industrialized and seemingly unfair environmental strategies pursued by many Western states.

This rejectionist stance is perhaps best embodied by attempts to create a cognitive understanding of a region called 'East Asia'. This understanding is largely predicated on a rejection of the Asia Pacific Economic Co-operation (APEC) definition of a region that includes not only the Asian states of Asia, but also the Australasian states, and those states on the Pacific seaboard of the Americas. The proposals of the then Malaysian premier Mohammed Mahathir to establish an East Asian Economic grouping (now formally the East Asian Economic Caucus within APEC) is a good example of defining a region by what it is not (Higgott and Stubbs 1995). So too was the impulse to decide on an Asian entity that would negotiate with the European Union in the Asia Europe Meeting (ASEM) process, which perhaps for the first time forced 'Asia' to decide what it was – and in the process, rejected both the Indian sub-continent and Australasia as comprised in Asia.

So what the Asian values debate helps clarify is what Asia is not – it is not the advanced industrialized and democratized West. It is also framed by a world-view in many Asian governmental elites that is suspicious of the motives of the West in trying to condition developments in the region. And in many cases, the West is synonymous with the United States; and for many regional critics of globalization, it is nothing more than Americanization. But while it might help us understand what Asia is not – what it rejects – it does not help us understand what Asia is. On one level, the concept that there is a single set of Asian values that spans the entire region obfuscates more than it clarifies. At worst, it leans towards an assessment of democratization in the region that treats it as a single entity, rather than reflecting the immense diversity that exists.

On another level, the search for explanations in traditional Asian values can be rather problematic. For example, in searching for the roots of liberal thoughts in Confucianism, Goldman (1994) concludes that the basic tenets of Confucianism are not necessarily incongruent with concepts of human rights. This may indeed be true, and Sen (1997) has argued forcefully against the Asian values concept as a justification for authoritarianism. But in some respects, searching for the roots of contemporary authoritarianism or contemporary democracy in *The Analects* is akin to searching for the roots of democracy in Britain in the belief systems of the Druids. In the intervening years, the structure of state power in China and in other states has done much to shape the way in which traditional ideas have become transformed into contemporary state systems. So rather than emphasize too strongly the historical philosophical roots of contemporary policy and intellectual discourse, it is worth turning to other factors that should inform the way in which we study contemporary democratization in East Asia, and which, in turn, could help us understand some of the preconditions upon which studies of democratization in the West are constructed.

The comparative method and democratization

First, we should simply not ignore the fact that comparative analyses need to take care when they decide on the unit of comparison. Taking democracy in the West as our benchmark could lead to a tendency to compare other parts of the world *now* with democracy in the West *now*. I suggest that this can lead to a false set of comparisons, and we should rather consider the correct temporal comparison. The emergence of democracy in the West was a slow and protracted evolutionary process. So too was the Western industrial revolution. Analyses of democratization and human rights in, for example, the United Kingdom during the industrial revolution would not necessarily generate favourable comparisons with the situation in the UK today. Accordingly, and in keeping with the general orientation of this book, we should consider comparison between comparable processes of democratization *qua* processes, accepting that the experience in the West *at similar phases of the national and industrial revolutions* might generate sounder foundations for comparison than judging unlike with unlike within an arbitrarily chosen common temporal framework.

We have noted above the disparities that exist within Asia – ranging from the relatively liberal political and economic system of Japan to the authoritarian (by any comparison) Burmese system. Leaving aside the most 'advanced' industrialized economies of Japan, Korea and Taiwan, and ignoring the rather strange anomalies of city states like Singapore and Hong Kong, gives us a situation where three key transitions have yet to take place in much of Asia – economic revolution, national revolution and a Polanyiesque great transformation (after Polanyi 1944).[1]

First, we need to recognize that economic underdevelopment remains the major context for politics in much of the region. We must not be too heavily influenced by the growth rates recorded by many Asian states in the last two decades – if you produce one tractor one year, and two the next, you register a growth rate of 100 per cent, but still have only three tractors. For example, despite near-double-digit growth rates in China for two decades, and the fact that the sheer size of the country generates an enormous Gross Domestic Product (GDP), per capita GDP is still below Russia's – widely considered to be the stock negative comparison in terms of economic fortunes in the transition from socialism.

And of course, in 1997, the Asian financial crises placed a new dimension on this issue of economic development. On one level, the crises promoted the importance of democratization, in terms of a reaction against the 'crony capitalism' that some argued had at least contributed to the crises (Wei and Dievers 2000). Crises and economic recession in many regional states impacted on the newly expanded middle classes, who had been the beneficiaries of the pre-crises boom. It is from within these groups that many of the pressures for change now emanate in Thailand, Indonesia and Malaysia. Similar pressures from the middle class can be observed in Hong Kong, where the educated middle classes are feeling the impact of economic recession for the first time in generations. Business elites too have been forced to rethink their position and their relationship with the state as a result of the crises – indeed, in Thailand a representative of the business elite was elected to lead the country. Rather than allow politicians to run the country on their behalf, the Thai elites appear to have decided to run it themselves!

There have also been uncertain or ambivalent consequences of crisis. Hewison (2001) notes that in Thailand there has been a turn towards local identities and localism as a response to national crisis. Such localism could provide the basis for a more participatory democratization at the grass-roots level. But it is also predicated on a concern that Thai culture is under attack from the agencies of international capitalism in the shape of World Bank and IMF recovery projects – projects that 'impose' alien Western values and practices. In this respect, nationalism as a response to crises has been an important political change in three main ways, as state elites have tried to turn the blame for crises away from themselves and on to 'outside' groups. First, the blame for the crises has been placed on foreign banks and investors, who moved their portfolios out of the region at speed, triggering financial chaos. Second, with the support of state elites, it has reinforced the rejectionist stance towards the West detailed above. Third, and again with the support of state elites, most notably in Indonesia, it has generated a wave of ethnic violence against minority groups – particularly the overseas Chinese.

For observers it is easy to point to the role of the state in attempting to deflect criticism for their own actions or inactions – and to an extent this is a valid argument. But we should not simply ignore the real concerns of many within the region – real concerns on one level that the West is imposing its values on countries with different historical, philosophical, cultural and political roots. But also real concerns that this thing called globalization is really impinging on sovereignty, or political self-determination. What point is there in voting for one party or another if the fundamental economic strategy of whichever government is elected is shaped by the IMF and the World Bank, or by the investment and disinvestment strategies of major external corporations and investment brokers? In this respect, there is a real feeling of disempowerment amongst many in the region, and a concern that globalization has resulted in a 'democratic deficit' – particularly amongst many in the intellectual community, as is perhaps best articulated by the work produced in connection with the 'Focus on the Global South'.[2]

Finally, the crises have impacted hardest on rural farmers and the urban working classes – many of whom are now the urban unemployed. These groups are the least represented in democratic politics, both in terms of formal political parties and organizations, and in terms of participation in pressure groups and civil society organizations. While they were perhaps never particularly well represented in many regional states, their under-representation now at a time when they need it more than ever is an important consideration in democratic politics.

Of course, it is entirely right and justifiable to consider the growth of civil society as an indicator of democratization and progress. But in doing so, we should not ignore the issue of the balance of representation and the extent to which democratization permeates all sectors of society. I suggest, then, that much of the activity of civil society in the region represents the interests of the middle classes – perhaps even over-represents those interests, while business elites retain an even stronger access to the political process and the representation of interest. A key challenge that remains is to ensure that democracy becomes more inclusive, more participatory, and more representative of the interests of those who may not be formally disenfranchised, but are often largely excluded from the political process.

We should remember that the national revolution in many Asian states is incomplete. Or at the very least, the processes of nation-building and state consolidation in many Asian states are still ongoing. The concept of a Vietnamese nation, for example, is still relatively new by historical standards, and largely a consequence of the dual processes of colonization and decolonization. Indonesia, as a political entity, has been challenged by the secession of East Timor, raising the fear in some (and hope in others) that the Indonesian state may further fragment into ethnically defined nation-states. And in Korea and China, there is the spectre of rival regimes claiming (though not always reciprocally) jurisdiction over a disputed national entity. Without a clear understanding of what constitutes the *demos*, constructing democracy is inherently problematic.

This immature realization of nationhood and statehood is often explained in terms of the end of the Cold War. And indeed, the end of the Cold War has played a key role. But in many respects, these issues are pre-Cold War in nature and owe much to the incomplete process of decolonization and nation-building that the onset of the Cold War interrupted.

Ethnic tensions – often closely related to this incomplete national revolution – also impinge on the evolution of democracy. The ethnic tensions that emerged during the financial crises, most notably in Indonesia, have already been mentioned. But even in more peaceful 'normal' times, resentment at the control of political power by dominant ethnic groups in Malaysia, Singapore and Indonesia, to name but three, undermines the legitimacy of the democratic polity.

But perhaps most fundamentally, we need to revisit the question of the way in which we study democratization and the basic premises on which many analyses are made. Take as a starting-point the classic text by Polanyi (1944). Almost implicitly, many studies of democratization assume the 'great transformation' as a given. The separation of public and private, of state and market, that occurred in Europe and other industrialized democracies established the basis of an understanding of the relationship between the state and non-state in which conceptions of democratization largely exist. In particular, when moving beyond an over-simple equation of elections with democracy, this separation of public and private becomes an essential component for understanding the state–society relationship.

But in reality, it was the 'great transformation' of industrialization in Europe in the nineteenth century that marked the 'singular departure' from the dominant norm by creating the institutional separation of society into an economic and a political sphere. For large parts of the world – not just in Asia – this transformation has not taken place, or is at best incomplete. The most obvious examples of this lack of separation are found in the communist party states within the region, where the socialist system all but demanded state control over society and economy. But it is also evident in other states – states that at first glance might appear to be Western-type democracies.

Van Wolferen (1990), for example, has long argued that analysts from the 'West' fail to understand Japan because they start with false assumptions. The concept of a separation between 'public' and 'private' that lies at the heart of some investigations of political economy is, according to van Wolferen, absent in Japan. Some have argued that this is a consequence both of the traditional understanding of 'economy' in East Asia and of the way in which market economies were established there. In Taiwan, where the residual authoritarian Guomindang government has been replaced through democratic elections, the former holders of a monopoly on state power retain strong control over key economic functions, through their ownership of large sections of the means of production.

Should this concern us as students of democratization, or is it an issue that we should leave for the political economists? Perhaps the details of state control and influence over the economy are best discussed elsewhere. But the important point is that analytical divisions between the national and the international, and between the political and the economic, obstruct a more nuanced understanding of domestic political processes and their impact on democratization in the contemporary world. As Gamble *et al.* (1996: 10) argue, 'The separation between the global and the local no longer holds, as the new hierarchies of the global economy cut across regional and national boundaries.' This being so, we should accept that a key, and neglected area of study in analyses of democratization is the ability of the *demos* to influence, through political processes, economic policy-making that impinges on the lives of national citizens – either through the structure of domestic political economies, or through the influence of external 'international' factors. In particular, a central concern here is the ability of those outside a narrow section of state elites and their allies to influence policy through democratic means, and the related question of transparency.

Robison (1988), for example, takes issue with claims that the Indonesian system does not work effectively. The point Robison wants to drive home is that political systems are designed to serve specific political interests. The Indonesian system might not have worked as external observers thought it *should*, but was in fact very successful in delivering the fruits of economic growth to members of the Indonesian elite. In particular, the politico-economic system was constructed to ensure that former President Suharto's family utilized political power to advance their economic status and control.

The Indonesian system, then, was deliberately opaque, and constructed to ensure that an elite group of insiders utilized a linkage between political power, economic policy-making, and state or family control over major sectors of the economy, to deliver rewards to themselves. The title of Harold Lasswell's *Politics: Who Gets What, When and How?* (1936) still offers an insightful starting-point for considerations of how political leaders make policies designed to benefit specific interests.

Perhaps Indonesia is an extreme case, though one that is remarkably similar in its deliberate opaqueness to the one that is emerging in China, as the transition from socialism creates a similar close relationship between elite policy-makers and the beneficiaries of those policies (many of whom emerge from within the party-state system itself). However, even in the most 'liberal' – in that it looks like a Western democratic system – democracy in the region, in Japan, an understanding of the functioning of the domestic political economy raises a number of questions over the validity of deploying 'traditional' understandings of democratization.

It is helpful here to consider the conception of a 'capitalist developmental state' (CDS). The CDS system proved to be remarkably successful in generating economic growth in Japan and the newly industrialized countries (NICs) – policies that were partially emulated by later generations of developing states in the region. For Chalmers Johnson, a key component in this developmental strategy was the 'relative state autonomy' of elite bureaucrats who planned economic strategy (albeit in market-conforming manners) around perceived national interests – politicians reign but bureaucrats rule (Johnson 1987: 152). Irrespective of the result of democratic elections, an elite group of professional bureaucrats made economic policy based on their conceptions of the national interest, unconstrained by considerations of electoral popularity and insulated from the demands of societal interest groups. The politicians could worry about getting re-elected – in the Japanese case, by considering the interests of their local constituency rather than issues of wider national importance – and the bureaucrats would get on with running the economy. Thus, electors might be able to influence local developmental issues through the democratic process – to win a new train link with Tokyo, for example – but the overall direction of national economic planning continued unhindered by the inconvenience of democratic politics.

This system was facilitated by the eradication of powerful interest groups at the end of the Second World War – through, first, defeat and then the US occupation in Japan, which resulted in the suppression of business and then workers' interests. The Japanese occupation in Korea resulted in weak societal or interest groups in the new South Korea. Meanwhile in Taiwan, similar groupings were eliminated following the arrival of the Guomindang and with the resulting party-state control of society and the economy. In all three cases, the state was emboldened by proclaimed strategies of national renewal and national mobilization to defend the new statist entities in the face of possible communist aggression in the region (Cumings 1987). And of course, in this Cold War context, being authoritarian, but anti-communist authoritarian, was often enough to qualify for considerable US economic aid, and Western tolerance of the lack of democratic forms.

In the case of Japan, the national interest was defined, according to Johnson (1981), by a policy community that encompassed a triad of bureaucrats, business interests and leaders of the LDP – the hegemonic party until the 1990s. A system of *amakudari* (descent from heaven) ensured that retired bureaucrats enjoyed second careers either within the business community or the LDP, while the industrial bureaux of the Ministry of International Trade and Industry (MITI) provided a formal framework within which business interests could influence the conception of national interest, and subsequently national economic planning.

What this means for students of democratization is that the opaque decision-making process was difficult for outsiders to penetrate. Elections, pressure groups and wider civil society had little chance to influence key economic policy-making that obviously impinged on the lives of national citizens. The system did not go unchallenged, as is perhaps best exemplified by the sporadic and violent protests in South Korea under military rule – perhaps most notably the Kwangju Incident of May 1980. But while it delivered significant economic growth, and as long as influential sectors of the populations were rewarded in the process, then the system was one that was at least tolerated by enough people to ensure its continuity. Even after the initial transition to democracy – albeit 'low intensity democracy' (Gills, Rocamora and Wilson 1993) in South Korea and Taiwan – the decision-making process that created national economic strategy remained largely not transparent, and continued to be dominated by a relatively small group of insiders (though not everyone agrees with this assessment).

To be sure, this system has been challenged by the financial crises that highlighted the failings of crony capitalism – in states where transparency is not the norm, and the relationship between state and economy remains strong. Nevertheless, many Asian states do not have transparent policy-making processes in the Western mould (where there are limitations of transparency too). Thus of major importance to anyone wishing to consider the real extent of democratization in Asia should be those issues that often would fall under the ambit of political economy perspectives. It is there that, elections and the evolution of civil society groups notwithstanding, forces affecting the ability of the *demos* to influence the polis are most salient.

This also means that we should pay more attention to the influence of external factors, and not simply to the way that international human rights organizations, for instance, try to press for domestic political change. Those pressures are of course significant, not least because of the way in which the end of the Cold War has removed a key impediment to pressures for democratic change – particularly from the United States. But alongside those 'traditional' forms of pressure we need to consider the democratic implications of other external factors. For example, if transparency is important in democracy, then the policy initiatives of the IMF, the World Bank, and the WTO – all of whom call for greater transparency from governments – potentially have important implications. So too do the less overt pressures to conform to international norms of economic activity that largely reflect Western practices and interests. Their intention may not be explicitly to promote domestic democratization, but their consequences could have implications for democratization.

Moreover, the hand of the state is not just evident in the economy; judicial power – or more correctly, judicial independence – is relatively weak in many East Asian states. Furthermore, it can be, and is, used to prosecute political opponents – a notable recent example being the trial of the former Malaysian Deputy Prime Minister, Anwar Ibrahim, for calling for reform to the authoritarian system. According to the likes of Human Rights Watch, the Anwar case illustrates how, despite a *prima facie* legitimate judicial process, four notable features undermine the real democratic nature of the system: the lack of independence of judges appointed by the government, and dependent on them for promotion and advancement; the treatment of defence witnesses and defendants; constraints on the defence's chances of preparing adequate responses to the frequently changing charges; and the political atmosphere in which the trial was taking place.

On this last issue, we should focus on the extent to which democracy is constrained by a lack of free and plural information. Or in other words, can democracy exist without a fully informed *demos*? In the Malaysian case, Eng (1999) notes that a media that was once supportive of Anwar soon turned against him once the political atmosphere from the national government signalled an anti-Anwar turn. Only the relatively small *Aliran Monthly*, with an average circulation of 8,000 (which doubled during the Anwar trials) maintained a pro-Anwar stance during the trials, as other journals responded to government pressure and mounted a character assassination on Anwar (Eng 1999). Similarly, in Singapore, journalistic and academic freedom are strictly curtailed, with criticisms of the government and government policy frequently leading to censure and the termination of academic contracts (Rodan 2000).

Such limitations of information do not require state ownership of media or state control of academia – though they clearly help. In many respects, self-censorship results in an equally unfree and biased provision of information. Indeed, the more successful authoritarian states probably do not need to use heavy-handed tactics, as informal self-censorship does the job of authoritarianism for them.

The China syndrome

At the risk of privileging the study of one regional state over others, it is worth considering the process of, and prospects for, democratization in China. This is partly because the Chinese case allows us to consider what democratization is *for*, and partly because it allows us to question some of the more traditional assumptions about the relationship between economic and political change.

First, then, we need to consider the purpose of democratization. Take as an example the introduction of competitive elections at county levels of authority since 1998. It might be the case that such elections allow Chinese voters to choose representatives who are not simply the candidates presented to them by the Chinese Communist Party (CCP). And indeed, in some cases, officially sanctioned CCP candidates have been defeated in these elections. Of course, critics can point to the fact that these county-level elections have little impact on the overall distribution of power in China – and it is a fair criticism. But even if such change in the distribution of power does occur in the long run, my concern here is with *intentions* rather than *outcomes*. In inception, and like the previous experiments with local-level elections in 1980, officially sanctioned processes of democratization in China are not intended to pave the way for a challenge to CCP rule, but rather to strengthen it (Goodman 1997). For Kelliher (1997), they were based on an understanding that the political legitimacy of the CCP in the countryside had been eroding. Thus providing greater degrees of self-government was a key means of rebuilding legitimacy – not just in local governments in themselves, but more importantly in a political system dominated by one-party rule in general. Consequently, what might look like a move away from single-party rule from the outside is conceived as a means of strengthening single-party rule by its initiators.

A similar argument can be deployed for understanding the growth of civil society groups in China (Howell 1998). The original growth of civil society groups in China in the 1990s occurred because the CCP wanted to allow more leeway for officially sanctioned groups to act as a buffer between government and society. As with the introduction of elections, the growth of civil society in the long run may have unintended consequences for CCP rule. But again, the intention was not to weaken single-party rule, but to strengthen the legitimacy of single-party rule.

Second, the fact that China is in the process of a transition from a socialist economy and continues to enjoy impressive rates of economic growth and modernization allows us to test hypotheses formed to explain the relationship between economic and political change (see the discussion by Addison in Chapter 3). In contrast to the idea that economic reform and material advancement will lead to pressures for political reform from either an emerging middle class or the increasingly abandoned working class (or both), there are at least two possible alternative scenarios. For the time being, at least, rather than China's workers applying pressure for a more liberal political system, much of the evidence suggests that they are a force for conservatism. On one level, many workers, particularly from the state-owned sector, resent the fact that marketization has resulted in loss of jobs and the concomitant reduction of welfare provision. What many of them want is the *certainty* and basic standards of welfare associated with the old – not a return to the harsh days of the Cultural Revolution, but instead to a time after Mao when market reforms had been introduced, but their harsh impact on unprofitable producers had yet to become apparent. This seems far preferable to the uncertainty that the new economic order now appears to offer, or the even greater uncertainty that democratic political transformation could bring. Partly because of the example of former communist party states elsewhere, most notably the former Soviet Union, and partly as a result of official policy to reinforce the message, a transition from authoritarianism to democracy is often equated with economic decline and political chaos. It is not seen as a progressive and beneficial process.

On another level, the emergence of a new entrepreneurial class has also yet to translate into pressure for liberal democratic political reform. Indeed, many of the 'new class' have emerged from within the party-state system – they have used their positions within the political elite to create new positions as economic elites. And for the time being, using political power (or connections) to protect or enhance their economic position results in, at the very least, a continued acceptance of the established political system. At the same time, the growth of CCP membership to around 66 million is in large part due to emerging non-party economic elites joining the party to protect their own positions. They want to benefit from the connections and security offered by being 'part of the club' and insure themselves against residual suspicion directed at the role of private enterprise. As such, there is a coalescing of new and old elites around mutually beneficial political and economic orders.

Of course, not all new elites join the party. And ultimately, the new economic elites may no longer need the support of the party to guarantee their economic position. It would be rash to say that pressures for political reform and political pluralism will never emerge as a consequence of economic growth and market reforms. However, for now the relationship appears not to be clear-cut, and there is a range of potential scenarios that could take precedence as China evolves.

(Are there any) conclusions

The path of democratization has not moved smoothly in Asia – indeed, it has not always moved in a single direction. Many regional states share similar challenges – not least the challenge of economic recovery in the wake of the financial crises. But the responses have been very diverse. There is certainly no convincing evidence that a common form of democracy is emerging across the region, nor that democratic politics is necessarily the best or the only way forward. As has been noted above, many people in China are at least prepared to tolerate political authoritarianism if it continues to provide a context in which economic advancement occurs.

Even in electoral systems in the region, the type of democracy that has evolved is often constrained by a lack of real choice, a lack of real societal freedom, and state control over sources of information and ideas. It is also constrained by opaque decision-making systems that result from a lack of a separation between public and private, between state and non-state, and between state and market – distinctions that are almost implicitly accepted as the basis for democratization in the West. Accordingly, studies of democratization in East Asia, while not ignoring 'normal' processes of democratization, should also consider the importance of political economy, and that marrying democratization perspectives with those in international political economy specifically offers a particularly appropriate and useful framework for future analyses.

Notes

1 It is in some ways a great disservice to Polanyi (1944) to reduce the 'Great Transformation' to a single concept. But the key issue of relevance here is his concept of how the industrial revolution fundamentally changed the previous system, where economic relationships were embedded within societal relationships. In particular, this transformation resulted in the separation of economy activity from community-based action, developing into a new institutional separation of politics and economics.

2 The 'Focus on the Global South' can be found on www.focusweb.org.

12

The European Union

ALEX WARLEIGH

Democratization has suddenly become a fashionable theme in both the practice and the study of European integration.[1] Since the Treaty on European Union (TEU) of 1991, which both raised the profile of the integration process and substantially extended the scope of powers enjoyed by the European Union (EU; the Union), the Union has become far more controversial. Received wisdom dictates that it suffers from a (generally unspecified) 'democratic deficit', which was scarcely noticed beforehand. Paradoxically, however, in the last decade several attempts to render the EU more democratic have actually been made, a good example being the significant empowerment of the European Parliament (EP). Moreover, the TEU made member-state nationals EU citizens, an unprecedented step in world history, even if EU citizenship remains rather limited. Indeed, the EU is preparing for both further enlargement and the next round of Treaty reform (due in 2004) by launching a process of 'civil dialogue' and a quasi-constitutional convention. These are supposed to provide suggestions about increasing the legitimacy and democratic credentials of the Union system.

This chapter explores the particularities and difficulties of the EU's democratization, and argues that the way forward is to construct a set of democratic practices based on deliberative democracy and active citizenship, cemented in and reflected by institutional reform. The EU case indicates much of interest to scholars of democratization in general, as it points towards the need both for innovative mixtures of experimentation and deliberative democracy and to re-think the links between the 'domestic' and the 'international'. First, however, it is necessary to examine the context in which EU democratization must be undertaken.

Framing the issue: EU democracy as a quadruple balancing act

Democratization of the EU is a very complex and unusual process. As a transnational system, the Union is unlikely to be suited to the straightforward application of models based on the nation-state, requiring instead innovations in the theory and practice of democratic governance (Schmitter 2000). Additionally, reformers must recognize that the EU is deeply coloured by a path dependency that affects both the nature of the EU system and the attitudes of actors within it about the possibilities for reform. Attempting to make common policy in the absence of a hegemon, Union decision-making has always been characterized by the search for consensus between key actors in the elites at national and EU levels, even though the elites' composition has changed as the inter-institutional balance of power has evolved. Lord (1998) observes that this 'extreme consensus democracy' has been at the expense of mass democracy, which explains both how perceptions of a democratic deficit have arisen and why the EU's legitimacy crisis of the last decade surprised many in positions of power. However, this culture of consensus usefully demonstrates that the EU must in fact balance different kinds of legitimacy and the demands of different groups of actors in order to be democratic. Thus, although the equilibrium between these different sources and types of legitimacy is clearly in need of revision, it is necessary to acknowledge that the approach itself – the instinct for balance – is both a reflection of the EU's own political culture and likely to remain necessary.

The first balancing act that the EU must perform is between different competing national views of what a democratic Union would constitute. The member states continue to want different things from integration in terms of both specific policy areas and its ultimate end-point, the so-called *finalité politique*. Consequently they differ in the degree of sovereignty they are prepared to exercise jointly with their partners, and also over the specific regime they would consider legitimate to erect at EU level. Member states may agree that a certain policy area should be an EU competence, but differ enormously about the nature of the legislation to be made and the constitution of the relevant decision rules. Furthermore, there are differences in political culture that often shape national elite responses to any given issue, as is demonstrated most notoriously by the diametrically opposed German and British understandings of the term 'federal' (respectively a decentralized system based on strict separation of powers and a strong rule of law, versus a centralized superstate). Moreover, national elite views about the desirable outcomes of the integration process change over time. For example, Italy under Prime Minister Berlusconi appears far less viscerally pro-integration than formerly. Thus it is clear that this first balance must be constantly revisited; no particular view has an inherently superior legitimacy. Each state that joins the Union has formal equality with all other member states, so there is no a priori reason why, for example, Denmark's reluctance to sign up to the Schengen agreements on freedom of movement is less legitimate than Belgium's enthusiasm.[2]

The second balancing act is between the different levels of governance within the EU system. The Union has not replaced or superseded national systems, which continue to reflect different national balances between centre and periphery and various approaches to the welfare state; rather, the EU has 'fused' with them (Wessels 1997), leaving (sub)national governments to implement EU policy according to national dictates. In for instance Germany, Austria, Belgium and Spain, regional/local government is powerful, bolstered by strong normative claims to legitimacy based on the principle of local self-government, often enshrined in national constitutions. As a complex and varied system of multi-level governance the EU needs to reflect the demands and roles of governance at local/regional, national *and* European levels if it is to be legitimate. Moreover, democratizing the Union cannot be accomplished solely at EU level, but also requires change at (sub)national level, given that it is through actors and institutions there that most citizens will experience the Union as a policy-maker.

The third balancing act is between output legitimacy and input legitimacy. Traditionally, output legitimacy has been preferred, in the hope that loyalties would be transferred to the Union as a result of its production of public goods perceived to increase the general welfare. But this approach has been insufficient for two main reasons. First, the EU's inability to develop the necessary redistributive policy, the member states having refused to give it the necessary competence and budget (despite the growth in relative importance of EU cohesion policy). Second, the Union's lack of attention to public participation, which has created, or at best done nothing to remove, a situation in which citizens are generally alienated from the integration process (Eurobarometer 54, Autumn 2000).[3] Thus democratization will require a shift in favour of input legitimacy, which will not be easy in the absence of a Europeanized civil society (Warleigh 2001). However, without the emergence of a self-conscious European *demos*, institutional change at EU level will not be perceived as legitimate but rather as the imposition of a false majoritarianism unrooted in (political) identity (Chryssochoou 2000[1998]).

The fourth balancing act is between different normative views of democracy. There are many different views about how democracy can be possible in the context of the EU, which may colour the different and changing national elite positions on the Union's *finalité politique*. However, this issue increasingly goes beyond national cleavages at the elite level to academic and popular debates on the best way to develop institutions like EU citizenship or the principles on which policy in newly-vigorous fields (such as justice and home affairs, or security and defence) should be based. In terms of political theory, this boils down to debates over the most appropriate way to mix principles of cosmopolitanism and communitarianism, both of which are relevant to the Union given its multi-level and 'fused' nature.

Particularities and difficulties: democratization in a quixotic polity[4]

The novel nature of the EU – its location at an uncertain and fluctuating point on a spectrum between classic international organization and supranational federation – means that it has numerous particularities. With regard to democratization, the first of these is the need to specify a suitable comparator for analysis. As the first case of institutionalized transnational democracy, however flawed, the EU is a paragon of legitimacy compared with traditional international diplomacy or international organizations. National models are unlikely to be suitable as direct comparators, given their dependence on a range of features and structures that the EU does not possess (see Schmitter 2000: 15–19). In addition, unfavourable comparisons with the nation-states may exhibit an overly rosy view of democracy in contemporary Western states, ignoring trends like the shift to the executive and the emergence of a 'post-parliamentary' system.

Given that the Union is developing in terms of its competence, geographical scope, and modes of policy-making, a further particularity is the requirement to marry democratization to a system that is rather more obviously evolutionary and process-based than those operating in member states. There is an unusual clarity in the EU case of the need to be experimental with forms of democratic governance. Additionally – and partly as a result – the EU's democratization process is uncommon in its blunt revelation of the links between *state power* and democracy. This can be seen in the repeated and ongoing attempts to elaborate the principles of subsidiarity, proportionality and flexibility as means of marrying national interest with collective need. It can also be seen in the crude, but nonetheless instructive, trade-off between different types of sovereignty: 'national' sovereignty (understood as the power of national governments), and 'popular' sovereignty (understood as either that of a nation or of the collectivity of EU citizens).

A further particularity of the EU context is the failure of most of the concerned actors to appreciate the implications of the EU's quixotic nature for models of democratization. Although other models of reform have been articulated, most strategies tend to rely to an unhelpful degree on what can be called the 'liberal democratic blueprint' (LDB). This is not to say that liberal democracy has no virtues which could be remodelled for the EU; as Lord and Beetham (2001) point out, certain classic features of liberal democracy are certainly capable of such adaptation. However, the LDB, with its emphasis on majoritarian parliamentary systems, ultimately provides a zero-sum choice about democratization as a yes-or-no response to the question whether the EU should become a federal state. This tends to reduce issues of democratization to arguments about the desirability or otherwise of federalism, which tend to be circular and incapable of solution. As Schmitter (2000) points out, there is a danger that citizens: (a) equate democracy as a set of principles and practices with one particular (albeit dominant) democratic tradition, namely *liberal* democracy; (b) decide that the EU cannot therefore be democratic on the grounds of national sovereignty; and (c) decide that the EU is therefore at best an undemocratic necessity to be suffered grudgingly, or at worst a system to be rejected in its entirety.

This pre-eminence of the LDB thus in fact creates the key difficulty of democratization in the EU: the centrality of the principle of national/state sovereignty in the debate. Creativity is thereby stifled; moreover, the 'Europeanization' of civil society – necessary to create a supportive and responsive arena for institutional reform (Pérez-Díaz 1998) – is thereby rendered more difficult. This is because citizens often simply fail to perceive when they need to engage with the EU to secure their objectives, as their horizons remain predominantly national. Moreover, given the pre-eminence of the LDB 'frame', they may consider that such mobilization is impossible in the EU system. Successful campaigning activity at EU level by non-governmental organizations has so far failed to change this situation (Warleigh 2001). Developing a meaningful set of common European values and principles requires more than their proclamation by treaty; without further popular interaction, citizens will continue to experience those values primarily as national phenomena.

A further difficulty is the need to address the fact that EU democratization is part of a general reconfiguring of the European state. Certain commentators have gone so far as to say that the integration process actually 'rescued' the idea of the nation-state in western Europe by allowing its successful rearticulation after the Second World War (Milward 1994[1992]). Whether or not this is true, it remains to be seen whether the Union can do as much for the new nation-states of Central and Eastern Europe as they accede. Nonetheless, it is clear that the EU is both a response to, and a cause of, the changing form of the nation-state in Europe. It has a similar relationship with the view that the exercise of sovereignty is often best achieved through its 'pooling' – witness the euro currency. However, this means in turn that democratization of the EU is part of a process of re-thinking the state itself. This has had two principal manifestations to date. First, the neoliberal tendency to use the EU as a means of 'rolling back the state' at national level while failing to reintroduce the same state controls or functions at EU level. The success of the single European market and the weakness of Union social policy are illustrative. Second, the fact that the EU has opened a Pandora's box in terms of centre–periphery contestation, at least in some parts of some member states. This does not prove that the EU must always privilege neoliberal tendencies or lead to a 'Europe of the regions'. However, it does demonstrate that the EU's democratization is all the more difficult for its impact on intra-, as well as inter-, state relations, and its use as a means of rethinking what the state can, or should, do. This means that support for integration can wax and wane according to current perceptions and comparisons with relevant states. As an example, recall the difficult relationship between the EU and Britain's political left. In the 1960s and 1970s, the Union was considered part of a capitalist project to exploit the working classes; in the late 1980s, when Jacques Delors led the European Commission, there was a shift towards seeing it as a potential source of social democracy; and now, although the mainstream of the Labour Party remains relatively pro-European, the EU's failure to develop its competences in social policy has triggered a return to Euroscepticism on the left.

The way forward: towards deliberative democracy?

There are of course various positions taken about the way forward. Communitarians often argue that EU democracy is a contradiction in terms, given that it depends on the existence of a *demos*, which can be found at national but not 'European' level. Others argue in a more cosmopolitan manner that the way out of the impasse is to apply the strictures of Western liberal democracy to the EU, making it a federation and hoping that the new institutions will cause *demos*-formation over time. However, most scholars are seeking to find a way between these two extremes. For there is an urgent need for some kind of further democratization of the Union to protect the benefits to date of the integration process, yet no great will at elite or popular levels to turn the EU into a state in its own right (see *inter alia* Chryssochoou 2000[1998]; Schmitter 2000).

Many analysts argue that the most suitable way to address the particularities and difficulties of democratizing the European Union is to apply a reform model based on deliberative democracy. This is because the principal problem is the lack of a Europeanized public sphere. That reflects the lack of a European political identity and solidarity between member-state nationals, their status as EU citizens having so far failed to alter significantly their sense of political identity. At popular and elite levels, there are substantial differences in perspective about both 'big picture' and more particular policy issues. There is no real sense of community, or *demos* (even civically-defined) at the EU level. Liberal democracy, with its dependence on a tightly-bound *demos* and over-reliance upon representative mechanisms that sit ill in the non-majoritarian EU context, is of limited help. Instead of implicitly assuming the existence of an EU political community, reformers must pay attention to the generation of one. Deliberation is a means by which this sense of community can be created by a process of difference management. It is also open-ended and process-based – which sits well with the evolutionary nature of the European integration process.

Deliberative democracy argues that the best form of democratic governance is one in which all those affected by a public policy engage in a process of deliberation: that is, they exchange views, try to understand other actors' needs and perspectives, and thereby reach a mutually acceptable outcome (Dryzek 2000). Thus, it is a process of constructing a common interest by learning and mutual accommodation. It is *not* a process of bargaining or interest aggregation; deliberation envisages the formation of a consensus through dialogue, not a package deal whereby actors reach strategic accommodations through processes of log-rolling.

To facilitate this, deliberative democracy envisages that issues should be treated in isolation from each other. Thus, participation is privileged over representation; the franchise is considered not just the right to vote but rather the ability to participate effectively in the formation of public policy, based on principles of pluralism, free debate and mutual recognition as political equals. Deliberative democracy thus favours input legitimacy over output legitimacy, and as a corollary depends on transparency and accountability, so that those who have engaged in deliberation can ensure that their input has been reflected in public policy (J. Cohen 1997). As a key asset in this context, deliberative democracy expects differences to exist, and seeks to provide a mechanism for actors to co-operate and build mutual understanding despite these differences. It is a means by which community can be built from the bottom up, and by which socialization can occur at both popular and elite levels through active citizenship, iterated contact, and social learning (Christiano 1997).

Further assets of deliberative democracy in the EU context are its adaptability, ability to generate a culture of voluntary compliance, and correspondence with the EU culture of informal politics and inter-institutional dialogue (see Dryzek 2000). Deliberation can be a means of making decisions in every policy regime, but is capable of providing different solutions to each issue and involving different groups of stakeholders as appropriate. This is in keeping with the EU, whose various competences are subject to different decision rules and involve many different actor sets. The ability to generate voluntary compliance is a particular benefit; EU policy depends on the member states (and their subnational governments and/or agencies) to implement policy, which leads to many gaps in the implementation of Union legislation. If legislation came from deliberation rather than log-rolling, the implementation deficit would probably diminish. In terms of inter-institutional dialogue, deliberation is of great relevance. It must be recalled that EU policy is generated through policy networks, given the unclear separation of powers and interdependence between the EU institutions and national equivalents. These networks function best when they engender a process of mutual understanding, such as the growing joint legislative culture between the EU Council and the European Parliament (EP) that is being established as a result of the codecision process[5] (Shackleton 2000). Such networks can be long-term or issue-specific. What matters is that they are successful when marginal utility becomes translated into a process of mutual understanding and collaboration.

Of course, deliberative democracy is not capable of application to the EU in unaltered form; like any theory it must be adapted to the real-world context. First, there is the obvious issue of communication capacity. Deliberation is impossible if citizens cannot understand each other. In the EU there is no popular *lingua franca*, despite the growing dominance of English at elite level. This means that at least in the medium term deliberative democracy will have to be tempered with representative democracy (Lord and Beetham 2001), accompanied by creative approaches to the language issue.

Deliberative democracy is so different from conventional liberal democratic views that citizens may simply fail to recognize it as 'democracy'. Others might find its uses limited; deliberative democracy is more than capable of reconciling differences of principle rather than policy preference, but even 'sincere reasoners (may) . . . find themselves in principled disagreements' (Gaus 1997: 231). This means that arbitration institutions will be necessary; deliberation will sometimes require some form of political decision-making institution, to be used sparingly but occupying the apex of the system. Deliberative democrats often consider that if no mutual accommodation can be reached the proposal in question should fall. If this happens regularly, however, citizens are likely to question the worth of the system, no matter how greatly they influence it (Gaus 1997). This is especially problematic for the EU, which does not have great reserves of legitimacy on which to draw *in extremis*.

Furthermore, a well-known feature of the EU system is its ability to produce unanticipated outcomes to policy decisions through the intervention of opportunistic actors (Pierson 1996); deliberative democracy would need to reduce the potential for such outcomes to occur in order to retain credibility (Lord and Beetham 2001). Moreover, there are likely to be limits to the amounts of time and resources individuals are prepared to commit to deliberation:

'deliberation fatigue' is a real possibility if there are no intermediary or representative mechanisms to channel the fruits of deliberation into the policy-making process. However, this should not be taken to mean that uniform solutions to EU problems are always necessary. Deliberation could be a very useful means of indicating where and how vague principles like 'proportionality' (the idea that the EU should act only to the minimum extent necessary to secure an objective), subsidiarity (whereby responsibilities are allocated to either the (sub)national or the EU level) and flexibility (the idea that integration need not be uniform but may instead require differentiated structures and policy regimes) should be operationalized (see Warleigh 2002).

Thus perhaps the chief virtue of deliberative democracy here is its reliance upon, and signalling of the need for, a more participatory political culture. As the EU becomes much more clearly a process of *political* unification, the need for a reform process that draws heavily on active citizenship is clear if citizens are to be socialized into the EU system and thereby enable it to develop in ways they consider legitimate. The recent process of civil dialogue and the 'constitutional convention' hold some promise in this regard.[6]

Conclusion: drawing lessons in democratization from the EU

The main lessons about democratization from the EU case should not be considered as a prescription automatically to be applied in other cases, but more a broad-brush indication.

The initial lesson is that EU democratization must produce a substantive rather than a Schumpeterian form of democratic governance. Institutional aspects of democratization, while certainly in need of further attention, are merely part of the complex problematic; indeed, a rather greater part is the absence of a Europeanized civil society. Without this, democratization will be impossible, for the existence of a public sphere is what makes it possible for institutional reform processes to deepen and resonate with the citizens subject to it (Pérez-Díaz 1998). However, in the EU's case this represents a particular challenge: civil society must 'Europeanize' (i.e. take on a specific EU rather than narrowly national element) in a context of a sustained legitimacy crisis and evidence of popular disaffection.

The second lesson is that deliberative democracy has a vital role to play in aiding this process of democratization-via-civil-society-Europeanization. Deliberative democracy places its emphasis on participation and input legitimacy. This is precisely the prescription needed by the contemporary EU, even if the nature of the Union as a polity places limits on the extent to which 'pure' deliberative democracy can be applied. Democratizing the EU requires the successful execution of a quadruple balancing act in which various sets of interests are entered into a process of dialogue and equilibrium generation. This should be conceived as a *process* that requires experimentation and creativity. The EU is an evolving polity, whose final contours are not yet clear and which appears to be subject to increasing differentiation in terms of its policy regimes and decision-making modes, as well as both its member states and their nationals. The struggle to democratize the EU is thus likely to be ongoing, perhaps requiring application of the deliberative method in different ways in order to reflect the changing status and composition of the Union and its citizenry.

The third lesson follows logically: it speaks to the need to reconsider the links between the 'domestic' and the 'international'. The EU is a particularly 'deep' form of regional integration. As such it reflects with great clarity a more general trend in contemporary politics, in which, thanks to globalization and interdependence, it is difficult to separate issues of domestic democratization from others like 'global justice' or 'ethical foreign policy'. In EU member states, national reform is restricted to some extent by EU norms such as the (albeit challenged) primacy of EU law. For the EU as a whole, democratization involves issues of political identity construction. These offer a laboratory for the study of how different communities can become part of a collective political culture.

Finally, and optimistically, the EU case suggests that democratization is a difficult, rather than an impossible, project. The Union has by no means succeeded in meeting all the challenges posed by its 'democratic deficit'. However, the latter crisis has acted as a catalyst for thought about why democracy matters, and how it can best be reconfigured, in the EU. This thought increasingly points towards the need for creative solutions and the adaptation of existing theories and practices of democracy to a contemporary context characterized by increased societal pluralism and a more diffuse system for the exercise of public power. Innovation is the key to democratization of the European Union. So perhaps the main lesson to be drawn here is that democratization is possible, but only if we are prepared to think 'outside the box'.

Notes

1 EU studies have taken a 'normative turn' in recent years. This is, first, a response to the perceived democratic deficit and the official attention that has begun to receive. Secondly, it reflects trends within EU integration theory, which has been going through a period of revision and reflexive thought combining normative with meta-theoretical issues. Thirdly, it follows increased interest from scholars outside the international relations and political science traditions, alerted by the Treaty on European Union to the EU as a polity-in-the-making and investigating it as a novel site of democratization.

2 These agreements were made on an extra-treaty basis in 1985, and incorporated into EU law by the Treaty of Amsterdam (agreed 1997; ratified 1999).

3 Eurobarometer under the aegis of the European Commission regularly samples citizens' opinions from all member states.

4 Some of these particularities are described as part of the 'quadruple balancing act' and are thus not revisited here.

5 Codecision is one of the three principal legislative procedures of the EU, which vary in the degree of power granted to the EP. Codecision gives the EP the right to both amend and veto legislation, making it the legislative equal of the EU Council.

6 The Convention on the Future of Europe was established in September 2001 by the EU member states' heads of government. The members of the Convention represented the member states' heads of government, but also the various national parliaments, the European Parliament and the European Commission. Their task was to deliberate on four specific issues (the separation of powers between the EU and national levels; the simplification of the various EU treaties; the status of the Charter of Fundamental Rights, which had been 'attached' to the Treaties by the Nice Treaty of 2001; and the role of national parliaments in the EU system). To that end, the Convention produced a Draft Constitution for the EU, on which the subsequent round of EU Treaty Reform (to take place in late 2003–early 2004) is based.

13

Latin America

GEORGE PHILIP

It is possible to argue that Latin America is no more than a geographical expression, and that, rather than trying to generalize across a range of different countries, we need to focus on the history of the individual republics. Certainly there are significant differences within the region, and path dependency is a factor in determining particular political outcomes. However, there are important similarities within the region as well. All Latin American political systems are presidential. No Latin American country has achieved a genuine 'first world' standard of living. Social inequality within the region is very high. Despite widespread poverty, most Latin Americans live in cities, and enjoy near-'first world' life expectancies. There are also similarities in religious tradition, legal system and language. The Latin American republics are also significantly influenced by the policies and outlook of the United States – almost completely so in the case of the small Central American republics, and significantly so in the countries of South America.

This discussion adopts a 'broad picture' approach to discuss efforts to conceptualize democracy and democratization in the region as a whole. Some common trends throughout the region as a whole make it plausible to do this. Toward the end of the 1970s, the vast majority of Latin American republics were under authoritarian rule. Now the vast majority have democratized. Some countries democratized much earlier than others, but Latin America can be included in the 'third wave' of democratic transition that also occurred in eastern Europe and some parts of Africa and Asia (Huntington 1991). In the 1980s, therefore, there was a significant literature on transitions to democracy, with a good deal of discussion of pacts and the general tactics of democratization.

The region as a whole also suffered from a severe economic setback, following the foreign debt crisis of 1982. Even today it has not fully recovered from the resulting problems, with the result that the region's record of strongly positive growth during 1945–82 was followed by a much more disappointing performance during 1982–2002. Discussions of political economy were inevitably dominated during the 1980s by issues concerning debt and economic stabilization. Later, when most countries in the region adopted market reforms, these became the main focus of discussion. Today this kind of approach has evolved into a literature on the relationship to be expected between market-oriented reform (or globalization) and democracy. The tone of the literature has become notably more pessimistic over the past few years.

If we abstract from economic issues (which is hard to do), then a positive case can be made for the consequences of democratization. The Latin American state now is responsible for far fewer abuses of human rights than it was in the authoritarian past. Violence against the person has probably diminished by less, owing to what most observers agree has been an increase in organized crime since the early 1980s. Some civil conflicts, notably those in Central America, have come to an end under the impact of democratization. However, other civil conflicts, most notably in Colombia, have continued and perhaps intensified under democracy. Even so, it is possible to argue that democracy has made Latin America more peaceful than it once was. Politics has also become much more inclusionary. The emergence into active politics of indigenous organizations, especially in Bolivia, Ecuador and – most dramatically of all – southern Mexico is one of many possible examples.

In the end, though, there is no getting away from the fact that economic progress under democracy has been disappointing, thus far at least. Furthermore, democracy itself has not operated particularly smoothly. There have been many constitutional crises, more in some countries than others. Ecuador saw the removal of one president by congress for 'mental instability' in 1997 and the enforced resignation of another president in 2000 owing to military intervention. The current president of Venezuela, Hugo Chávez, was largely unknown to the general public when as Colonel Chávez he led a coup attempt against a democratically-elected government in February 1992. This did not stop him being elected to the presidency in 1998. Peru's Alberto Fujimori, though democratically elected in 1990 and 1995, looked to be on the point of imposing a kind of full-scale authoritarianism when he finally lost power in 2000. Argentina saw a sequence of economic disasters, riots and dramatic presidential resignations late in 2001.

It is true that some countries of the region have endured much less political turbulence than others. However, it is not easy to devise general hypotheses to explain why some countries should have had more problems than others, except for the fact of greater United States influence in Central America and the Caribbean than further south. Levels of development within the region do not seem to relate to anything much. Argentina has one of the highest levels of per capita income in the region, but suffered severe political problems during 2001–2. The durability of electoral democracy is also not easy to generalize. Venezuela and Colombia have been free of overt authoritarian government since the 1950s, but the first elected a former coup leader to the presidency and the second is suffering from what seems like an interminable civil war. The experience of democratic rupture has been varied too. Chile has had fewer political upheavals and more policy successes than most democratic countries in the region; but the Chilean transition was for a long time the most constrained, owing to the continuing role of its previous president, General Pinochet. Only Pinochet's arrest in London in October 1998 completely punctured the threat of a military veto. Whatever may have explained Chile's relatively successful transition in the 1990s, it was not any kind of dramatic rupture with the past. Yet Peru, where there has also been substantial continuity between military and democratic government, is one of the most politically troubled cases in the whole region. There probably is a relationship between marked cyclical economic decline and political crisis; but that observation is not particularly remarkable.

The issue of democratic consolidation in Latin America

What has, therefore, to be explained is a rather ambiguous outcome. Democracy has indeed survived in the region, despite policy problems and political crises. However, the policy problems and political crises that might eventually threaten democracy and are already reducing its benefits have not gone away. The concept of democratic consolidation, or more precisely non-consolidation, seems helpful in this regard. There is a considerable literature on democratic consolidation in Latin America, but (like the subject-matter itself) it is ambiguous. According to some definitions, Latin America is mostly made up of consolidated democracies. According to other definitions, including the one preferred by this author, this is not the case. Either way, we have to try to explain how democracy has survived without being consolidated or alternatively how it has remained consolidated (by virtue of its survival) despite many problems with its operation.

At least four different ideas or approaches can be detected in the literature on democratic consolidation in Latin America. They are, first, the game-theoretical idea; second, longevity; third, legitimacy; fourth, the 'checklist' approach. Take each in turn. The game-theoretical idea considers a democracy to be a set of rules and adopts rational choice techniques to discuss both rule-making and participatory strategies. Przeworski's (1991: 26) famous claim that 'democracy becomes consolidated when under particular political and economic conditions a particular set of institutions becomes the only game in town' precisely uses the word 'game'. Przeworski's point is that consolidated democracy can be analysed as a system because political actors can be relied upon to follow the established rules. This happens when it becomes in the interest of all parties to accept the constraints of the democratic process. Failure to do this in a consolidated democracy is less a threat to democracy than evidence of irrationality and self-destructiveness. This need not mean that every political actor obeys all the rules all the time, but it does mean that successful rule-breaking requires concealment. It is bad news for a politician in a consolidated democracy to be found with his hand in the till.

Few Latin American democracies are fully consolidated according to Przeworski's criterion. There are many cases in which politicians who are openly corrupt and barely trouble to deny it have won important elections. More important still, open defiance of the national constitution by figures such as Chávez, Fujimori and the Peronist majority in the Argentine congress (which in December 2001 effectively forced President de la Rúa's resignation though it had no official power to do this) has often worked. It is not at all obvious in Latin America that political actors improve their chances of success by obeying the rules of the game. It happens much more often that cynics prosper, while those who observe the rules finish last.

On Przeworski's definition few Latin American democracies are consolidated. Instead of the institutionalization of uncertainty, there is 'law of the jungle' politics. A pure Hobbesian logic (after Thomas Hobbes, 1588–1679) indicates that a failure to institutionalize democracy would lead to the breakdown of democracy and the imposition of government by force. However, although this did indeed happen many times in the region prior to 1980, it has not really happened since. Empirically, non-consolidated democracies in Latin America do not tend to break down, but instead stagger on from crisis to crisis. Latin American democracies, therefore, are non-consolidated in Przeworski's sense, but they are stable in a much broader and possibly more eclectic sense. The question is why?

A second approach to consolidation, following O'Donnell (1996) and Schedler (1998), is to regard consolidation as longevity. A consolidated democracy is a democracy that does not break down. However, the notion is otherwise tautologous unless it implies that longevity is itself a factor that sustains democracy. The problem with the longevity argument is that it has not worked well in the region. We have already noted that Colombia and Venezuela, counties that have held contested elections for many years, have very problematic democracies. Moreover, during the 1970s authoritarian governments took power in some countries, most notably Uruguay and Chile, in which democracy had in earlier times appeared fully established. In both of those countries the appearance of stability gave way to crisis and democratic breakdown. The problem of democratic stability has not gone away since 1980, but democratic instability has not thus far led to democratic breakdown. That is a significant difference, and one that needs more explanation.

There is more to say about the notion of consolidation as longevity; but we now turn to the third approach, exemplified by Diamond (1999) and Lagos (1997) among others. These authors draw on public opinion surveys, which have become increasingly sophisticated during the past decade. Their core concept of consolidation is based on Lipset's earlier (1983) claim that legitimacy and efficiency are keys to the stability of democracies. Public opinion surveys routinely measure popular preference for democracy and popular satisfaction with the performance of democratic systems. Until recently, most Latin American samples expressed fairly strong preferences for democracy, but much less satisfaction with the performances of their political systems and institutions generally. According to the notion of consolidation as legitimacy, one could regard a country as democratically consolidated if the vast majority of its citizens preferred democracy as their system of government. This is obviously an important political fact in itself, and it is also a fact with explanatory potential. If most people want democracy, then it is likely that they will vote for democrats and against anti-democrats. This might not be enough to stop a hypothetical group of committed authoritarians from seeking or retaining power, but it should certainly reduce their chances.

There are, though, two reservations worth making. First, as noted, the surveys showing popular support for democracy as a concept do not show anything like the same kind of support for democracy as a set of institutions. On the contrary, there is often a deep-rooted cynicism about the workings of congress, the judiciary, the police, the presidency and the political parties. This outlook can easily translate into a situation where, although democracy may be the only political concept in town, the legal rules are not the only rules. When Fujimori closed the Peruvian congress by force, his popularity went up. The resulting situation is a complex one. Plebiscitary democracy is not stable democracy. Mass support can produce precisely those increasing returns to power that are most dangerous for democratic stability. What is to stop this from happening in Latin America?

Earlier in the 1990s some political scientists expressed the fear that what O'Donnell (1994) referred to as 'delegative democracy' (that is, elective dictatorship) might become common in the region. This has not really happened. In part the reason may be that Latin American publics are capable of recognizing some political leaders as excessively authoritarian, and reacting against them. This is clearly what happened to Fujimori in 2000. However, not every rule-breaker or aspiring dictator is necessarily going to be inhibited by fear of unpopularity. There seem to be complex institutional reasons preventing ambitious political leaders from using a temporary burst of popularity as a means of overthrowing democratic institutions altogether. A positive popular orientation toward democracy, unless expressed in terms of specific support for a particular set of institutions, may not be sufficient guarantee of the stability of a democratic system. There is therefore something further to explain that cannot be explained by popular orientations toward democracy alone.

The other reservation is that public opinion is capable of changing over time. The most recent surveys (for example, in *The Economist* 26 July 2001) have shown a marked decline in popular support for democracy across much of Latin America. When asked whether authoritarian government could under certain circumstances be preferable to democracy, a majority of respondents in 2001 still said 'no', except in the single case of Paraguay. However, the very wide margins of approval given to democracy in 1996 and 1997 are starting to reduce. Almost certainly this can be attributed to worsening economic circumstances.

Again, there is more that can be said about the notion of consolidation as legitimacy; but this is a good place to introduce the fourth approach to democratic consolidation, which is associated with Linz and Stepan (1996). Their argument is complex, but best known for attempting to develop a 'checklist' approach to democratic consolidation. In other words, a democracy is consolidated if it is organized in accordance with some general principles (laid down by political scientists) of what democracy should be. Linz and Stepan refer to five arenas of contestation: the political, administrative, legal, social, and economic. There must be free and fair elections, a Weberian civil service governed by a concept of state impartiality, an effective and impartial rule of law, interest group participation in the context of an active civil society, and respect for property rights.

Linz and Stepan, like Diamond, seek empirical indicators of democratic consolidation; but those of Linz and Stepan are empirically far more demanding. Diamond and others look largely at the state of public opinion – information that can in principle be acquired in a self-contained way. In contrast, Linz and Stepan pay more attention to a whole series of empirical conditions that, they believe, are likely to underlie the state of public opinion and its orientations toward a particular status quo. As we move from the first (game-theoretic) to the fourth of the approaches to consolidation, we move from an analytically neat but empirically problematic approach to more and more demanding empirical specifications. But can we be sure that they are the right empirical specifications?

Questioning the approaches

All four approaches can be subjected to the key question 'how can we know whether a democracy is consolidated or not?' The Przeworski test – is open violation of the democratic process unthinkable? – cannot be verified absolutely. We cannot be sure that public opinion plus the state authorities will rally to the support of the democratic order under any conceivable set of circumstances. Since we cannot know this, we cannot confirm that any system is necessarily consolidated for all time. However, Przeworski's condition of consolidation can in principle be falsified. In fact it has been falsified in a number of Latin American countries. If a president closes congress and finds that his popularity has increased, or if congress exceeds its authority and overthrows an incumbent president on a pretext, then the rules of the democratic system can no longer be regarded as the 'only game in town'. The problem for Latin Americanists is that we still need some explanation of why non-consolidated democracy does not break down altogether when these things occur. Przeworski does not really tell us why it hasn't, though he does suggest that the reasons for the non-breakdown of non-consolidated democracy are likely to be different from the non-breakdown of consolidated democracy.

The definition of consolidation as stability over time is also open to a rather similar objection. It is serviceable descriptively and has the merit of being simple, but there is no explanation. An explanation sometimes given is that the electoral arena is privileged in Latin America, in the sense that the electoral process is sealed off from the abuses of the system that occur at the level of the bureaucracy, the judiciary or civil society. However, this explanation is empirically unconvincing. There have been many examples of elections that have been contested, but nevertheless influenced by rule-breaking. For example in Mexico in 2000, the presidential candidate of the Institutional Revolutionary Party (the PRI) received significant election funding from the state oil monopoly Pemex. In Peru in 2000 a close ally of President Fujimori was caught on video bribing a legislator to change sides. In Paraguay in 1999 the president was impeached by congress on charges that included the murder of the vice-president. These are clearly interferences with the electoral process. Overall, to say that consolidated democracy is long-lived democracy risks tautology.

The idea of consolidation as legitimation has the merit of being testable. The fact that popular orientations toward democracy in Latin America have become more negative in recent years may make further testing necessary. We have discovered what is in principle a new fact, namely growing popular disillusionment with democracy. But we have not yet learned its significance. We have yet to establish if this will eventually threaten democracy. However, the idea that democratic consolidation can be judged by whether or not the polls convey a positive message about popular attitudes to the system still seems rather limiting. As social scientists we presumably believe that there is some kind of relationship between underlying structural realities and people's systems of belief.

The Linz and Stepan approach therefore has a great deal going for it, but there are problems as well. For their criteria for consolidation are very demanding. Taking them strictly then, Spain (because of the violent opposition of Basque nationalists), Northern Ireland (because of violence from republican sympathizers) and the Old South of the United

States (because of racism) would have to be considered non-consolidated. The non-consolidated democracies of Latin America would find themselves in rather distinguished company.

The Linz and Stepan approach also involves problems of verification. In this case, the problem has to do with the significance of democratic non-consolidation. Even if we could somehow abstract from problems of measurement and devise a single scale, all we could know is how country X stood in respect of the criteria for democratic consolidation. We could not be absolutely sure whether this fact was significant or not. It would not be self-evident that local public opinion would endorse the view suggested by the criteria. Even if it did, we cannot be sure that a negative public opinion would fatally wound democracy (though we could be pretty sure that it wouldn't do it much good). For example, Linz and Stepan themselves discover that there is significantly less popular support for democracy in Chile than might have been expected in view of that country's very successful post-1990 policy performance. The question is: why? Possibly there is more latent popular support for the Pinochet regime than people want to tell opinion pollsters. Certainly the arrest of Pinochet in London was soon followed by a considerable boost in the fortunes of the right-wing candidate for the 1999 presidential elections. The right has remained strong in Chilean opinion polls. Idiosyncrasies of perception may not be the whole story, but they are probably a part of it.

In the end, we have a continuing puzzle. Why have Latin American democracies neither truly stabilized nor broken down altogether? When trying to understand this we should look at a range of factors. These include the opinion polls, the historical record (which tells us that politically motivated law-breaking is nothing new in the region), and the gap between what an idealized form of democracy should look like and what Latin American politics actually does look like. Then we may still want to remain agnostic about ultimate causes, but we should at least have a reasonable 'common sense' understanding of the main political problems facing the region. This understanding should also help us keep track of growing popular disillusionment that might translate into something more sinister but has not as yet done so.

Institutional aspects of non-consolidation

At an institutional level, the criteria supplied by Linz and Stepan are extremely useful. They do help to explain non-consolidation. Most Latin American countries (Uruguay being the only really significant exception) fill the top positions of their state bureaucracies via patronage. It is somewhat true that patronage criteria play a part in filling the United States' public bureaucracy as well, but not to anything like the same extent. If we exclude those state bureaucrats with tenured positions who do not show up to work at all, the ratio of patronage to permanent appointments in Latin American bureaucracies can be as high as 1 to 12. That is vastly higher than in the United States.

In addition, judicial power is relatively weak in Latin America. Elected presidents sometimes simply refuse to implement the findings of the courts. Fujimori was notorious for not doing this in Peru, while Argentina's president Eduardo Duhalde in January 2002 responded to an adverse Supreme Court decision on his government's economic policies by decreeing non-implementation for 180 days. Meanwhile, the Argentine congress set about impeaching the Supreme Court, with whose verdict it disagreed. Other criteria, notably those of civil society activism and a secure institutionalization of the economic decision-making process, also tend to show up weaknesses.

Interestingly, Linz and Stepan's work on democratic consolidation has little to say about core executives, although Linz earlier made a scathing critique of presidentialism (Linz 1994). In fact, the nature of Latin American presidentialism may be of central importance, and although Linz's scepticism about presidentialism has been criticized in the literature there is much to be said in its support. Critics point out, quite rightly, that presidentialism has its advantages as well as disadvantages. Quite apart from anything else, most Latin Americans evidently prefer presidential government, and there is therefore no chance of introducing a fully alternative system. Furthermore, there are many different types of presidentialism, and quite detailed provisions relating to (say) budgetary policy can make a difference between a system that works and one that on the whole does not.

Finally, if there is a climate of political good will, then any specific problems with any particular variant of presidentialism can be dealt with by introducing reform.

However these objections do not really deal with the main problem of presidentialism: while Latin American presidentialism may operate within a set of formal institutions that are similar to their US counterpart, these have generally been informed by quite different concepts. US presidentialism was invented in the eighteenth century as a means of limiting the power of the state. In contrast, Latin American presidentialism developed a few decades later as a means of asserting state authority. Madisonian presidentialism (after James Madison, 1751–1836) was not and is not the same thing as Bolivarian presidentialism (after Simon Bolivar, 'the Liberator'). One might roughly identify the first with checks and balances and the second with a leadership principle that is its antithesis.

As a result, the formal institutional system of checks-and-balances does not really describe how Latin American presidentialism works. There is much more of a crude battle for power in Latin America. Even under normal political circumstances, Latin American presidents have rights (to decree legislation, to interpret legislation, to refuse to spend the national budget) that do not easily fit Madisonian notions of checks-and-balances. When presidents are powerful enough, they may try to close congress outright (Peru in 1992). They may develop new constitutions that reduce congressional power to a minimum (Venezuela in 1999, and Peru in 1993). Alternatively, they may try to change the rules to permit their own re-election. In the past, the power of Latin American presidents was generally restricted by term limits. However since 1990 constitutions have been changed to permit presidential re-election in Brazil, Argentina, Peru and Venezuela. On the other hand, anti-government majorities in congress have also shown an increased willingness to go over on to the attack. Before 1990 presidential impeachment was virtually unheard-of in Latin America. However, in 1992 Brazil's Collor de Mello was impeached and removed on corruption charges and Venezuela's Carlos Pérez was impeached and briefly imprisoned in 1993. In these cases (and also with the impeachment of Raúl Cubas in Paraguay in 1999) there can be no doubt that congress was concerned with criminal acts. However, in 1997 Ecuador's Abdala Bucaram was removed from office by congress on the ground of mental instability, and in 2001 Argentina's de la Rúa was forced by congress to resign even though there was no suggestion of corruption or mental instability.

Democratization and international involvements

Almost all the literature on democratic consolidation treats the main issues as endogenous. But perhaps the main factors that have prevented renewed democratic breakdown are exogenous. This is not to deny that most Latin Americans still want democracy; but it could still be the case that institutional weaknesses could be exploited by manipulative authoritarian leaders. The Ecuadorian coup attempt of January 2000 ultimately failed, though not before deposing the president. But in acknowledging failure, the coup leaders stated that Ecuador could not afford the international isolation that a coup would create. Ironically, survey evidence shows that a successful coup might have been popular in Ecuador, at least in the short run.

In diplomatic terms, there is little doubt that the US government and other international bodies prefer democracy in Latin America. In economic terms, it has generally been believed that Latin American countries gain material advantages from being democratic. The point is not whether or not democracy works better in principle, but rather that non-democracies would incur bad will in Washington, and this would hurt their reputation in financial markets. They would come to be regarded as political risky. It is not entirely clear that this logic is unbreakable. The Argentine crisis that began in 2001 has already severely damaged the market credibility of many Latin American economies. There is now much less hope in the region than there was even a few years ago that market reform will bring about sustained economic progress.

What South America does not have, and Central America plus Mexico essentially does, is an opportunity to tie in its future to a larger international community. There can be little doubt that the prospect of joining the European Union has made a significant difference to the development of democracy in both southern and eastern Europe. Even Turkey, which is unlikely to join the European Union soon, has gained considerable material benefit from its international position. The United States could not regard the financial bankruptcy of a strategic ally like Turkey with the same equanimity with which it has regarded the Argentine default and economic crisis that came to a head in 2002. It is true that international financial institutions like the World Bank and the International Monetary Fund play a (controversial) part in economic policy-making in the region. However, such involvement is no substitute for the prospect of joining a powerful collective. Even the North American Free Trade Agreement, which is a far looser kind of organization than the European Union, has demonstrably influenced the process of institutional change in Mexico.

Conclusions

Latin American countries returned to democracy sooner than other 'third wave' countries in the developing world. Latin America raises issues concerning democratic consolidation and might be expected to teach us more about that aspect than can countries in, say, Africa, where the contemporary agenda more closely resembles the trials and tribulations of political and democratic transition. The discussion of consolidation in this chapter has moved from a discussion considering concepts to one based more on analysing the workings of institutions. This is a necessary progression. It is not possible easily to understand consolidation in purely conceptual terms without understanding more of the real world to which the concept relates. However, there can be no certainty either about whether any particular set of institutional conditions will prove to be little more than transient obstacles to the strengthening of democracy, or instead will ultimately make stable democracy unviable. We can, though, hope to tease out some of the ambiguities involved both in the concept of democratic consolidation and in the empirical realities of Latin American politics through the study of these countries.

Finally, Latin America – more so than some other regions – raises in quite a sharp way the tensions created when the international diplomatic and 'human rights' community seeks to exert influence in one direction and a business and financial community tries to influence in a different direction. Although they both refer to such concepts as 'good governance', they tend to mean different things by them. Markets will often welcome a decisive show of political leadership, while human rights activists may worry about democracy being put in danger. The controversy surrounding the US-supported anti-drugs and anti-insurgency 'Plan Colombia', in 2002, illustrates the point. Only in Mexico and Central America is there a coherent project of institutional transformation, and this (broadly speaking) means integration with the North American economic zone and political system. The international community as a whole clearly matters to Latin America, but tends to send out different messages. That, too, is a factor working against any secure form of institutional consolidation.

14

South Asia

GURHARPAL SINGH

In the theorization and general discussion of democratization South Asia occupies a distinctive space. The region,
comprising India, Pakistan, Bangladesh, Sri Lanka, Nepal,
Bhutan, and the Maldives, is home to 1.4 billion people
(almost 22 per cent of the world's population), of whom
around 550 million live below the poverty line. As recent
events have demonstrated, in the popular imagination South
Asia is commonly characterized as suffering from chronic
political instability, protracted ethnic conflicts and the ever-
present threat of nuclear war. But South Asia also boasts
some of the oldest democracies in the developing world.
India remains – despite its many limitations – the premier
example, the 'largest democracy' in the world, and Sri Lanka,
its current difficulties notwithstanding, is a reasonably
strong contender as a viable developing democracy. Pakistan
and Bangladesh, though sharing a common ancestry, have
had prolonged periods of alternation between civilian and
military rule. And Nepal has managed a transition from
a monarchy to a parliamentary democracy. In one form or
another democratic governance in South Asia has taken
root against formidable odds, and while the post-colonial
history of these states is not one of linear progress, it would
be misleading to suggest that democratization is essentially
a short-term contemporary phenomenon.

Directly or indirectly, democratization has been central
to the study of South Asian politics over the last decade.
Coinciding with the 'third wave', it reflects seismic changes
within the governance of South Asian states. These changes
embrace the collapse of dominant party systems, the transition from military or monarchical regimes (Pakistan,

Bangladesh and Nepal), the rise of violent ethnic conflicts, the social mobilization of previously excluded groups, economic liberalization, the emergence of a vibrant civil sector, regionalization and localization in the face of globalization, international pressure, and domestic demands for political reform. The old certainties that defined the post-colonial order are fast disappearing; the new order is yet to emerge. Transition best represents South Asian politics today, and democratization as an overarching theme most appropriately encapsulates this change.[1]

Key issues

Although the sheer size and diversity of the region – India is itself of continental dimensions – defies any meaningful generalizations, the common experience of statehood has given rise to similar concerns in the efforts to establish viable democracies (Jalal 1995). At the risk of a great deal of simplicity – and violence – the most important of these concerns as identified in the literature are: political consolidation; structural social change; democratic transition; and the impact of international developments.

In the last decade much of the analysis of South Asian politics has been preoccupied with the rise of ethno-national movements – in Kashmir, Punjab, and the North-Eastern States, the emergence of the Hindu right (India), Sindh (Pakistan) and the Tamil–Singhalese conflict (Sri Lanka). Explanations of these movements have ranged from standard accounts of political management to those that question the very bases of political consolidation broadly understood as both institutionalization and statehood (Singh 2000). Inasmuch as these movements are resilient, speak the language of ethno-nationalism and lay claim, rightly or wrongly, to self-determination, they have magnified the failures of South Asian states to build legitimate democracy that commands consent freely given (Tambiah 1996). Indeed, violent peripheral ethno-nationalist movements – and the aggressive mainstream reaction to them – have, in large measure, undermined 'official' nationalism while simultaneously throwing into doubt the post-colonial project in which nation- and state-building were envisaged as the handmaidens of democracy. For some writers, this confrontation has revealed the state-centric nature of 'official' nationalisms in South Asia and the limited progress made in democratizing the state in the half century since independence (Jalal 1995). For others, ethnocracies or ethnic democracies, it is suggested, are the more appropriate way to conceptualize the South Asian democratic experience (Singh 2000: 35–55). Despite these disagreements, the problems of political consolidation are real. Whether it is the more relatively institutionalized democracies like India or Sri Lanka or more fragile polities in transition in Bangladesh and Nepal, the inability to overcome permanent threats to the stability of existing regimes has retarded the processes of consolidation. At best it has made consolidation uneven and partial; at worst a frequent prey to institutional decay, mismanagement and political populism. In a region in which the understanding of the nation and the state is deeply contested, the idea and practice of democracy is similarly compromised by the inability firmly to resolve these differences in durable constitutional designs.[2]

The second major trend evident in the literature is the focus on social change as the key variable in explaining recent developments. Epitomized in the novelist Naipaul's phrase as 'a million mutinies' (Naipaul 1990), it captures graphically the tumultuous social mobilization of previously quiescent classes – peasants, lower castes, the petit bourgeoisie – who were the silent spectators during the transfers of power from colonial rule. Modernization, urbanization, economic liberalization and affirmative action policies have brought these classes/groups into the political systems, and thereby have altered fundamentally the character of existing institutions and state policies. This mobilization has been associated with populist styles and idioms in political life in which personalities and symbolism have replaced effective delivery. According to Varshney (2000: 12–13), on the other hand, the change signifies the emergence of 'plebeian politics' along the lines of social democracy in Europe in the late nineteenth century. A visible transfer of power is taking place from the upper to lower castes, from the privileged to underprivileged and from the Western-educated elites to 'sons of the soil' (Corbridge and Harriss

2000). Such change is most apparent in the populous northern states of the Indian Union. In Pakistan, Sri Lanka, Bangladesh and Nepal 'plebeian politics' has also made itself felt, though perhaps less so in terms of representation than in generating demands upon the respective political systems. In sum, social change is 'reinventing' South Asian polities by creating new pressures for change through gradually displacing the traditional elites who have so far managed the post-colonial settlement.

In Bangladesh, Nepal and Pakistan the democratization literature (Waseem 1996; Talbot 1999; Baral 2001) has also been concerned with the theme of transition. While in Pakistan the post-1988 transition suffered a dramatic reversal in 1999, when a military coup led by General Parvez Musharraf overthrew the government of Nahwaz Sharif, Nepal's transition has been disturbed by a widespread Maoist insurgency. Bangladesh's parliamentary democracy remains precarious, in spite of having experienced two alternations of power between the leading political parties. In these three states the transition has been influenced by the efforts of previous regimes to frame the processes of democratization. Pakistan's embedded 'praetorian state' effectively scuttled the post-1988 phase of democratization (Waseem 2001); it is currently in the process of fashioning a new polity that establishes a permanent status for the armed forces. Likewise Nepal's monarchy reluctantly conceded parliamentary democracy in 1990, but against the backdrop of the palace massacre (2001) and the insurgency it has been trying to rein in politicians through the emergency and the anti-corruption drive (Singh 2002). Bangladesh's difficult transition has been shaped primarily by the bitter contest between the Awami League and the Bangladesh National Party – an entity sponsored by the earlier military regimes.

The impact of international developments is a recurrent theme in the literature on democratization in South Asia (Chadda 2000). The end of the second Cold War coincided with the Soviet withdrawal from Afghanistan and redefined the geopolitics of the region, which had been locked in proxy superpower rivalries. The Soviet Union's collapse, which undermined the Nehruvian settlement in India, precipitating the end of centralized planning and the beginning of economic liberalization, created new openness in a unipolar world. Simultaneously the development of new communications technologies eroded the strict control on political communications that had been a characteristic feature of South Asian states (Rajagopal 2001). Combined, these changes generated two sets of external pressures that directly affected democratization in the region. First, some writings recognize that the 'good governance agenda' arising from the Washington consensus has imposed prescriptive requirements for public policy based on accountability, transparency and decentralization (Ahmed 2001). Sri Lanka, Bangladesh, Pakistan and Nepal have felt the conditionality of this agenda, particularly in dealing with the World Bank and the International Monetary Fund (Singh 2002). And if India thus far has avoided such blandishments, it is because some of the major initiatives, such as those in the reform of local government, have anticipated these developments in some measure. The second area where international developments have made a significant contribution, according to some analysts, is in creating a transnational wedge of local and international activists who have, through non-governmental organizations (NGOs) and other organizations, created a vibrant civil society sector committed to deepening democracy and establishing international norms in such fields as human rights, women's rights, and environmental protection. South Asia is sometimes described as the 'NGO capital of the world' (Kudva 1996:1), where social and political conditions are ideal for non-state organizations, and all the more so as the capacity of the state to influence social change is undergoing serious decline.

South Asian experience and democratization

Given the range and depth of the themes currently analysed by specialists studying democratization in South Asia, what do these studies have most to offer a critical understanding of democratization as process in a broader sense? There are many empirical and theoretical lessons that cannot be adequately covered in a short survey; but taking the region as whole five aspects merit more detailed consideration.

First, the overwhelming concern of analysts of democratization in South Asia regarding political consolidation
suggests a profound disquiet about the teleology of democratization. In a region in which democracy preceded nation
and state-building the challenges have been correspondingly
difficult. The experience of South Asian states – of India in
particular, it is asserted – offers a revisionist interpretation
of accounts in which state and nationhood are seen as seen
the *sine qua non* of effective democratization. According to
some (Chadda 2000; Kohli 2001: 1–19) the Nehruvian state
and its progeny appear to have successfully managed the
challenge of building a developing democracy while reconciling a plural conception of nationhood, even if it is bitterly
contested in the peripheral regions. In Sri Lanka, too, the
consociational arrangement between Singhalese and Tamil
elites appears to have broken down only in the late 1970s
(Tambiah 1986). Moreover, if statehood and nationhood are
seen as necessary pre-requisites of effective democratization, then Bangladesh, Nepal and, to lesser extent, post-1971
Pakistan should have been more successful in managing the
transitions. Even allowing for the fact that some readings
suggest that a 'centralised state' (Kohli 2001: 19) might be
the efficient secret of Indian democracy's success, or that
the shortcomings of transitions in Bangladesh, Nepal and
Pakistan can be attributed to failures of nation- and state-
building, the South Asian experience, by and large, does not
conform to the European ideal or the experience of democratization in Southeast Asia.

Second, the problems of political consolidation that beset
most states in South Asia highlight a more basic concern
with the effectiveness of post-transition democracy: that
is, the substantive nature of democracy and its varied
experience. Political decay, de-institutionalization and
malgovernance have become the familiar lament of those
who have attempted to explain away the tenuousness of
post-transition regimes. Yet more considered responses
have sought to rework Moore's (1981) thesis in the light of
comparative South Asian experience. In India, for instance,
the effectiveness of provincial democracy varies enormously,
with populous states like Bihar on the verge of anarchy,
while others like Kerala have become models of social
democracy. These variations, notes Heller (2000) – and the

argument is applicable to other Indian provinces as well as to post-transition regimes in Bangladesh, Nepal and Pakistan (1988–99) – can be understood if we revisit Moore's thesis, paying close attention to constitutional design and the configuration of class forces in contributing to a 'virtuous cycle of democratization'. Kerala's case, Heller argues, demonstrates that a hierarchical, caste-ridden society can be transformed into one in which associational life and class organizations flourish within a democratic culture. Indeed 'if democracy works better today in Kerala, it is because its citizens are active and organised and because horizontal associations prevail over vertical (clientelistic) forms of association' (Heller 2000:501). The emergence of civil society there is not the function of elite engineering or regional cultural tradition but the outgrowth of conflict and social mobilization over the last half-century. In a region where even the best models of democracy function without substantive horizontal associations, Kerala offers a salutary counterfactual example.

Third, there is a broad consensus that within South Asia the 'third wave' has coincided with 'democratization from below'. Whereas the 'second wave' was primarily elite-driven and reflected a colonial bequest, developments since 1989 have had a greater impact in encouraging political participation and decision-making at the village level and upwards. Institutional changes made as a result of external pressure – or in anticipation of it – have radically transformed the nature of local government, which had largely been left in abeyance since decolonization. In India the 73rd Constitutional Amendment Act (1993), which established *panchayati raj* (village rule), with delegated funds and reservation for backward classes/castes and women, has created a new cadre of trained democrats in India's 800,000 villages. Ironically, although *panchayati raj* was originally intended to undermine the states and to centralize power in New Delhi even further, its actual consequences have been to rework local democracy in ways that now engage the previously excluded and underprivileged. Reforms of local government in Bangladesh and Pakistan have also had similar unintended consequences by providing new structures that have unleashed decades of frustration, though in Pakistan the current military regime has sought to use local power to legitimize its

rule. But perhaps the most significant impact of 'democratization from below' has been to foster, along with the
activities of NGOs, a transparency and accountability
culture that manifests itself in manifold forms of citizen
activism – in local movements against corruption in the
disbursement of development funds, and increasing demands
to audit government programmes. These movements have
increasingly international sponsorships, and some have been
quite successful in influencing policies at the local level.
The growing culture of democratic accountability, more
than anything, is likely to provide the firm bedrock for a
systemic transformation of governance from below in South
Asian states.

Fourth, the strength of 'democratization from below' in
some ways can be attributed to the impact of social movements or social activism, particularly, though not exclusively, since the early 1990s. Social movements have been
identified as an important component of democratization
in Latin America, but their contribution in South Asia has
tended to be overlooked because of the state-centric nature
of much of the analysis. As the effectiveness of political parties at all levels has declined, social movements have begun
to take over the discursive and organizational space between
state and society (Katzenstein *et al.* 2001). These movements, of course, vary enormously, from some whose vision
is transformative to others that are essentially single-issue
organizations. Among the most prominent are women's,
environmental and local movements, with a variety of
agendas at the local, regional, national or international level,
often collaborating with multinational organizations and
NGOs to bring their demands to the international audience.
Some academics have interpreted the rise of the Hindu right
as a social movement that does not only seek political power,
but also aims to effect long-term social change in values
through the advocacy of *Hindutva* (Hinduness) (Basu 2001).
The same in a sense could be argued of other revivalist or
fundamentalist movements in other faiths. Nonetheless,
taken collectively the influence of these movements far
exceeds their numbers. Interestingly, social movements have
tended to eschew electoral politics, which have become the
arena for 'representing and endorsing essentialised identities and institutionalising them' (Katzenstein *et al.* 2001:

269). Instead, they frequently articulate interests within the judicial-administrative apparatus of the state primarily because the latter is far more receptive to the demands of interest rather than identity, and allows the state to negotiate the diversity of interests that 'perform a very different democratic function than party or electoral politics' (Katzenstein et al. 2001: 269). If institutional sclerosis sometimes seems to typify most South Asian states, then it is in the sphere of the social, we are informed, that the real resilience of democratization is to be found. Social activism may not always meet the threshold of institutional significance, but in South Asia it provides an important 'discursive space in which new and transformative meanings are constantly being generated' (Katzenstein et al. 2001: 269). Such social movements provide a crucial element of renewal and cohesion, and the most promising prospects for enduring reform.

Finally, critiques of democratization have generated a lively debate about the relevance of the process in South Asia. Much as Marxist analysis provided a counterpoint to modernization theory in the 1960s and 1970s, today an equivalent intellectual space in South Asia is occupied by post-structural analysis that combines the traditional anticolonial agenda with critiques of 'Western-style' democratization. At one level there is the frontal assault on the 'good governance agenda' and its political prescription as 'the new political economy', in which, it is claimed, concepts like social capital have masked the actual appropriation – through liberalization – of capital through the obfuscating discourse of neoliberal economics (Rajasingham-Senanayake 2001). At another there is a fundamental effort to interrogate key concepts and assumptions that sustain democratization. For instance, drawing on the experience of South Asian societies, Kaviraj and Khilnani (2001) have highlighted how unhelpful a concept like 'civil society' can be in understanding the politics of developing societies. They question whether civil society *can* be politically manufactured in the ways that appear to be implicit in some of the writing on democratization and explicit in the work of multinational agencies engaged in development. That this kind of engineering might be tantamount to inflicting violence on South Asian societies is also a point noted by Nandy (2001), a psychologist turned political scientist. For him the project of democratization has to be located in a deeper understanding of how modernity has impacted on traditional societies through secular states. Much of the *anomie* present in South Asian politics and societies, insists Nandy, is the result of renewed searches for certainty manifest in the appeal of Hindu, Islamic and Singhalese 'fundamentalism'. These uncertainties have been compounded by globalization and economic liberalization, introducing dimensions of personal development that are at odds with traditional precepts. For Nandy, any meaningful understanding of such changes cannot be structured within familiar paradigms such as mass society: they require, above all, a recognition of the relevance of indigenous knowledge systems, which are refusing to die but are at the mercy of secularizing states. The need to realign the cultural and the political in South Asia might be suggestive of a 'clash of civilizations' in which the whole project of representative democracy is being called into question. But for Nandy the failure to recognize the potency of indigenous knowledge systems and to structure political institutions accordingly – the state, representative institutions, electoral systems – is the root cause of social and political dissonance, of schizoid political cultures that mimic modernity while exuding xenophobic fundamentalisms.

Constraints on democratization in South Asia

There is little doubt that today democratization in South Asia has become a multifaceted process that is both deepening in its form and extending across the region. Even when there have been recent reversals, as in Pakistan, these setbacks have had to acknowledge the need to restore the democratic process. Yet in a wider sense we need to be wary of arguments that predict an ever-onward march of democratization: in reforming or establishing new institutions to meet the challenge of change, South Asian political elites have proved quite adept at producing outcomes that can be profoundly undemocratic. In the light of this, what are the major constraints on democratization in the future?

As developments in Afghanistan and Kashmir have illustrated, the problem of political consolidation afflicts all

South Asian states, and holds the potential to undermine or arrest progress towards more open and participatory regimes. Because South Asia's 'soft states' cannot guarantee territorial integrity, there is always the temptation to resort to violence or encourage majoritarian nationalisms as legitimizing ideologies. These weaknesses arise mainly from the failure to evolve viable polities that combine democracy and social pluralism in ways that reject majoritarian impulses. It may well be that we are witnessing a peaking of the idea of homogenizing nationalism in the region, of the idea of 'one nation, one state'. Equally, there is sufficient evidence to suggest that such a judgement is probably premature. In India the ruling right-wing Bharatiya Janata Party recently established a constitutional review commission with a view to assessing the efficacy of the 'Westminster model', a decision that its critics alleged was an attempt to move the country towards a presidential system that would make it more possible for the party to implement its Hindu nationalist agenda. In Sri Lanka the externally sponsored peace accord aimed at resolving the Tamil insurgency is facing increasing difficulties from parties representing the Singhalese majority. In Nepal the parliamentary regime and the conduct of the counter-insurgency against Maoist guerrillas have failed to adequately recognize the extreme social diversity of the country. In Bangladesh the newly elected Bangladesh National Party is said to be promoting Islamicist policies. And in Pakistan Musharraf proposed changes to the constitution make few concessions to plural governance. In short, with perhaps the notable exception of some states in India, there has been remarkably little new innovation in the shape of new forms of governance that promote and institutionalize diversity. This major shortcoming is remarkable, given that South Asia is the most socially diverse region in the world. For democratization in South Asia to become a self-perpetuating process, it would seem that the challenges of political consolidation have to be met by reconciling the needs of the process of governing plural societies at all levels.

The tensions between social pluralism and political majoritarianism that plague South Asian states are rooted in the political elites' mindsets, which are singularly lacking in alternative visions of political reform. In contrast with other regions – eastern Europe and the former Soviet Union – the post-1989 changes have not generally produced, with one or two provincial exceptions, political elites, either traditional or new, with radically alternative visions of democratic futures – visions where the secular trends of 'downsizing', 'decentralization' and 'deregulation' and 'right-sizing' the state are embraced as reforming projects capable of mobilizing new constituencies. Perhaps, as Lustick (1993) observes, the threshold costs for counter-elites to be able to undertake these kinds of reforms are currently too high. But given the size of the sub-continent and the range of problems of governance, such alternative agendas should have found natural appeal. That they have not, or have been imposed piecemeal by external agencies, indicates that for political elites in South Asia the concept of statecraft is largely one founded in the post-colonial transition, with nation- and state-building as a sacred testament. Naturally, this outlook has created an innate conservative attitude towards reform, where often change is conceded only when the pressures becoming unmanageable. Change, moreover, has sometimes taken place by default (for example, as, in the case of regionalization in India), rather than as a result of conscious political design. In contemporary South Asia it could be reasonably surmised that elite inertia rather than overt hostility to political reforms is the main constraint on further democratization.

Lastly, it has been suggested that the effectiveness of democratization as a process is much richer in societies where class politics with horizontal associations is the norm (Heller 2000). In so far as this hypothesis can be applied to South Asia, it offers sobering lessons. Traditionally left-wing parties, including the communist parties, have found it difficult to establish constituencies, despite the widespread poverty throughout South Asia. Communist parties have been successful in creating enclaves in some provinces, such as West Bengal, Tripura and Kerala, largely, though not exclusively, by championing regional nationalisms or, as in Nepal, by undertaking an anti-establishment struggle. In a region where caste, language, religion, and tribe mediate class-consciousness, horizontal associations of the kind found in developed capitalist societies have been very thin on the ground. Systematic and rapid industrialization might

erode vertical loyalties, but at current rates this is likely to
be a very gradual process. In the absence of class politics
some commentators have noted a healthy development
from clientelism to identity politics (Heller 2000). Whether
this presages class politics remains to be seen, for there is
no certainty that industrialization will supplant the politics
of identity. In so far as class politics articulates a 'modern'
politics of interest, with attendant demands for equity, it
would constitute a profound challenge to current state policies of affirmative action and representation that combine
pre-modern conceptions of identity with modern, democratic notions of distributive justice.

Conclusion: future trends

In one form or another the theme of democratization will
continue to preoccupy scholars of South Asia for the foreseeable future. National peculiarities will, of course, qualify
how democratization is adapted, improved and subsequently
revised. Nevertheless, in the light of the past and recent
developments several broad areas can be identified that are
likely to remain the focus of study.

Political consolidation and the effectiveness of the democratic process are likely to remain the key area of research.
In the medium term it is unlikely that we will see a dramatic transformation in the concerns of territorial integrity
that bedevil South Asian states. In fact the possibilities
that some of the 'soft states' might implode, be 'right-sized'
(have their boundaries changed) or re-sized (have their
internal boundaries changed) as a result of internal and/or
external pressures cannot be ruled out (Singh 2001). Barring
such outcomes, the concerns with consolidation are likely
to persist with those regimes currently negotiating or in
the throes of transition – Nepal, Pakistan and Bangladesh.
In more established democracies (India, Sri Lanka) the concern with consolidation is likely to be reflected in the evalu-
ation of effectiveness: in a study of the social and political
factors that explain variations at national and regional levels,
and the growing pressure, from external and internal quar-
ters, for accountability and transparency, democratic audits

and the need to meet international standards in key areas such as human rights, anti-discrimination legislation, and environmental protection. Although international agencies are increasingly imposing 'good governance' conditionality in their dealings with South Asian states, it remains to be seen whether such intervention complements ongoing processes or becomes a source for counter-mobilization.

There is also every likelihood that in South Asia the province will become the key unit of analysis. To be sure, the most challenging examination of democratization has focused on the provincial level; but comparisons between provinces and between South Asian states have been limited or beset by the nationalist polemics that are all too common. Given that there is a growing recognition of the need to view South Asia as a continental entity, a region that is increasingly interdependent in war and peace, with a tremendous economic potential if political stability is ensured, provincial successes and failures will become models to be emulated or avoided. In India Chandrababu Naidu in Andhra Pradesh has become the icon of new governance, delivering political reform and economic change in a way that marks a radical departure from established traditional norms in Indian politics. Developments elsewhere suggest that there are other provincial politicians for whom the agenda of transparency and accountability is appealing, if only to undermine opponents or the ruling political parties (Singh 2002).

The role that social movements play in encouraging the democratization of both the state and society will certainly come under greater scrutiny. As has been indicated previously, thus far this development has been explored mainly at the point of interface with state structures and in terms of how they have been reinvigorated and renewed. But social movements whose vision is tranformative have tremendous potential to democratize society as well. There is clearly a great need to examine how social relations are being transformed by systemic social change and the activities of social movements. Whether the erosion of traditional norms results in less hierarchical societies remains to be seen; but it should radically alter conventional social roles. The reluctant acceptance by most South Asian states of the need to address gender discrimination is recognition of these imminent changes, even if, at times, it is external pressures that have prompted policy initiatives. The iterative experience of these new participatory structures is likely to provide the opportunities and the demand for political reform along lines in which social change can be better represented.

Finally, given the rich intellectual tradition that underpins the analysis of the idea of democracy in South Asia over the last half-century, it is unlikely that the strength of the critiques of democratization will diminish in the future. Whereas such ideological critiques as the Marxist, Hindu, and Islamicist traditions have failed to provide effective counters to the broad processes currently under way, analysts reflecting on the wider implications of the South Asian experience have been to the fore in highlighting the limitations of key concepts such as civil society. This tradition is extremely rich and varied, and it is unlikely that it will concede to democratization as a hegemonic process without offering correctives or some basic revisions. At the same time, while these critiques are likely to draw attention to the shortcomings of democratization processes, their celebration of regional exceptionalism is likely to be tempered by an admission that at best they offer confusing intellectual road maps to achieving more tolerant, transparent and accountable societies. Hence Nandy's pining for neo-Gandhism is as utopian as the Taliban's political agenda in Afghanistan. Both in their own ways are trapped in timewarps of the pre-modern (undemocratic) age.

Notes

1 Governability has provided an alternative theoretical framework – see Kohli (1990). But given its association with the politics of order, governability as a concept is inherently limited in its ability to explain the multifaceted nature of the changes currently under way.

2 The problems of political consolidation are much more basic than those posed by the management of peripheral provinces. The rise of the Hindu Right in India, for instance, with its objective of a new constitutional design, suggests that the Nehruvian settlement has failed to become a hegemonic project.

15

The United States

FRANCISCO E. GONZÁLEZ and
DESMOND KING

Any discussion of the United States' political democratization is fundamentally complicated by its role since 1917 as a global model and defender of liberal democracy, a role that burgeoned after 1941. As a consequence of this responsibility, historically the United States' democratization has been both a domestic and international process. National and international politics have presented two trajectories that cohere into a common narrative of democratization (King 2004). This narrative is a continuing one.

Domestically, the hundred years after the Civil War (1861–65) were characterized by a gradual abandonment of narrow assimilationism and the enactment – in the 1960s – of legislation, prompted by the civil rights movement (Morris 1984), to uphold the rights of citizenship of all Americans. Addressing the legacies of pre-1960s discrimination and racism (Fields 1990; Jordan 1968; Kelley 1994) proved a platform for a multiculturalist reformulation of American national identity, or in David Hollinger's phrase a 'post-ethnic politics' (Hollinger 1995). The transformation of US politics from a narrowly based assimilationist and exclusionary system to a broadly defined and inclusive democracy is the major story of its twentieth-century politics. The historian Gary Gerstle characterizes this shift as a turn from 'racial' nationalism to 'civic' nationalism (Gerstle 2001).

There was a parallel international story. In 1917, President Woodrow Wilson decided to bring the United States into the European theatre of the First World War as an opportunity to 'make the world safe for democracy', and outlined his (unrealized) Fourteen Points for a post-war liberal order. In 1941, President Franklin D. Roosevelt responded to the

Pearl Harbor attack by both leading the United States into the Second World War and formulating (jointly with allies) the Atlantic Charter doctrine for the post-1945 world. This Charter was quintessentially American in its aspirations. Its renunciation of imperialism (a stance opposed by Great Britain) aligned the United States with a future world order of liberal democratic states. The Truman Doctrine, as effected in the defence of democracy in Greece in 1947, confirmed these values, while the other Western powers' post-war infirmity made the United States the key Western defender against communism. President Ronald Reagan articulated the keystone of his administration's foreign policy as the defeat of the 'evil empire', Soviet communism. These external postures were accompanied by foreign scrutiny and criticism of the United States' own democratic practices toward minorities and people of colour. Maintaining the United States' integrity abroad necessitated remedying its own democratic deficit; this duality illustrates the overlapping effects of domestic and international politics in the formation of American nationhood.

In the next section the conventional timing of the United States' democratization is assessed, a prelude to considering how best to conceive the core beliefs and values of American nationhood. The discussion then examines how international pressures influenced the democratization enacted in the 1960s. The present role of the United States as a domestic and international emblem of liberal democracy concludes the chapter.

First new nation or late democratizer?

Although commonly cited as the world's first liberal democracy (Lipset 1963, 1996; McElroy 1999), in many ways the United States was also a remarkably late democratizer. Not until the passage of the Civil Rights Act in 1964 and the Voting Rights Act in 1965 (and the related US Supreme Court judgment in 1971) did the United States fully guarantee the basic democratic right to vote to all its citizens and protection of civil rights, that is, the conditions for Robert Dahl's idea of polyarchy. In practice, until the mid-1960s the United States presented the picture of a restricted democracy with significant parts of its citizenry *de facto* or *de jure* excluded from democratic participation. This pattern subverted the triumph of the North in the Civil War. Reconstruction led to segregation, and this consolidated an exclusionary democracy in the United States, which persisted for one hundred years after the North–South conflict. The core values of American nationhood expressed in the Declaration of Independence and the Constitution were thus thwarted, and could not be a reality until the federal government was able to enforce the nationwide protection of civil rights and the guarantee of free and fair contestation and participation in genuine democratic elections. This did not happen until the late 1960s.

This picture is at variance with the conventional narrative presented in those accounts of America's political development reliant upon Alexis de Tocqueville's nineteenth-century survey and Louis Hartz's articulation of American 'individualist' liberalism (Hartz 1955). Foremost amongst this new, reflective, American scholarship is the work of the political scientist Rogers Smith, who wrote: 'for over 80 per cent of US history, its laws declared most of the world's population to be ineligible for full American citizenship solely because of their race, original nationality or gender. For at least two-thirds of American history, the majority of the domestic adult population was also ineligible for full citizenship for the same reasons. Contrary to Tocquevillian views of American civic identity, it did not matter how "liberal", "democratic", or "republican" those persons' beliefs were. The Tocquevillian story is thus deceptive because it is too narrow. It is centred on relationships among a minority of Americans (white men, largely of northern European ancestry)' (Smith 1993: 549). Rogers Smith's broadening of the historical narrative of American democracy offers one in which attention is given to the United States' 'multiple traditions' (Smith 1997). This multiple traditions thesis finds in US politics and history numerous examples of political elites attempting to define American identity as one rooted in inegalitarian ascriptive themes. It provides the ideational context in which co-existing political ideologies competed to win dominance (Stears 2001).

Another characteristic of standard accounts of the United States' political development to liberal democracy is their teleological form (Gerstle 2001). In this view, the United States shifted from a condition of imperfect individualism, the imperfections commonly reflecting discrimination against individuals because of their association with certain groups, to one of formal equality of individual rights, and in some accounts to multiculturalism. This influential version of the transformative narrative underestimates the endurance of group-based distinctions in American national identity. It neglects the continuing salience of issues once considered settled (as for instance in the movement for reparations for slavery) and overlooks how the United States' international presence, as a defender and model of democracy, exposes its domestic policy to foreign scrutiny.

Historians and social scientists have emphasized the 'exceptional' character of American democratization, a term with several implications. First, the weakness of class-based divisions – as expressed in political behaviour – compared with the effects of such divisions as race, region and religion distinguish the United States comparatively (Sombart 1976; Goldfield 1997; Nelson 2000). Second, the effects of federalism, which not only produced parallel party systems, rooted in local communities and then organized at state and federal level, but encouraged voters to maintain strong ethnic or regional loyalties. Ira Katznelson argues that a distinction between the politics of community and the politics of work is a feature of American politics, with significant effects (Katznelson 1981). A third factor, suggested by the 'third wave' democratization literature, is the distinctive character of the US state (González and King, forthcoming). The federal government or 'state' demonstrated a historical bias, between the 1880s and 1960s, in favour of segregationist policies, and instead of challenging the legality of 'separate but equal' arrangements (the system upheld by the US Supreme Court between 1896 and 1954) often fostered their diffusion (King 1999). As a set of bureaucratic resources and institutions, the US federal state also appeared weakly placed to advance democratization in comparison with other liberal democracies (González and King, forthcoming).

These sources of 'exceptionalism' identify distinct factors in the United States' national identity as a democracy,

but do not obviate the need to acknowledge the lateness
– comparatively speaking – of the establishment of full
democracy.

Nationhood, individualism and groups

One important implication of a broader, multiple traditions,
account of the United States' democratization path is the
need to re-consider the content of American national identity. This latter combines a rich individualism, guaranteed
in constitutional rights, with a reality of wide group loyalties and ties, based variously upon ethnicity, national background or race. Politically, a tension has endured between
the individualist and the group components of Americanism:
in practice, American nationalism has consisted in both
individualism and group identities. This is not quite the 'post
ethnic' identity envisaged by David Hollinger (1995); but
it is a richer conception than that expressed in traditional
accounts. The change is epitomized by the comments of
Woodrow Wilson in 1917 compared with those of President
George W. Bush in 2001. Wilson declaimed, 'you can not
become thorough Americans if you think of yourselves in
groups. America does not consist of groups. A man who
thinks of himself as belonging to a particular national group
in America has not yet become an American.' He condemned
'hyphenated Americans' as un-American. In contrast, within
days of the 11 September 2001 bombings George Bush pur-
posefully visited a mosque in Washington and, speaking in
Congress, expressed support to Arab and Muslim Americans.

Wilson's comments epitomize the contemporary expectation of assimilation promoted federally between the 1870s
and the 1960s. The political imperative to construct an
assimilationist conception of American national identity,
before the 1960s, arose from the United States' engagement
with Native Americans, openness to immigrants and acceptance of segregation. Historically, Americans worried about
threats to national identity arising from unsuitable immigrants. Between 1882 and 1965 the United States operated
a restrictionist immigration policy based in discriminatory
guidelines (King 2000). Since 1965, the United States has

established a non-discriminatory, liberal immigration regime that has included periodic amnesties for illegal immigrants.

The international context

Since 1917, but particularly from 1941, the United States has acted as the pre-eminent defender of liberal democracy in two senses. First, it has espoused democratic values in its political institutions and political culture and offered them, at times explicitly, as suitable for emulation by other states. Second, it has served as the principal military enforcer of democracy against totalitarianism, in its various guises.

The Truman presidency (1945–52) rejected US isolationism, both for pragmatic reasons (the Soviet Union and China would exploit such a withdrawal through expansionism) and for ideological motives, the 'imponderable, but nevertheless drastic effects on our beliefs in ourselves and in our way of life of a deliberate decision to isolate ourselves' (in Etzold and Gaddis 1978: 432). President Truman's National Security Council (NSC) articulated the worth of defending the United States because of its profound commitment to individual liberty and a free society: 'the idea of freedom is the most contagious idea in history, more contagious than the idea of submission to authority' (in Etzold and Gaddis 1978: 388). Anti-communism and anti-totalitarianism drove US foreign policy from 1947 and dictated the content of 'Americanism' as the defence of individualism and democracy. This agenda is signalled in a 1950 memorandum from the National Security Council describing Americanism as a doctrine adhered to at home and abroad: 'The fundamental purpose of the United States is . . . to assure the integrity and vitality of our free society, which is founded upon the dignity and worth of the individual. The free society attempts to create and maintain an environment in which every individual has the opportunity to realize his creative powers. It derives its strength from its hospitality even to antipathetic ideas' (in Etzold and Gaddis 1978: 386, 387–8). This characterization of American democracy – and there are numerous comparable formulations – is a complement to the external cold war strategy of containing communism (and for critical reviews of NSC 68 see Schilling *et al.* 1962 and Hammond 1969). It emphasizes individualism and democratic rights of citizenship. But this very defence influenced external commentary about the United States.

Scholars have increasingly recognized one of the surprising and unintended consequences of America's global role as a model of liberal democracy in the Cold War years: it exposed domestic practices and policies to external scrutiny, to an extent that intensified the reform of civil rights in the 1960s (Dudziak 2000; Klinkner and Smith 1998; Kryder 2000; Layton 2000; Plummer 1996; Von Eschen 1997). The main object of this scrutiny was the United States' egregious treatment of African Americans and other minorities. (Already in 1919, Woodrow Wilson's articulation of his 14-point programme for a new world order was challenged by Black Americans setting out their 14-point programme for the achievement of democracy at home (Rosenberg 1999).) Writing from jail in Birmingham, Alabama in 1963, Martin Luther King Jr. angrily declared: 'we have waited for more than 340 years for our constitutional and God-given rights. The nations of Asia and Africa are moving with jetlike speed toward gaining political independence, but we still creep at horse-and-buggy pace toward gaining a cup of coffee at a lunch counter.' Both the United Nations' agenda-setting in human rights and the rapid decolonization of the European empires' former colonial peoples created a context for advancing civil rights in the United States.

British and French newspapers provided detailed coverage of African Americans' civil rights struggles in the post-1945 decades. Correspondents both reported new developments in respect to lynching, segregation, presidential initiatives and Supreme Court decisions; and provided detailed historical portraits of the experience of Black Americans and the obstacles they faced. Of the latter sort for instance *Le Monde* ran a lengthy six-part series by Henri Pierre, 'Les noirs aux Etats-Unis', over a week in June 1950 (the first of which was tellingly entitled 'Problème "Noir" ou problème "Blanc"?'); comparable series appeared in *Le Figaro* and *La Croix* in France and the *Manchester Guardian* and *The Economist* in Britain. Individual lynchings received detailed coverage overseas, as in due course did both the *Brown* decision (1954) and 'Little Rock crisis' (1955).

To some extent French interest in African Americans' conditions was informed by anti-Americanism. Particularly during the period when the Parti Communiste Français (PCF) was a powerful presence in French politics, an eagerness to unearth defects in American politics and society was not uncommon. In 1946 Jean Paul Sartre, the doyen of the French intellectual left, published a critical account of Black Americans in the PCF's *Combat*. But to explain French interest in the civil rights of Blacks solely by anti-Americanism would produce a partial account for several reasons. Black Americans, such as Josephine Baker and Sidney Bechet, had been important figures in French cultural life during the inter-war decades, and in the post-war years Paris-settled writers such as Richard Wright and James Baldwin maintained this interest.

Indeed, French affection for Americans was strong after 1918, as the role of the United States in contributing to France's victory was recognized. Black American soldiers served alongside French soldiers at the end of the Great War, a role they did not achieve within the US military force. In Britain during the Second World War American GIs were welcomed, but many British people found African American soldiers far more polite and interesting than the white recruits, and were often disturbed by the beatings whites meted out to their black colleagues. This positive view contributed to subsequent British interest in civil rights in the United States.

Despite the passage of civil rights legislation in the 1960s, aspects of the United States' race politics continue to engage foreign commentary and engagement. The debate about the possible racial bias of prison inmates facing capital punishment has been widely aired in Europe, and the retention of capital punishment itself has been criticized (instanced by French protests about the intention of the Attorney General to seek it in respect of terrorist suspect Zacarias Moussaoui, a French national, post-'September 11'). The use of racial profiling by state and local police forces is another aspect of the United States' domestic practices analysed abroad.

Events, internal and external, inevitably exert pressure on the balance of these individualist and group tendencies. Engagement in foreign conflicts has commonly had integrative effects – they have heightened Americans' sense of shared national identity – though in the long term such interventions have also effected profound social and political changes. For instance, the Japanese attack on Pearl Harbor, in 1941, and the terrorist bombing of the World Trade Center and Pentagon, in 2001, had integrative effects: Americans disregarded differences between internal groups to forge common responses. In contrast, the United States' entry into the Great War and the Vietnam War had significant disintegrative consequences: German-Americans suffered during the first event, giving up their identity, while in the latter the fabric of American society was challenged and changed irreversibly. And of course even those events that were outwardly most integrative had significant lines of division: in 1941 Japanese Americans encountered swift retribution for the Hawaiian bombing, with 120,000 interned under emergency legislation.

US foreign policy has often elicited distinct responses from different groups of Americans. Ethnic lobbying on foreign policy is longstanding: for instance, Jewish Americans' interest in the Middle East or Irish Americans' advocacy of Irish nationalism. African Americans have often found themselves at odds with US foreign policy, opposing US support of South African apartheid more vigorously and earlier than many policy-makers. In an earlier period, African Americans were dismayed by the failure of the United States to object to the Italian invasion of Ethiopia in the 1935. But the 2001 terrorist attack is unlikely to garner any such divisions among Americans.

The continuing narrative

Democratization is a continuing process as the internal boundaries of American nationhood are challenged and redrawn in various ways, for instance by the Japanese American movement to win compensation for wartime incarceration, and by the United States' international roles in defending liberal democracy against alternative ideologies and belief systems – what the political scientist Samuel Huntington calls the 'clash of civilizations' (1996). Domestically some scholars – such as Robert Putnam – argue that the multiplicity of groups in US society and the diversity of experience between rural and urban America and between immigrants and non-immigrants harms the level of social capital, therefore damaging the resilience of democracy. Other scholars have emphasized how variations between states about voter registration may discriminate between citizens (for example, the disbarring of former felons in some states). Globally the United States' role as a defender of Western democracy against extremist ideologies has both fanned the resurgence of anti-Americanism and underlined its international presence. We consider these domestic and international roles in turn.

Democracy at home

The notion of 'one people' expressed in American nation-hood has been a constant for over two centuries; but the parameters of who is included, who is excluded and how these relationships are defined is never fixed. Negotiating these inclusions and exclusions creates unexpected issues. For instance, since the late 1960s Native Americans have restructured their relationship to the United States. On Thanksgiving Day in 1970 a group of Native Americans sailed a replica of the Pilgrims' *Mayflower* ship and threw a dummy of a pilgrim in the water. The event was declared the first National Day of Mourning in commemoration of the victims of the European conquest of the United States. It has become an annual pilgrimage. It signalled a wider set of issues about the relationship between Native Americans and American nationhood. In the last decade and a half the repatriation of American Indian human remains has become integral to the way in which Native Americans configure their relationship to the American nation. Stretching back to the nineteenth-century traditions of ethnology, physical anthropology and phrenology, scientists have collected thousands of skulls and other remains from American Indians, often from battle sites. Many were stored in the Smithsonian Institution, which opened in 1846. Some of these were acquired with appropriate permission, but many were taken fraudulently or by stealing from mass grave-sites. Native

Americans have increasingly sought the return of these human remains for proper burial in appropriate places in ways that respect tribal cultural beliefs. Especially those remains of American Indians who died on battlefields need the full honours of a traditional burial. The Pan-Indian Repatriation Movement lobbies for federal and state laws to permit repatriation and to proscribe further dissipation of human remains. These demands have had some success with the passage of both the Native American Grave Protection and Repatriation Act in 1990 (requiring all federal institutions to compile inventories of their collections of Indian human remains and artefacts for repatriation where appropriate) and laws in over ten states (Thornton 2001: 159–61). The National Museum of the American Indian, created in 1989, is required also to inventorize its cultural and sacred objects with a view to repatriation.

One of the most influential meditations upon the state of American democracy in the last quarter of the twentieth century is found in the political scientist Robert Putnam's *Bowling Alone* (2000). Building on his and other scholars' arguments about the need for high levels of trust generated through voluntary civic participation as the basis for a strong civic society, Putnam finds a decline in the social capital necessary for such processes to function. Putnam's book charts a decline in community involvement and social connectedness in the US polity. He argues that a combination of structural changes in American society – such as changing family household arrangements, suburbanization, and the diffusion of television as the main medium of entertainment – have coincided with a marked decline in civic engagement by Americans measured in terms of participation in voluntary organizations and membership of social activities. This decline in social capital matters, Putnam maintains, because it has fundamental effects upon social and political interactions. High social capital implies the existence of high interpersonal trust, which permits the resolution of collective action problems through co-operation rather than formal contracts; it also reduced the demand for government in certain areas of life, thereby curbing tax demands. Putnam emphasizes the political costs of the decline in social capital in America, writing that 'nowhere is the need to restore connectedness, trust, and civic engagement clearer than in the now often empty public forums of our democracy' (2000: 412). He calls for reform of campaign finance rules, an aspiration met by the Congress in March 2002 when both houses enacted a fundamental revision of the rules governing 'soft money' donations to electoral campaigns.

There has been much criticism of and debate about Putnam's work. Some critics find his social capital agenda unattractive, while others remain sceptical about the causal status of the correlation between the general social trends he sets out and levels of civic engagement. The national and patriotic response to the bombings of 11 September seemed to mark a potential resuscitation of community-based engagement of the sort Putnam advocated. What is not in doubt is either the enormous impact of his concept of 'bowling alone', as a description of reduced civic engagement, among many Americans or the international diffusion of the concept (Putnam 2002).

Democracy abroad

Despite making little of foreign affairs during his electoral campaign, President George W. Bush has reverted, since 11 September 2001, to the tradition begun with Woodrow Wilson in 1917 of articulating a distinct global role for the United States, one rooted in the beliefs valued in domestic politics. The cornerstone of the Bush administration's approach is a war against global terrorism and the states that support terrorist activity. Bush has specified an 'axis of evil' aligned aggressively against Western democracy. On 20 September 2001 he told Congress that every country fell into one of two camps: 'either you are with us [the US] or you are with the terrorist'.

Citing values closer to those of his Democratic predecessor Bill Clinton than those of many Republicans, President Bush has stressed the diversity of the United States and its openness to all religions and beliefs within the twin context of loyalty to the American nation and the constitutional separation of church and state. Bush declared, 'in a free society, diversity is not disorder. Debate is not strife. And dissent is not revolution. A free society trusts its citizens to seek greatness in themselves and their country.' He presents this conception of a 'free society' as a model for international emulation. In his state visit to China in February 2002, President Bush used his live broadcast as an occasion to proselytize to Chinese people the virtues of democracy and American values: 'life in America shows that liberty, paired with law, is not to be feared'. The US is conducting a global war of ideas both to promote democracy and to revise the received views of American institutions. To this end, a new position, under-secretary of state for public diplomacy and public affairs, has been created at the State Department.

The international stance of the Bush administration towards human rights originates with the policy initiated during President Jimmy Carter's incumbency of the White House (1977–80). Carter campaigned on and implemented a foreign policy for the United States sensitive to international human rights and ethics (Foot 2000). Speaking in December 1974, the future Democratic president proclaimed his dream that 'this country set a standard within the community of nations of courage, compassion, integrity, and dedication to basic human rights and freedoms' (quoted in Foot 2000: 43). The United States was also associated during the Carter presidency and subsequently with devising mechanisms to enshrine this priority in the federal government's own institutions. At the Department of State, the Bureau of Human Rights and Humanitarian Affairs was created. The Bureau's staff were responsible for compiling human rights assessment reports on every country receiving US aid, a brief extended later to other countries who were members of the United Nations. Carter appointed Patricia Derian, a veteran of the civil rights movement, to serve as Assistant Secretary in charge of the Bureau. This initiative was continued by the Reagan administration and over twenty years later – by the time of President George W. Bush's presidency – the agency had been renamed the Bureau of Democracy, Human Rights and Labor (still located in the Department of State, website: www.state.gov/www/global/human_rights/). It issues an annual human rights report that receives wide publicity in the international community and media. Its report on 2001 singled out human rights abuses in China, Russia and Saudi Arabia; but the Bureau's remit was set broadly, with the government of the Republic of Ireland, for instance, finding itself criticized for poor standards in prisons.

Conclusion

External attacks upon the American state heighten Americans' sense of unity and shared nationhood. This effect is pronounced or deflated according to how Americans behave toward their fellow citizens: if there are groups of Americans whose ethnicity or national background render them vulnerable to association with the external enemy, and that connection is drawn, then any fresh unity is dinted. The September 2001 terrorist bombings failed to stir up such internal group divisions (though a number of suspicious deaths may have been motivated by anti-Arab sentiment, and close to a thousand suspects, overwhelmingly immigrants, were arrested). This gave them a unique significance as a mechanism of political integration in the US polity.

Initially, a striking effect of the September 2001 bombings has been to transcend domestic divisions based in race, class, ethnicity or national background. The United States has historically been riven with internal cleavages drawn along lines of race, ethnicity, national background and region. These cleavages have not evaporated, but their political salience declined in the wake of the Islamic bombings. Americans *per se* were the objects of the Islamic terrorists. And because the United States has advanced politically so much since the civil and voting rights acts enacted in the 1960s in terms of black political participation and achievement, it is an integrated polity and people that experienced this onslaught. The massive sales of the American flag illustrate national unity and the sense of patriotic inclusion.

The September bombings forged Americans' sense of national identity in another way too: they underline the existence and strength of an ideology of anti-Americanism present in certain parts of the world. Anti-Americanism is not new.

Several threads to this ideology need to be disentangled. First, during the Cold War years communist states and their supporters engaged in immense efforts to cultivate anti-Americanism, especially in West European democracies and in Third World countries. This strand has declined in significance. Second, emerging during the Cold War years, but retaining its influence, is a set of anti-American critiques linking US economic and political power with the main-tenance of undemocratic regimes and governments. The writers of such intellectual analyses – for instance, those of orientalism or post-colonialism or dependency theory – have not always singled out the United States explicitly, but have often done so implicitly. Third, in the 1990s American-ization has been equated with globalization, and the anti-global capitalism movement has therefore often explicitly attacked the United States and its policies. Critics of the International Monetary Fund, the World Bank and other international organizations such as the World Trade Organ-ization have often equated these organizations' policies with those of the United States. This tendency has encouraged simplistic explanations of Third World problems that blame the United States. Fourth, American culture is a continuing source of critique by Western intellectuals. Despite the huge success of American mass culture, a dichotomy endures abroad between elite hostility to American values and cul-tural products and popular embracing of them. In many Arab countries, significantly, the dichotomy is reversed: the edu-cated elites welcome Americanization, for its association with democracy, while the increasingly fundamentalist masses despise American values and culture. Finally, anti-Americanism has been stirred by the ultramontane fanatic-ism espoused by some Islamic fundamentalists. Both religion (for instance, anti-Christianity) and politics (for example, anti-Israeli proclamations) feature in this coagulation.

The combined effect of these threads constitutive of anti-Americanism has been to render anti-Americanism an ideological world-view, a way of seeing the world and inter-preting international events (Christie 2002). The United States' economic power, political democracy, and cultural influence are assimilated into a single entity, the object of hatred and criticism for anti-Americans dispersed through-out the world. In its most sinister form, anti-Americanism is paraded out as an explanation for all evils – political, economic or cultural – and anti-American ideology enables its advocates to explain how unrelated phenomena are in fact part of an integrated ideology and world presence. While this anti-Americanism is a continuing challenge to the values of the United States at home and abroad, it has also proved, in the short term, a source of strengthened nationhood.

16

Conclusion

PETER BURNELL

The authors of this book were invited to address a number of key questions in respect of their discipline or region of special interest, such as: What does it most have to offer a critical understanding of democratization? In respect of the disciplines, how is democratization understood and what conceptual lenses are used to interrogate the subject? In regard to the regions, what does democratization mean to the inhabitants, what has been their experience, the main constraints or limitations and future prospects? The chapters address these prompts each in their own way. In doing so they reveal not just the issues for which their discipline or area studies demand priority but also their own insights and answers. Collectively, they illustrate a combination of different and overlapping frameworks of analysis for making sense of political processes generally, and democratization together with democratic possibilities more specifically, in a wide range of settings. What is abundantly clear is that democratization does not have to be a discipline's central preoccupation or, even, a cherished value in order that it provide interesting and important analytical insights, relevant theoretical propositions and empirically-testable observations.

A bibliometric analysis would show that not only do the contributors draw on disparate literatures but, more unexpectedly, very few authors or texts concerning democratization are so central as to be cited everywhere. Samuel P. Huntington and Seymour Martin Lipset are confirmed as being among the most ubiquitous (Huntington's 'waves' metaphor has become almost universally embedded in the discourse, notwithstanding various criticisms of his analysis), and even more so in the comparative areas studies literature; Anthony Giddens's work resonates too. The variety of perspectives, themes and issues presented by the chapters holds out a mirror to the very qualities of pluralism, diversity and respect for difference that, together with a commitment to inclusiveness, constitute hallmarks of most theories of democracy. At the same time it is clear that we should navigate carefully between the two sound tenets articulated through historical observation and comparativism respectively. On the one side Calvert is right to say that uniqueness in the detail does not mean that different approaches are not referring to the same thing or cannot be treated as belonging to the same family of 'descriptions'. On the other we should beware of judging unlike with unlike within a common temporal dimension – especially any eras that are chosen more or less arbitrarily (Breslin).

Significantly the chapters provide some major points of convergence and shared understandings as well as clear points of contrast. Just as none of the disciplines have stood still but have evolved over time, so they *all* exhibit their own domestic disputes concerning democracy and its relationship to surrounding factors. Even in Cerny's conclusion on the relatively youthful study of international political economy (IPE) we find different accounts of the future possibilities for democracy and democratization in a globalizing world. More particularly, at regional levels such as Latin America Philip tells us that the very meaning of democratic *consolidation* is very far from being settled. In parts of Africa and Asia where *Western* notions of democratization *tout court* are essentially contested, not only is democratic consolidation a remote prospect or problematic, but politics *per* se is in flux, 'in transition' to an unknown future.

Even the most mathematically rigorous of the social sciences betrays considerable disagreement over such matters as the true relationship between democracy, economic growth and political change, let alone the controversies in other much more discursive branches of inquiry. Economists like Addison show an especial sensitivity to issues of sequencing and to how different time-horizons can affect the results gleaned from multivariate analysis. But perhaps it is fitting that it is a sociologist (Wood) who reminds us that even as problems persist over how to reconcile democratic principles with (widening) social inequality and (increasing) concentrations of economic power, we must not lose sight of the centrality of state power to democratic concerns. Even anthropology, influenced by the rise of non-Western scholars, now grapples increasingly with 'state effects', chiefly at the local level. That said, the stuff of politics generally and the concerns of democratization specifically clearly extend far beyond state institutions, as is evident in the anthropologists' concern with power – whether located in formal organizational structures and more informal relationships or when manipulated through the political rhetorics. For one thing, in democratization there is contestation (Wood) and struggle – which Rai shows to be especially prominent in the feminist discourse – and the quest for consensus across a much broader plane. For another, and as International Political Economy makes abundantly clear, contemporary forms of organization of social and economic life among non-state actors at both sub-state and supra-state levels, transnational and transgovernmental, pose multiple challenges to the traditional instruments of state authority, as they manipulate and bypass state legal systems. Conventional democratic legitimacy appears to be seriously challenged. By comparison, democratization's consequences for globalization seem to have been the focus of far less critical inquiry by political scientists and others.

All the regions have been touched unevenly by political transformation, and more specifically by liberal democratic advance, and even within individual countries there are signs of both forwards and backwards movements, as well as overall situations of very little change. Apart from there being one common observation of regional diversity, it may be as challenging a task (although not impossible) to establish sound and significant generalizations within regions as between regions. The contrasts between different parts of a single country like India, or, say examination of the impact that inter-state or supra-state relations make at the local level, can be every bit as revealing as comparisons between much more distant points of departure. So, for example, a comparison of South Africa or Israel with their neighbours and inquiry into the bearing that relations with the region have on the internal politics could be every bit as rewarding as an attempt to compare the convoluted history of democratic trends in those two named states.

Of course, history is always open to reinterpretation, not least in the light of present-day issues and the way more proximate circumstances are perceived and the particular concerns these give rise to. And if democratizing states individually cannot be understood outside their specific historical contexts and capacities (Grugel 2002: 90), then neither can democratization as a contemporary world historical phenomenon be fully grasped in isolation from debates over the political and intellectual well-springs of where it all began. Put crudely, of the different revolutionary traditions, which is the more authentic?; do theories based around the rights and freedoms of the individual, or ideas of political equality and popular sovereignty, supply dominant genes? In practice it seems that when providing us with the raw material even the most celebrated historians can do no more than bequeath their own versions of rationality and orderly – or sometimes chaotic – development (Calvert). Yet as is shown in many places, for example in Africa, society's memories of the past (not least of any previous failures to sustain democracy or to move democratization further forwards) can be vital to making sense of present-day developments and the attitudes taken towards those developments and future prospects. Myths relating to women, for instance, can be just as potent, and may be singularly damaging (Rai). And as South Asia today illustrates all too well, the legacies of old hostilities can continue to bedevil the possibility of registering democratic progress through beneficial co-operation and mutual support among states within a region, in addition to exerting a negative influence within countries individually. Yet even in much older democracies the democratic content is being reconfigured as we speak. Witness the impact European Union membership is now having on shifting the boundaries of judicial power in Britain, where, as McEldowney shows, we need a historical awareness to understand the antecedents and to appreciate the full significance of more recent advances in the 'justicialization of government'. And it is also worth repeating, as Gonzales and King usefully remind us, that the United States made a quantum leap forward in respect of civil rights really only very recently – within the lifetime of American citizens now endeavouring to export their democracy abroad.

The chapters display the particularities within a common concern for institutional structures and their performance, ranging over the representation of women, electoral systems and constitutions (in Africa) and presidentialism (in Latin America). These objects span the borders of politics and legal affairs; to which can be added the economists' interest in democracy's institutional guarantees more broadly defined, most notably investment in education (Addison). South Asia appears exceptional in terms of the inertia displayed by formal political institutions and traditional actors, but the picture takes on a different colour once we turn the spotlight on the vibrant social sphere (Singh). The various chapters detail a variety of types of social grouping, including especially social movements, but not necessarily political parties, as being in the vanguard pressing for change. The weakness of class conflict relative to other social divisions such as those involving race, ethnicity and religion is remarked on in several countries and not just the more prosperous United States and European Union, notwithstanding growing middle-class interest in political reform in certain East Asian countries.

At the same time the impact of international influences is found by most to be ambivalent, not least because of a widely-shared suspicion of the more adverse consequences of globalization and the hegemony of the neo-liberal economic agenda especially – and for women specifically (Rai). In contrast, there is the welcome contribution that international organizations' pressures are making to greater transparency in governments' management of the public finances, although national controls over the flows of private monies are becoming considerably weaker. So far the European Union's influence on accession candidates (and their rejection of the past in the shape of Soviet domination) constitutes a special case of benign external influence, although Lewis and Warleigh offer differing views on the EU's capability to help with their democratization in the future. Yet the tendency of these accession candidates to identify democratization with Europeanization jars somewhat with the essentially inward-looking focus of the EU itself, as the constituent parts grope towards deciding what kind of political entity the EU should become and whether, or how, it could be made more democratic.

The potential for ordinary people to influence through political processes the economic vectors that can make so much difference to their daily lives emerges as a central topic that seems ripe for further study (the key question being not what political economy perspectives might have to offer but whether it is any longer meaningful to isolate for purpose of analysis the purely *domestic* political economy). This interdependence of political trends and economic and social development (or lack of development), inescapable everywhere and especially salient in the poorest countries of Africa, is given extra meaning in post-communist societies. That is because of the transformative approach to economic management there, combined in some cases with the additional imperatives of nation- and state-building. This provides a clear contrast with the nostalgia for socialism and distrust of capitalist individualism that Southall reports in parts of Africa. Perhaps it is all the more remarkable to find group tendencies bidding for a place among the defining features of American nationalism too. And if democracy only thrives where there is some shared identity equivalent to nationhood (*demos*), that too must feature in the building plans for the EU (Warleigh) – as well as being a vital issue in countries emerging from the dismantling of former socialist states and in Asia too. Thus issues of both state and nation feature prominently in alternative scenarios depicting the democratic possibilities, but with distinct regional particularities.

Similarly, both Europe and North America present in their different ways a kind of bridge between domestic and international dimensions of democratization. But perhaps most intriguing of all is the colouring of American attitudes towards their own polity, and thereby the consequences for political progress in the United States. On the one side are the carefully crafted myths about America's past, noted by Calvert. On the other, paralleling the reservations some Americans have about the country's democratic pretensions owing to its dubious Cold War engagements abroad (Gould), foreign perceptions of democracy in the United States prompted by its claims to leadership of the free world have reverberated inside the country (Gonzales and King). This makes the United States absolutely unique. There, external factors appear to have worked to the benefit of societal integration. That contrasts starkly with the disintegrative and possibly very divisive impact of global economic integration and marketization on the domestic social structures of many developing countries, including those in Latin America whose political systems have long been attuned to US influence (Philip), and in East Asia. The potentially adverse consequences for democracy are well rehearsed.

The future

The rapid accumulation of political studies of democratization in the 1990s came about as a result of political developments on the ground. The one tracked the other; and it is worth asking now what are the implications for the future. The evidence so far has been of dynamism in the study of democratization. There is scope for further advances in theory and in practice, such as by moving away from the standard liberal state model of 'democratic accountability' – queried in the sociological and anthropological literatures and regarded as increasingly obsolete from within IPE – towards consideration of new possibilities. More truly participatory forms of political engagement and the elevation of meaningful empowerment are obvious examples. The 'democratization from below' that Singh finds on the rise in India could be one source of inspiration. The democratic development of the European Union offers speculative possibilities for innovation (Warleigh). Even in Africa – with few obvious 'champions' of democracy and a conviction that political science largely fails to offer the sort of version of democracy that Africans are said to want and need – democracy remains very much 'on the agenda' (Southall).

Yet in large parts of the world the democratic openings of the 1980s and early 1990s and the optimism they gave rise to have given way to a more sober judgement: the most sanguine is that we are now seeing a period of democratic stabilization, or survival without consolidation ('trendless fluctuation'). Many 'transitions' proved unsuccessful – they were not transitions to liberal democracy – or remain glaringly incomplete. For many societies and communities the 'deepening' of democracy in any meaningful sense still lies a long way off. The possibility of democratic regression in some countries cannot be ruled out. Hence, even if his demo-pessimism regarding China is overstated, Breslin's caution against 'concept stretching' has value far beyond just East Asia. And looked at through the lens of IPE in a gathering climate of globalization, the early rose-tinted view of a third, or even fourth wave of democratization now looks to have been only partially sighted, even though the widespread collapse of old-fashioned autocracies was so evidently under way.

Furthermore, that democracy has its own limitations is also now more freely acknowledged: democracy is neither an instant solution for all *political* ills nor an answer to every major problem, social, economic, or environmental; moreover it seems incapable of confronting some pressing and major global issues. Democracy may simply be unsuited to some countries, for the foreseeable future anyway. The concept of democracy and the route map of democratization mapped out in the West do not necessarily offer useful templates for organizing our understanding of the politics of diverse societies elsewhere. In some situations they can actually derange productive analysis. Such reflections as these certainly resonate well in Africa, where now is not the first time that attempts have been made to transfer Western political aspirations, and where current perceptions are coloured by recollections of a troubled past and the expectation that unfavourable social and economic conditions will persist. Even in eastern Europe it seems that democratization studies have shown an inclination to create their own image of what is happening, so departing from the evidence of 'objective reality' (Lewis).

If the outlook for democratization looks increasingly insecure, is that a bad omen for studies of democratization? Are we doomed to come to the view that, the more we know, the less we think we understand? Critical scrutiny, adherence to Karl Popper's injunction, in *The Logic of Scientific Discovery* (1934), for social scientists to seek out falsifying rather than corroborating evidence, and the temptation of academics to accentuate the significance of negative findings, could all put at risk the gains we think we have made. Of course, the elimination of errors and misconceptions should not as such be a cause for concern – after all, democratic progress has itself been defined in terms of disillusionment or an evaporation of the blind confidence formerly placed in the rulers by the ruled (Huntington 1991: 262). But that is no reason for not trying to aim for more constructive forms of progress than simply the discovery that there are more puzzles for which we do not have adequate explanations than was previously realized. In Latin America Philip reminds us that institutionalized *uncertainty* (concerning who will govern after the next or subsequent elections) is considered by some a defining feature of consolidated representative democracy. Yet in terms of our comprehension of democratization, the quest for *greater certainty* still constitutes a legitimate ambition, a motivating force. That claim is made more realistic, not weakened, by including in the ambit of democratization studies the slowing of democracy's progress and the conditions for democratic weakening or regression, not to mention the so-called 'hybrid' polities. Diamond's (2002: 34) remark that issues in comparative democratic studies now run to the forms and dynamics of 'electoral authoritarianism' can also be seen as lending support. So to conclude, here are at least two reasons to 'think positive'.

First, the increase in pessimism about the future for democratization owes in some measure to the fact that we now redefine democracy in more exacting ways (Burgess 2001: 58). More correctly, we are simply rediscovering democracy's basic values, which had briefly been lost sight of in the early enthusiasm that greeted the political developments of the late 1980s and early 1990s. Then, surface developments captured the imagination, overshadowing more substantive considerations and time-honoured controversies over political ideals. More than a decade later, attention has shifted from the half of the glass that we formerly thought was full to the half-empty portion of what is now more often agreed to be a significantly larger glass. That development is a testimony of the evolution of the literature, not a teleological statement, and certainly not grounds for complaint. Anyway, in politics more generally history tells us the reality all too often falls short of the dream: so democratization – no exception – at least is in good company.

Finally, we can be positive about the future study of democratization *even if* there is going to be only a small and dwindling number of new, unambiguous democracies to study. There is a readily available solution in the event that political science show signs of running out of steam. The fact is that political studies have always needed other disciplines, in order to optimize the chances of making further advances. The evidence displayed by the looking-glass reveals the potential to create more 'added value' by expanding the vision. That means seeking a closer engagement among disciplines and increasing the scope for broad-based comparative analysis, thereby highlighting distinctive cases, confirming important variations, and enhancing the quest for cross-cultural generalizations, both intra- and cross-regional. And for activists, including but not only activists in the women's movement, there is even the possibility of sponsoring more fruitful exchanges over effective strategies for achieving sought-after political change. That put on one side, and regardless of whatever reservations we might have about democratization as a practical vision or a normative undertaking, the possibilities for increasing our understanding that are offered by adopting a more holistic approach are clearly there for the taking.

References

Acemoglu, D. and Robinson, J. A. (2000), 'Why did the West extend the franchise? Democracy, inequality and growth in historical perspective', *Quarterly Journal of Economics*, 115:4, 1167–99.

Acemoglu, D. and Robinson, J. A. (2001), 'A theory of political transitions', *American Economic Review*, 91:4, 938–63.

Addison, T. and Rahman, A. (2003), 'Why is so little spent on educating the poor?', in Van der Hoeven, R. and Shorrocks, T. (eds), *Perspectives on Growth and Poverty*, Tokyo, UNU Press for WIDER, 93–112.

Ahmed, I. (2001), 'Crisis in democracy: the experience of Bangladesh', paper presented at the conference 'Dialogue on Democracy and Pluralism in South Asia', India International Centre, New Delhi, March 14–17 (unpublished).

Ali, S. S. (2000), 'Law, Islam and the women's movement in Pakistan', in Rai (2000), 41–63.

Allison, L. (1994), 'On the gap between theories of democracy and theories of democratization', *Democratization*, 1:1, 8–26.

Almond, G. and Verba, S. (1965), *The Civic Culture: Political Attitudes and Democracy in Five Nations*, Boston, MA, Little Brown.

Aman, A. C. Jr. (1999), 'Administrative law for a new century', in Prakash, A. and Hart, J. A. (eds), *Globalization and Governance*, London, Routledge, 267–88.

Amin, A. (ed.) (1994), *Post-Fordism: A Reader*, Oxford, Basil Blackwell.

Anderson, B. (1991), *Imagined Communities*, London, Verso.

Anderson, P. (2000), 'Renewals', *New Left Review*, 1:239, 5–24.

Ankersmit, F. R. (1983), *Narrative Logic: A Semantic Analysis of the Historian's Language*, The Hague, Martinus Nijhoff.

Archibugi, D. and Held, D. (eds) (1995), *Cosmopolitan Democracy: An Agenda for a New World Order*, Oxford, Polity.

Arensberg, C. M. and Niehoff, A. H. (1964), *Introducing Social Change: A Manual for Americans Overseas*, Chicago, Aldine.

Ashworth, G. (1986), *Of Violence and Violation: Women and Human Rights*, London, Change.

Bailey, F. G. (1969), *Stratagems and Spoils: A Social Anthropology of Politics*, Oxford, Blackwell.

Bailey, T. A. (1940), *A Diplomatic History of the American People*, New York, Appleton-Century-Crofts.

Baker, B. (2000), 'Who should be called to account for good governance in Africa?', *Democratization*, 7:2, 186–210.

Baral, L. R. (2001), 'Nepal: democracy and diversity', paper presented at the conference 'Dialogue on Democracy and Pluralism in South Asia', India International Centre, New Delhi, March 14–17 (unpublished).

Barro, R. (1996), 'Democracy and growth', *Journal of Economic Growth*, 1:1, 1–27.

Barro, R. (2000), 'Democracy and the rule of law', in Bueno de Mesquita, B. and Root, H. L. (eds), *Governing for Prosperity*, New Haven, CT, Yale University Press, 209–31.

Barry, B. (1999), 'The study of politics as a vocation', in Hayward, J., Barry, B. and Brown, A. (eds), *The British Study of Politics in the Twentieth Century*, Oxford, Oxford University Press for The British Academy, 425–67.

Basu, A. (2001), 'The dialectics of Hindu nationalism', in Kolhi, A. (ed.), *The Success of India's Democracy*, Cambridge, Cambridge University Press, 163–89.

Bemis, S. F. (1937), *A Diplomatic History of the United States*, London, Jonathan Cape.

Blacklock, C. and Macdonald, L. (2000), 'Women and citizenship in Mexico and Guatemala', in Rai (2000), 19–40.

Blondel, J. (2001), 'Greetings for the new journal', *European Political Science*, 1:1, 3–9.

Bratton, M. and van de Walle, N. (1997), *Democratic Experiments in Africa: Regime Transitions in Comparative Perspective*, Cambridge, Cambridge University Press.

Brinton, C. (1952), *The Anatomy of Revolution*, New York, Vintage Books.

Bunce, V. (2000a), 'Comparative democratization: big and bounded generalizations', *Comparative Political Studies*, 33:6/7, 706–19.

Bunce, V. (2000b), 'The place of place in transitions to democracy', in Dobry (2000a), 71–90.

Burgess, A. (2001), 'Universal democracy, diminished expectation', *Democratization*, 8:3, 51–74.

Burke, P. (1991), *New Perspectives on Historical Writing*, Cambridge, Polity Press.

Buzan, B. (2001), 'The big picture', *Bulletin of the Centre for the Study of Democracy*, 8:2, 12.

Callinicos, A. (1997), 'Where does political power lie?', *International Socialist Review*, 206, at www.istendency.org/sr206.html.

Castells, M. (1998), 'Interview conducted by Bregtje van der Haak', *DNW*, September 1998 edition, n.p., at www.globetrotter.berkeley.edu/people/castells.

Cerny, P. G. (1995), 'Globalization and the changing logic of collective action', *International Organization*, 49:4, 595–626.

Cerny, P. G. (1998), 'Neomedievalism, civil wars and the new security dilemma: globalization as durable disorder', *Civil Wars*, 1:1, 36–64.

Cerny, P. G. (2000a), 'Political agency in a globalizing world: toward a structurational approach', *European Journal of International Relations*, 6:4, 147–62.

Cerny, P. G. (2000b), 'Restructuring the political arena: globalization and the paradoxes of the competition state', in Germain, R. D. (ed.), *Globalization and Its Critics: Perspectives from Political Economy*, London, Macmillan, 117–38.

Cerny, P. G. (2000c), 'The new security dilemma: divisibility, defection and disorder in the global era', *Review of International Studies*, 26:4, 623–46.

Chabal, P. and Daloz, J. (1999), *Africa Works. Disorder as Political Instrument*, Oxford, James Currey.

Chadda, M. (2000), *Building Democracy in South Asia: India, Nepal and Pakistan*, Boulder, CO, Lynne Rienner Publishers.

Chanock, M. (1985), *Law, Custom and Social Order: The Colonial Experience in Malawi and Zambia*, Cambridge, Cambridge University Press.

Chazan, N. (1979), 'African voters at the polls: a re-examination of the role of elections in African politics', *Journal of Commonwealth and Comparative Politics*, 71:1, 136–58.

Cherry, J. (1999), 'Traditions and transitions: African political participation in Port Elizabeth', in Hyslop, J. (ed.), *African Democracy in the Era of Globalisation*, Johannesburg, University of the Witwatersrand Press, 393–413.

Cheru, F. (1996), 'New social movements: democratic struggles and human rights in Africa', in Mittelman, J. H. (ed.), *Globalization: Critical Reflections*, Boulder, CO and London, Lynne Rienner, 145–64.

Christiano, T. (1997), 'The significance of public deliberation', in Bohman, J. and Rehg, W. (eds), *Deliberative Democracy: Essays on Reason and Politics*, London and Cambridge, MA, MIT Press.

Christie, C. (2002), 'US hate: a designer prejudice for our time', *Times Higher*, 1521, 18 January.

Chryssochoou, D. (2000[1998]), *Democracy in the EU*, London, Tauris.

Clague, C., Keefer, P., Knack, S. and Olson, M. (1996), 'Property and contract rights in autocracies and democracies', *Journal of Economic Growth*, 1: June, 243–76.

Clayton, R. and Pontusson, J. (1998), 'Welfare-state retrenchment revisited: entitlement cuts, public sector restructuring, and inegalitarian trends in advanced capitalist societies', *World Politics*, 51:1, 67–98.

Cohen, B. J. (1996), 'Phoenix risen: the resurrection of global finance', *World Politics*, 48:2, 268–96.

Cohen, D. (1983), 'Elections and election studies in Africa', in Barongo, Y. (ed.), *Political Science in Africa: A Critical Review*, London, Zed Press, 72–93.

Cohen, J. (1997), 'Deliberation and democratic legitimacy', in Bohman, J. and Rehg, W. (eds), *Deliberative Democracy: Essays on Reason and Politics*, London and Cambridge, MA, MIT Press.

Corbridge, S. and Harriss, J. (2000), *Reinventing India: Liberalisation, Hindu Nationalism and Popular Democracy*, Oxford, Polity.

Cox, M., Ikenberry, J. and Inoguchi, J. (eds) (2000), *American Democracy Promotion: Impulses, Strategies and Perspectives*, Oxford, Oxford University Press.

Craig, P. (2000), 'Public law, political theory and legal theory', *Public Law*, 211–39.

Crouch, C. (1979), 'The state, capital and liberal democracy', in Crouch, C. (ed.), *State and Economy in Contemporary Capitalism*, London, Croom Helm, 13–54.

Cumings, B. (1987), 'The origins and development of the Northeast Asian political economy: industrial sectors, product cycles, and political consequences', in Deyo, F. C. (ed.), *The Political Economy of the New East Asian Industrialism*, New York, Cornell University Press, 44–83.

Cutler, A. C. (forthcoming), *Private Power and Global Authority*, Cambridge, Cambridge University Press.

Daniel, J. and Southall, R. (1999), 'Electoral corruption and manipulation in Africa: The case for electoral monitoring', in Daniel, J., Southall, R. and Szeftel, M. (eds) (1999), 37–56.

Daniel, J., Southall, R. and Szeftel, M. (eds) (1999), *Voting for Democracy: Watershed Elections in Contemporary Anglophone Africa*, Aldershot, Ashgate.

Darnolf, S. (1997), *Democratic Electioneering in Southern Africa: The Contrasting Cases of Botswana and Zimbabwe*, Goteburg, Goteburg University.

Davis, J. C. (2001), *Oliver Cromwell*, London, Arnold.

Deleuze, G. and Guattari, F. (1988), *A Thousand Plateaus*, Minneapolis, MN, University of Minnesota Press.

Diamond, L. (1999), *Developing Democracy: Toward Consolidation*, Baltimore, MD, Johns Hopkins University Press.

Diamond, L. (2002), 'Thinking about hybrid regimes', *Journal of Democracy*, 13:2, 1–35.

Dietz, M. (1992), 'Context is all: feminism and theories of citizenship', in Mouffe, C. (ed.), *Dimensions of Radical Democracy*, London, Verso, 63–85.

Dobry, M. (ed.) (2000a), *Democratic and Capitalist Transitions in Eastern Europe: Lessons for the Social Sciences*, Dordrecht, Kluwer.

Dobry, M. (2000b), 'Introduction: when transitology meets simultaneous transitions', in Dobry (ed.) (2000), 1–16.

Dogan, M. (1996), 'Political science and the other social sciences', in Goodin, R. E. and Klingemann, H.-D. (eds), *A New Handbook of Political Science*, Oxford, Oxford University Press, 97–130.

Drewry, G. (1996), 'Political institutions: legal perspectives', in Goodin, R. E. and Klingeman, H.-D. (eds), *A New Handbook of Political Science*, Oxford, Oxford University Press, 191–204.

Dryzek, J. (2000), *Deliberative Democracy and Beyond: Liberals, Critics, Contestations*, Oxford, Oxford University Press.

Dudziak, M. (2000), *Cold War Civil Rights*, Princeton, NJ, Princeton University Press.

Durkheim, E. (1933), *The Division of Labour in Society*, Glencoe, IL., The Free Press.

Duverger, M. (1966), *The Idea of Politics*, trans. North, R. and Murphy, R., London, Methuen.

Easterly, W. (2001a), *The Elusive Quest for Growth*, Cambridge, MA, MIT Press.

Easterly, W. (2001b), 'The middle class consensus and economic growth', *Journal of Economic Growth*, 6:4, 317–35.

Easterly, W. and Levine, R. (1997), 'Africa's growth tragedy: policies and ethnic divisions', *Quarterly Journal of Economics*, 112:4, 1203–50.

Einhorn, B. (2000), 'Gender and citizenship in the context of democratisation and economic reform in East Central Europe', in Rai (2000), 103–24.

Elson, D. (1989), 'How is structural adjustment affecting women', *Development*, 1, 67–74.

Eng, P. (1999), 'Malaysia: A Small Magazine Defies a Despot', *Columbia Journalism Review* (January/February).

Englund, H. (2002), *From War to Peace on the Mozambique–Malawi Border*, London, Edinburgh University Press.

Eschle, C. (2001), *Global Democracy, Social Movements and Feminism*, Boulder, CO, Westview Press.

Escobar, A. (1995), *Encountering Development: The Making and Unmaking of the Third World*, Princeton, NJ, Princeton University Press.

Eskridge Jr., W. N. (1994), *Dynamic Interpretation*, Harvard, MA, Harvard University Press.

Etzold, T. H. and Gaddis, J. L. (eds) (1978), *Containment: Documents on American Policy and Strategy, 1945–1950*, New York, Columbia University Press.

Ewing, K. D. (2001), 'The unbalanced constitution', in Campbell, T., Ewing, K. D. and Tomkins, A. (eds), *Sceptical Essays on Human Rights*, Oxford, Oxford University Press, 103–17.

Fanon, F. (1970), *The Wretched of the Earth*, Harmondsworth, Penguin.

Ferguson, J. (1991), *The Anti-politics Machine: 'Development', Depoliticization, and Bureaucratic Power in Lesotho*, Minneapolis, MN, University of Minnesota Press.

Fields, B. J. (1990), 'Slavery, race and ideology in the United States of America,' *New Left Review*, 181, 95–118.

Fish, M. S. (1998), 'Democratization's requisites in the postcommunist experience', *Post-Soviet Affairs*, 14:3, 212–47.

Fligstein, N. (2001), *The Architecture of Markets: An Economic Sociology of Twenty-First-Century Capitalist Societies*, Princeton, NJ, Princeton University Press.

Foot, R. (2000), *Rights Beyond Borders*, Oxford, Oxford University Press.

Freedom House (2002a), 'Survey of Freedom Country Scores', at www.freedomhouse.org/ratings/.

Freedom House (2002b), *Freedom in the World 2001–2002: The Democracy Gap*, New York: Freedom House (www.freedomhouse.org/research/survey2002.htm).

Fukuyama, F. (2000), 'The end of history', in Burns, R. and Rayment-Pickard, H. (eds), *Philosophies of History*, Oxford, Blackwell.

Fuss, D. (1989), *Essentially Speaking: Feminism, Nature, Difference*, New York, Routledge.

Gamble, A., Payne, A., Hoogvelt, A., Dietrich, M. and Kenny, M. (1996) 'Editorial: New Political Economy', *New Political Economy*, 1:1, 5–11.

Gaus, G. (1997), 'Reason, justification and consensus: why democracy can't have it all', in Bohman, J. and Rehg, W. (eds), *Deliberative Democracy: Essays on Reason and Politics*, London/Cambridge, MA, MIT Press.

Gearty, C. (ed.) (1997), *European Civil Liberties and the European Convention on Human Rights*, The Hague and London, Martinus Nijhoff.

Geddes, B. (1999), 'What do we know about democratization after twenty years?', *Annual Review of Political Science*, 2, 115–44.

Geertz, C. (ed.) (1963), *Old Societies and New States: The Quest for Modernity in Asia and Africa*, New York, Free Press of Glencoe.

Gerstle, G. (2001), *American Crucible*, Princeton, NJ, Princeton University Press.

Giddens, A. (1971), *Capitalism and Modern Social Theory: An Analysis of the Writings of Marx, Durkheim, and Max Weber*, Cambridge, Cambridge University Press.

Giddens, A. (1998), *The Third Way: The Renewal of Social Democracy*, Oxford, Polity.

Giddens, A. (2000), *The Third Way and its Critics*, Cambridge, Polity.

Gills, B., Rocamora, J. and Wilson, R. (1993), *Low Intensity Democracy*, Oxford, Pluto.

Goldfield, Michael (1997), *The Color of Politics*, New York, Free Press.

Goldman, M. (1994), *Sowing The Seeds of Democracy in China: Political Reform In the Deng Xiaoping Era*, Cambridge, MA, Harvard University Press.

González, F. E. and King, D. (forthcoming), 'The state and democratization: the United States in comparative perspective', *British Journal of Political Science*.

Gooch, G. P. (1952), *History and Historians in the Nineteenth Century*, London, Longman.

Goodman, D. (1997), 'Can China change?', in Diamond, L., Plattner, M. F., Chu, Y. and Tien, H. (eds), *Consolidating the Third Wave Democracies*, Baltimore, MD, The Johns Hopkins University Press, 250–7.

Goodman, J. B. and Pauly, L. W. (1993), 'The obsolescence of capital controls? Economic management in an age of global markets', *World Politics*, 46:1, 50–82.

Gradstein, M. and Milanovic, B. (2000), 'Does liberté = egalité? A survey of the empirical evidence on the link between political democracy and income inequality', Washington DC, World Bank, at www.worldbank.org/research/transition/pdf/gradmilanovic.pdf.

Greenleaf, W. H. (1968), 'The world of politics', Inaugural lecture, 5 March 1968, University College of Swansea.

Griffith, J. A. G. (2000), 'The brave new world of Sir John Laws', *Modern Law Review*, 63:2, 159–76.

Grugel, J. (2002), *Democratization. A Critical Introduction*, Basingstoke, Palgrave.

Habermas, J. (1989), *The New Conservatism*, Cambridge, Polity.

Habermas, J. (1990), *Moral Consciousness and Communicative Action*, Cambridge, Polity.

Hammond, P. Y. (1969), *The Cold War Years: American Foreign Policy since 1945*, New York, Harcourt, Brace and World.

Hansen, T. B. and Stepputat, F. (eds) (2001), *States of Imagination. Ethnographic Explorations of the Postcolonial State*, Durham, NC, Duke University Press.

Harman, C. (1998), 'For democratic centralism', *International Socialism Journal*, 80, at www.internationalsocialist.org/resource.html.

Hartz, L. (1955), *The Liberal Tradition in America*, New York, Basic.

Held, D. (1991), 'Democracy, the nation-state and the global system', *Economy and Society*, 20:2, 138–72.

Held, D. (1995), *Democracy and the Global Order: From the Modern State to Democratic Governance*, Oxford, Polity.

Heller, P. (2000), 'Degrees of democracy: some comparative lessons from India', *World Politics*, 52:4, 484–519.

Helliwell, J. (1994), 'Empirical linkages between democracy and economic growth', *British Journal of Political Science*, 24:2, 225–48.

Hertz, L. (2001), *The Silent Takeover: Global Capitalism and the Death of Democracy*, London, Heinemann.

Hewison, K. (2001), 'Nationalism, populism, dependency: old ideas for a new Southeast Asia?', *City University of Hong Kong Southeast Asia Research Centre Working Papers Series No 3*.

Higgott, R. and Stubbs, R. (1995), 'Competing conceptions of economic regionalism: APEC versus EAEC in the Asia Pacific', *Review of International Political Economy*, 2:3, 549–68.

Hirst, P. and Thompson, G. (1999), *Globalization in Question: The International Political Economy and the Possibilities of Governance*, Oxford, Polity, 2nd edn.

Hobsbawm, E. (1994), *Age of Extremes: The Short Twentieth Century, 1914–1991*, London, Michael Joseph.

Hollinger, D. A. (1995), *Post-Ethnic Politics*, Berkeley, CA, University of California Press.

Horowitz, D. (1991), *A Democratic South Africa? Constitutional Engineering in a Divided Society*, Berkeley, CA and Oxford, California University Press.

Howell, J. (1998), 'An unholy trinity? Civil society, economic liberalisation, and democratisation in post-Mao China', *Government and Opposition*, 33:1, 56–80.

Hülsemeyer, Axel (ed.) (forthcoming 2003), *Globalization in the 21st Century: Convergence and Divergence*, London, Palgrave.

Humm, M. (1989), *The Dictionary of Feminist Theory*, London, Harvester-Wheatsheaf.

Huntington, S. P. (1968), *Political Order in Changing Societies*, London, Yale University Press.

Huntington, S. P. (1988), 'One soul at a time: political science and political reform', *American Political Science Review*, 82:1, 3–10.

Huntington, S. P. (1991), *The Third Wave. Democratization in the Late Twentieth Century*, Norman, OK and London, University of Oklahoma Press.

Huntington, S. P. (1996), *The Clash of Civilizations and the Remaking of World Order*, New York, Simon & Schuster.

Hyslop, J. (ed.) (1999), *African Democracy in the Era of Globalisation*, Johannesburg, University of the Witwatersrand Press.

Ihonvbere, J. (2000), *Africa and the New World Order*, New York, Peter Lang.

Jaggers, K. and Gurr, T. (1995), 'Tracking democracy's Third Wave with Polity III data', *Journal of Peace Research*, 32:4, 469–82.

Jalal, A. (1995), *Democracy and Authoritarianism in South Asia*, Cambridge, Cambridge University Press.

Jayawardena, K. (1986), *Feminism and Nationalism in the Third World*, London, Zed Press.

Jenkins, K. (1995), *On 'What is History?', from Carr and Elton to Rorty and White*, London, Routledge.

Jessop, B. (2001a), 'Series preface', in Jessop, B., *Regulation Theory and the Crisis of Capitalism*, Volume 1, London, Edward Elgar.

Jessop, B. (2001b), 'Introduction: developments and extensions', in Jessop (2001c).

Jessop, B. (2001c), *Regulation Theory and the Crisis of Capitalism*, Volume 5, London, Edward Elgar.

Johnson, C. (1981), *MITI and the Japanese Miracle: Industrial Policy 1925–1975*, Stanford, CA, Stanford University Press.

Johnson, C. (1987), 'Political institutions and economic performance: the government–business relationship in Japan, South Korea, and Taiwan', in Deyo, F. C. (ed.), *The Political Economy of the New East Asian Industrialism*, New York, Cornell University Press, 136–64.

Jordan, W. D. (1968), *White Over Black*, Chapel Hill, NC, University of North Carolina Press.

Joseph, R. (1991), 'Africa: the rebirth of African freedom', *Journal of Democracy*, 2:4, 11–24.

Junger, E. (1970), *On Marble Cliffs*, London, Penguin Modern Classics.

Kamrava, M. (1995), 'Political culture and a new definition of the Third World', *Third World Quarterly*, 16:4, 691–701.

Karatnycky, A. (ed.) (2001), *Freedom in the World: The Annual Survey of Political Rights and Civil Liberties*, New York, Freedom House.

Karl, T. L. (1991), 'Dilemmas of democratization', *Comparative Politics*, 23:1, 1–21.

Karlström, M. (1999), 'Civil society and its presuppositions: lessons from Uganda', in Comaroff, J. L. and J. (eds), *Civil Society and the Political Imagination in Africa: Critical Perspectives*, Chicago, University of Chicago Press, 104–23.

Katzenstein, M., Kothari, S. and Mehta, M. (2001), 'Social movement politics in India: institutions, interests and identities', in Kohli, A. (ed.), *The Success of India's Democracy*, Cambridge, Cambridge University Press, 242–69.

Katznelson, I. (1981), *City Trenches*, New York, Pantheon.

Kaviraj, S. and Khilnani, S. (eds) (2001), *Civil Society: History and Possibilities*, Cambridge, Cambridge University Press.

Kelley, R. D. G. (1994), *Race Rebels*, New York, Free Press.

Kelliher, D. (1997), 'The Chinese village debate over village self-government', *The China Journal*, 37:1, 31–62.

King, D. (1999), 'The racial bureaucracy: African Americans and the Federal Government in the era of segregated race relations', *Governance*, 12:4, 345–78.

King, D. (2000), *Making Americans: Immigration, Race and the Origins of the Diverse Democracy*, Cambridge, MA, Harvard University Press.

King, D. (2004), *America Abroad*, New York, Oxford University Press.

Kitschelt, H. (2001), 'Accounting for post-communist regime diversity: what counts as a good cause?', in Markowski, R. and Wnuk-Lipinski, E. (eds), *Transformative Paths in Central and Eastern Europe* (Warsaw, Institute of Political Studies of Polish Academy of Sciences), 11–45.

Klinkner, P. and Smith, R. M. (1998), *The Unsteady March*, Chicago, University of Chicago Press.

Kohli, A. (1990), *Democracy and Discontent: India's Growing Crisis of Governability*, Cambridge, Cambridge University Press.

Kohli, A. (ed.) (2001), *The Success of India's Democracy*, Cambridge, Cambridge University Press.

Kopecký, P. and Mudde, C. (2000), 'What has Eastern Europe taught us about the democratisation literature (and vice versa)?, *European Journal of Political Research*, 37:4, 517–23.

Kopstein, J. and Reilly, D. A. (1999), 'Explaining the why of the why: a comment on Fish's "Determinants of economic reform in the post-communist world"', *East European Politics and Societies*, 13:3, 613–24.

Kormendi, R. C. and Meguire, P. G. (1985), 'Macroeconomic determinants of growth', *Journal of Monetary Economics* 16, 141–63.

Kryder, D. (2000), *Divided Arsenal*, New York, Cambridge University Press.

Kubicek, P. (2000), 'Post-communist political studies: ten years later, twenty years behind?', *Communist and Post-Communist Studies*, 33:3, 295–309.

Kudva, N. (1996), 'Uneasy parternship? Government–NGO relations in India'. Working Paper 673, University of California at Berkeley, Institute of Urban and Region Development.

Kymlicka, W. (ed.) (1995), *The Rights of Minority Cultures*, Oxford, Oxford University Press.

Lagos, M. (1997), 'Latin America's smiling mask', *Journal of Democracy*, 8:3, 125–38.

Landman, T. (2000), *Issues and Methods in Comparative Politics: An Introduction*, London: Routledge.

Lane, J.-E. and Ersson, S. (1997), 'The probability of democratic success in South Africa', *Democratization*, 4:4, 1–15.

Laslett, P. (1970), *The World We Have Lost*, London, Methuen, 2nd edn.

Layton, A. S. (2000), *International Politics and Civil Rights Policies in the United States, 1941–1960*, New York, Cambridge University Press.

Lefebvre, R. (1966), *The Sociology of Karl Marx*, London, Penguin.

Leftwich, A. (1984), *What is Politics? The Activity and its Study*, Oxford, Basil Blackwell.

Lentz, C. (1998), 'The chief, the mine captain and the politician: legitimating power in Northern Ghana', *Africa*, 68:1, 46–67.

Leys, C. (1996), *The Rise and Fall of Development Theory*, London, James Currey and Nairobi, East African Educational Publishers.

Liddle, J. and Rai, S. M. (1998), 'Orientalism and feminism: the challenge of the "Indian woman"', *The Women's Journal of History*, 25:4, 495–520.

Lindblom, C. E. (1977), *Politics and Markets: The World's Political-Economic Systems*, New York, Basic Books.

Lindert, P. H. (2002), 'What drives social spending 1780–2020', in Kapstein, E. B. and Milanovic, B. (eds), *When Markets Fail: Social Policy and Economic Reform*, New York, Russell Sage Foundation.

Linz, J. J. (1994), 'Presidential or parliamentary democracy: does it make a difference?', in Linz, J. J. and Valenzuela, A. (eds), *The Failure of Presidential Democracy: The Case of Latin America*, Baltimore, MD, Johns Hopkins University Press, 3–87.

Linz, J. J. and Stepan, A. (1996), *Problems of Democratic Transition and Consolidation*, Baltimore, MD, Johns Hopkins University Press.

Lipietz, A. (2001), 'Geography, ecology, democracy', in Jessop (2001c).

Lipset, S. M. (1959), 'Some social requisites of democracy: economic development and political legitimacy', *American Political Science Review*, 53, 69–105.

Lipset, S. M. (1963), *The First New Nation*, New York, Doubleday Books.

Lipset, S. M. (1983), *Political Man: The Social Bases of Politics*, London, Heinemann.

Lipset, S. M. (1996), *American Exceptionalism*, New York, Norton.

Lister, R. (1997), *Citizenship: Feminist Perspectives*, Basingstoke: Macmillan.

Lord, C. (1998), *Democracy in the European Union*, Sheffield, Sheffield Academic Press.

Lord, C. and Beetham, D. (2001), 'Legitimizing the European Union: is there a "post-Parliamentary basis" for its legitimation?', *Journal of Common Market Studies*, 39:3, 443–62.

Loughlin, M. (2001), 'Rights, democracy and law', in Campbell, T., Ewing, K. D. and Tomkins, A. (eds), *Sceptical Essays on Human Rights*, Oxford, Oxford University Press, 41–60.

Luckham, R. and White, G. (eds) (1996a), *Democratization in the South: The Jagged Wave*, Manchester, Manchester University Press.

Luckham, R. and White, G. (1996b), 'Introduction: democratizing the South', in Luckham and White (1996a), 1–10.

Lund, C. (1998), *Law, Power and Politics: The Rural Code in Niger*, Hamburg, Lit Verlag.

Lund, C. (2002), 'Twilight institutions: public authority and political culture in local contexts – an introduction' (unpublished ms), Copenhagen: Centre for Development Research.

Lustick, I. S. (1993), *Unsettled States, Disputed Lands. Britain and Ireland, France and Algeria, Israel and West Bank–Gaza*, Ithaca, NY, Cornell University Press.

Lynch, C. (1998), 'Social movements and the problem of globalization', *Alternatives*, 23:2, 149–74.

MacEwan, A. (1999), *Neo-Liberalism or Democracy?*, London, Zed.

Madge, C. and Harisson, T. (eds) (1939), *Britain by Mass Observation*, Harmondsworth, Penguin Books.

Mair, P. (1996), 'Comparative politics: an overview', in Goodin, R. E. and Klingemann, H.-D. (eds), *A New Handbook of Political Science*, Oxford, Oxford University Press, 309–35.

Mamdani, M. (1996), *Citizen and Subject. Contemporary Africa and the Legacy of Late Colonialism*, Princeton, NJ, Princeton University Press.

Marglin, F. A. and Marglin, S. A. (eds) (1990), *Dominating Knowledge. Development, Culture and Resistance*, Oxford, Clarendon Press.

Matzner, E. and W. Streeck (1991), 'Towards a socio-economics of employment in a post-Keynesian economy', in Matzner, E. and Streeck, W. (eds), *Beyond Keynesianism: The Socio-Economics of Production and Full Employment*, Aldershot, Edward Elgar.

McCullagh, G. Behan (1998), *The Truth of History*, London, Routledge.

McElroy, J. H. (1999), *American Beliefs*, Chicago, Ivan R. Dee.

McMillan, J. (2002), *Reinventing the Bazaar: A Natural History of Markets*, New York, Norton.

Merkel, W. and Croissant, A. (2000), 'Defective democracies: concept and causes', *Central European Political Science Review*, 1:2, 31–47.

Miliband, R. (1972), *Parliamentary Socialism*, London, Merlin.

Mills, C. W. (1959), *The Sociological Imagination*, New York, Oxford University Press.

Milward, A. (1994[1992]), *The European Rescue of the Nation-State*, London, Routledge.

Minc, A. (1993), *Le Nouveau Moyen Age*, Paris, Gallimard.

Mitchell, T. (1999), 'Society, economy and the state effect', in Steinmetz, G. (ed.), *State/Culture: State Formation after the Cultural Turn*, Ithaca, NY and London, Cornell University Press, 76–97.

Moore, B., Jr. (1981), *Social Origins of Dictatorship and Democracy. Lord and Peasant in the Making of the Modern World*, London, Penguin Books.

Moore, S. F. (1986), *Social Facts and Fabrications: 'Customary' Law on Kilimanjaro, 1880–1980*, Cambridge, Cambridge University Press.

Morris, A. D. (1984), *The Origins of the Civil Rights Movement*, New York, Free Press.

Murphy, C. N. (ed.) (2002), *Egalitarian Politics in the Age of Globalization*, London, Palgrave.

Nader, L. (1969), 'Up the anthropologist – perspectives gained from studying up', in Hymes, D. (ed.), *Reinventing Anthropology*, New York, Vintage Books, 284–311.

Nagengast, C. (1994), 'Violence, terror, and the crisis of the state', *Annual Review of Anthropology*, 23: 109–36.

Naipaul, V. S. (1990), *India. A Million Mutinies Now*, London, Heinemann.

Namier, L. B. (1929), *The Structure of Politics at the Accession of George III*, London, Macmillan.

Nandy, A. (2001), *Time Warps: Silent and Evasive Past in Indian Politics and Religion*, London, Hurst and Co.

Navarro, M. (1989), 'The personal is political: las Madres de la Plaza de Mayo', in Eckstein, S. (ed.) (1989), *Power and Popular Protest: Latin American Social Movements*, Berkeley, CA, University of California Press, 241–58.

Nelson, B. (2000), *Divided We Stand*, Princeton, NJ, Princeton University Press.

Nelson, M. A. and Singh, R. D. (1998), 'Democracy, economic freedom, fiscal policy and growth in LDCs: a fresh look', *Economic Development and Cultural Change*, 46:4, 677–96.

Norris, P. (1997), 'Towards a more cosmopolitan political science?', *European Journal of Political Science*, 31:1–2, 17–34.

Nozick, R. (1984), 'Moral consciousness and distributive justice', in Sandel, M. (ed.), *Liberalism and its Critics*, Oxford, Basil Blackwell, 100–22.

Oakeshott, M. (1991[1947]), *Rationalism in Politics and Other Essays*, Indianapolis, IN, Liberty Press.

O'Connor, J. (1973), *The Fiscal Crisis of the State*, New York, St Martin's Press.

O'Donnell, G. (1994), 'Delegative democracy', *Journal of Democracy*, 5:1, 55–69.

O'Donnell, G. (1996), 'Illusions about consolidation', *Journal of Democracy*, 7:2, 34–51.

O'Donnell, G., Schmitter, P. and Whitehead, L. (1986), *Transitions from Authoritarian Rule*, Baltimore, MD, Johns Hopkins University Press.

Okoth-Ogendo, H. W. O. (1991), 'Constitions without constitutionalism: reflections on an African political paradox', in Shivji, I. (ed.), *State and Constitutionalism: An African Debate on Democracy*, Harare, Sapes Books, 3–24.

Olivier de Sardan, J.-P. (1995), *Anthropologie et Dévéloppement*, Paris, Karthala.

Olson, M. (1993), 'Dictatorship, democracy, and development', *American Political Science Review*, 87:3, 567–76.

Olson, M. (2000a), 'Dictatorship, democracy and development', in Olson, M. and Kahkonen, S. (eds), *The Not-So-Dismal Science: A Broader View of Economies and Societies*, Oxford, Oxford University Press.

Olson, M. (2000b), *Power and Prosperity: Outgrowing Communist and Capitalist Dictatorships*, New York: Basic Books.

Omoruyi, O. (1983), 'Teaching political science as a vocation in Africa', in Barongo, Y. (ed.), *Political Science in Africa: A Critical Review*, London, Zed Press.

Osborne, D. and Gaebler, T. (1992), *Reinventing Government: How the Entrepreneurial Spirit is Transforming the Public Sector, from Schoolhouse to Statehouse, City Hall to the Pentagon*, Reading, MA, Addison-Wesley.

Palmer, R. R. (1959), *The Age of the Democratic Revolution*, vol. 1, Princeton, NJ, Princeton University Press.

Palmer, R. R. (1964), *The Age of the Democratic Revolution*, vol. 2, Princeton, NJ, Princeton University Press.

Parpart, J. L., Rai, S. M. and Staudt, K. (2003), *Rethinking Empowerment, Gender and Development in a Local/Global World*, London, Routledge.

Pateman, C. (1983), *The Sexual Contract*, Cambridge, Polity Press.

Pérez-Díaz, V. (1998), 'The public sphere and a European civil society', in Alexander, J. (ed.), *Real Civil Societies: Dilemmas of Institutionalisation*, London, Sage.

Persson, T. and Tabellini, G. (1994), 'Is inequality harmful for growth? Theory and evidence', *American Economic Review*, 84:2, 600–21.

Phillips, A. (1991), *Engendering Democracy*, Cambridge, Polity Press.

Phillips, A. (1993), *Democracy and Difference*, Cambridge, Polity Press.

Pierson, P. (1996), 'The path to European integration: a historical institutionalist analysis', *Comparative Political Studies*, 29:2, 123–63.

Pierson, P. (2000), 'Increasing returns, path dependency, and the study of politics', *American Political Science Review*, 94:2, 251–67.

Plasser, F., Ulram, P. A. and Waldrauch, H. (1998), *Democratic Consolidation in East-Central Europe*, London, Macmillan.

Plummer, B. G. (1996), *Rising Wind: Black Americans and US Foreign Affairs 1935–1960*, Chapel Hill, NC, University of North Carolina Press.

Polanyi, K. (1944), *The Great Transformation: The Political and Economic Origins of Our Time*, Boston, MA, Beacon Press, reprinted 1957.

Poster, M. (1984), *Foucault, Marxism and History*, Cambridge, Polity.

Potter, D. (1996), 'Democratization at the same time in South Korea and Taiwan', in Potter, D., Goldblatt, D., Kiloh, M. and Lewis, P. (eds), *Democratization*, Oxford, Polity Press, 219–39.

Przeworski, A. (1991), *Democracy and the Market: Political and Economic Reforms in Eastern Europe and Latin America*, Cambridge, Cambridge University Press.

Przeworski, A. and Limongi, F. (1997), 'Modernization: theories and facts', *World Politics*, 49:2, 155–83.

Putnam, R. D. (2000), *Bowling Alone*, New York, Simon & Schuster.

Putnam, R. D. (ed.) (2002), *Democracies in Flux*, New York, Oxford University Press.

Rai, S. M. (1996), 'Women and the state in the Third World: some issues for debate', in Rai, S. M. and Lievesley, G. (eds), *Women and the State: International Perspectives*, London, Taylor and Francis, 5–22.

Rai, S. M. (ed.) (2000), *International Perspectives on Gender and Democratisation*, Basingstoke, Macmillan.

Rai, S. M. (2002), *Gender and the Political Economy of Development: From Nationalism to Globalisation*, London, Polity Press.

Rajagopal, A. (2001), *Politics after Television: Hindu Nationalism and the Reshaping of the Public in India*, Cambridge, Cambridge University Press.

Rajasingham-Senanayake, D. (2001), 'Conflict and a paradox of national democracy: rethinking the fetishism of institutions and constitutions for good governance', paper presented at the conference on 'Dialogue on Democracy and Pluralism in South Asia', India International Centre, New Delhi, 14–17 March (unpublished).

Randall, V. and Theobald, R. (1998), *Political Change and Underdevelopment*, Basingstoke, Macmillan.

Remmer, K. L. (1995), 'New theoretical perspectives on democratization', *Comparative Politics*, 28:1, 103–22.

Renou, X. (2002), 'A new French Policy for Africa?', *Journal of Contemporary African Studies*, 20:1, 1–27.

Reynolds, A. (1999), *Electoral Systems and Democratization in Southern Africa*, New York, Oxford University Press.

Roberts, J. M. (1997), *The French Revolution*, 2nd edn, Oxford, Oxford University Press.

Robison, R. (1988), 'Authoritarian states, capital-owning classes and the politics of NICs: the case of Indonesia', *World Politics*, 41:1, 52–74.

Rodan, Garry (2000), 'Asian crisis, transparency and the international media in Singapore', *Pacific Review*, 13:2, 217–42.

Rodney, W. (1972), *How Europe Underdeveloped Africa*, London, Bogle-L'Ouverture, and Dar es Salaam, Tanzania Publishing House.

Rose, R. and Shin, D. C. (2001), 'Democratization backwards: the problem of third-wave democracies', *British Journal of Political Science*, 31, 331–54.

Rosenberg, J. (1999), 'For democracy, not hypocrisy: world war and race relations in the United States, 1914–1919', *International History Review*, 21:3, 592–625.

Rubery, J. (ed.) (1988), *Women and Recession*, London, Routledge and Kegan Paul.

Rueschemeyer, D., Stephens, E. H. and Stephens, J. D. (1992), *Capitalist Development and Democracy*, Cambridge, Polity.

Ruggie, J. G. (1983), 'International regimes, transactions, and change: embedded liberalism in the postwar economic order', in Krasner, S. D. (ed.), *International Regimes*, Ithaca, NY, Cornell University Press, 195–231.

Rustow, D. W. (1968), 'Modernization and comparative politics: prospects in research and theory', *Comparative Politics*, 1:1, 37–51.

Sadurski, W. (2001), 'Conclusions: on the relevance of institutions and the centrality of constitutions in post-communist transitions', in Zielonka, J. (ed.), *Democratic Consolidation in Eastern Europe, Volume 1: Institutional Engineering*, Oxford, Oxford University Press, 455–74.

Saint-Paul, G. and Verdier, T. (1993), 'Education, democracy and economic growth', *Journal of Development Economics*, 42:2, 399–407.

Saul, J. (1997), 'Liberal democracy vs. popular democracy in Sub-Saharan Africa', *Review of African Political Economy*, 24:73, 339–52.

Schama, S. (2000 [1989]), *Citizens: A Chronicle of the French Revolution*, London, Viking.

Schatzberg, M. (1993), 'Power, legitimacy and "democratisation" in Africa', *Africa*, 63, 445–61.

Schedler, A. (1998), 'What is democratic consolidation?', *Journal of Democracy*, 9:2, 91–107.

Schilling, W. R., Hammond, P. Y. and Snyder, G. H. (1962), *Strategy, Politics and Defense Budgets*, New York, Columbia University Press.

Schmitter, P. (2000), *How to Democratize the European Union . . . And Why Bother?*, New York, Rowman and Littlefield.

Scott, J. W. (1992), 'Experience', in Butler, J. and Scott, J. W. (eds), *Feminists Theorize the Political*, London, Routledge, 22–40.

Scully, G. W. (1988), 'The institutional framework and economic development', *Journal of Political Economy*, 96:3, 652–62.

Seaman, L. C. B. (1966), *Post-Victorian Britain 1902–1951*, London, Methuen.

Sen, A. (1997), 'Human rights and Asian values', *The New Republic*, 14 July–21 July.

Sen, A. (1999), 'Democracy as a universal value', *Journal of Democracy*, 10:3, 3–17.

Sen, A. (2001), 'What is development about?', in Meier, G. M. and Stiglitz, J. E. (eds), *Frontiers of Development Economics: The Future in Perspective*, Oxford, Oxford University Press for the World Bank, 506–13.

Shackleton, M. (2000), 'The politics of codecision', *Journal of Common Market Studies*, 38:2, 325–42.

Shils, E. (1992), 'The universities, the social sciences, and liberal democracy', *Interchange*, 23:1/2, 183–223.

Shivji, I. (1976), *Class Struggles in Tanzania*, London, Heinemann Educational.

Shivji, I. (1991), 'Contradictory class perspectives in the debate on democracy', in Shivji, I. (ed.), *State and Constitutionalism: An African Debate on Democracy*, Harare, Sapes Books, 251–60.

Singh, G. (2000), *Ethnic Conflict in India. A Case-Study of Punjab*, London, Macmillan.

Singh, G. (2001), 'Resizing and reshaping the state: India from partition to the present', in O'Leary, B., Lustick, I. S. and Callaghy, T. (eds), *Right-Sizing the State: The Politics of Moving Borders*, Oxford, Oxford University Press.

Singh, G. (2003), 'South Asia', in Transparency International, *Global Corruption Report 2003*, Berlin.

Smith, H. (2000), 'Why is there no international democratic theory?', in Smith, H. (ed.), *Democracy and International Relations: Critical Theories, Problematic Issues*, Basingstoke, Macmillan, 1–30.

Smith, R. M. (1993), 'Beyond Tocqueville, Myrdal and Hartz: the multiple traditions in America', *American Political Science Review*, 87:3, 549–66.

Smith, R. M. (1997), *Civic Ideals*, New Haven, CT, Yale University Press.

Soboul, A. (1965), *A Short History of the French Revolution, 1789–1799*, Berkeley, CA, University of California Press.

Sombart, W. (1976), *Why Is There No Socialism in the United States?*, White Plains, NY, M. E. Sharpe.

Southall, R. (1999), 'Electoral systems and democratization in Africa', in Daniel, J., Southall, R. and Szeftel, M. (eds), *Voting for Democracy: Watershed Elections in Contemporary Anglophone Africa*, 19–37.

Southall, R. (2001), 'Opposition in South Africa: issues and problems', *Democratization*, 8:1, 1–24.

Spencer, J. (1997), 'Postcolonialism and the political imagination', *Journal of the Royal Anthropological Institute*, 3:1, 1–19.

Spruyt, H. (1994), *The Sovereign State and Its Competitors: An Analysis of Systems Change*, Princeton, NJ, Princeton University Press.

Stears, M. (2001), 'Beyond the logic of liberalism', *Journal of Political Ideologies*, 6:2, 215–30.

Streeck, W. (1996), 'Public power beyond the nation-state: the case of the European Community', in Boyer, R. and Drache, D. (eds), *States Against Markets: The Limits of Globalization*, London, Routledge, 299–315.

Streeck, W. and Schmitter, P. C. (eds) (1985), *Private Interest Government: Beyond Market and State*, London, Sage.

Strinati, D. (1982), *Capitalism, the State and Industrial Relations*, London, Croom Helm.

Stubbs, W. (ed.) (1866), *Select Charters and Other Illustrations of English Constitutional History from the Earliest Times to the Reign of Edward the First*, Oxford, Clarendon Press.

Sweet, A. S. (2000), *Governing With Judges*, Oxford, Oxford University Press.

Talbot, I. (1999), *Pakistan: A Political History*, London, C. Hurst and Co.

Tambiah, S. J. (1986), *Ethnic Fratricide and the Dismantling of Democracy*, Chicago, Chicago University Press.

Tambiah, S. J. (1996), *Levelling Crowds. Ethnonationalist Conflicts and Collective Violence in South Asia*, Berkeley, CA, University of California Press.

Tavares, J. and Wacziarg, R. (2001), 'How democracy affects growth', *European Economic Review*, 45:8, 1341–78.

Teske, R. L. and Tetreault, M. A. (eds) 2000, *Conscious Acts and the Politics of Social Change: Feminist Approaches to Social Movements, Community and Power, Volume One*, Columbia, South Carolina, University of South Carolina Press.

Thomson, A. (2000), *An Introduction to African Politics*, London, Routledge.

Thornton, R. (2001), 'Trends among American Indians in the United States', in Smelser, N. J., Wilson, W. J. and Mitchell, F. (eds), *American Becoming: Racial Trends and Their Consequences, Volume 1*, Washington, DC, National Academy Press, 135–69.

Tosh, J. (1991), *The Pursuit of History: Aims, Methods and New Directions in the Study of Modern History*, 2nd edn, Harlow, Longman.

Trouillot, M.-R. (2001), 'The anthropology of the state in the age of globalization. Close encounters of the deceptive kind', *Current Anthropology*, 42:1, 125–38.

UNCTAD (United Nations Conference on Trade and Development) (2000), 'UNCTAD/World Bank Partnership' Last update: November www.unctad.org/en/subsites/dmfas/english/worldbank.htm.

UNDP (United Nations Development Programme) (2000), *Human Development Report 2000*, New York, Oxford University Press for the United Nations Development Programme.

van Binsbergen, W. (1995), 'Aspects of democracy and democratization in Zambia and Botswana: exploring African political culture at the grassroots', *Journal of Contemporary African Studies*, 13:1, 3–33.

Van Wolferen, K. (1990), *The Enigma of Japanese Power*, New York, Vintage.

Varshney, A. (2000), 'Is India becoming more democratic?', *The Journal of Asian Studies*, 59:1, 3–25.

Von Eschen, P. M. (1997), *Race Against Empire*, Ithaca, NY, Cornell University Press.

Warleigh, A. (2001), 'Europeanising civil society: NGOs as agents of political socialisation', *Journal of Common Market Studies*, 39: 4, 619–39.

Warleigh. A. (2002), *Flexible Integration: Which Model for the European Union*? London, Continuum.

Waseem, M. (1996), 'Democratisation in Pakistan: the current phase', in Hampsher-Monk, I. and Stanyer, J. (eds), *Contemporary Political Studies, Volume 1*, Basingstoke, Macmillan, 257–64.

Waseem, M. (2001), 'Democratisation in Pakistan: problems and prospects', paper presented at the conference on 'Dialogue on Democracy and Pluralism in South Asia', India International Centre, New Delhi, 14–17 March (unpublished).

Waylen, G. (1994), 'Women and democratization: conceptualizing gender relations in transition politics', in *World Politics*, 46:3, 327–54.

Waylen G. (2003), 'Gender and transitions: what do we know?', *Democratization*, 10:1, 157–78.

Weatherley, R. (1999), *The Discourse of Rights in Modern China: Historical and Ideological Perspectives*, Basingstoke, Macmillan.

Wei, S. and Dievers, S. (2000), 'The cost of crony capitalism', in Woo, W. T., Sachs, J. D. and Schwab, K. (eds), *The Asian Financial Crisis: Lessons for a Resilient Asia*, Boston, MIT Press, 91–102.

Werbner, R. (1996), 'Introduction: multiple identities, plural arenas', in Werbner, R. and Ranger, T. (eds), *Postcolonial Identities in Africa*, London: Zed Books, pp. 1–25.

Wessels, W. (1997), 'An ever closer fusion? A dynamic macropolitical view on integration processes', *Journal of Common Market Studies*, 35:2, 267–99.

White, H. V. (1966), 'The burden of history', *History and Theory*, 5:2, 111–71.

Wiseman, H. V. (1969), *Politics The Master Science*, London, Routledge and Kegan Paul.

Wiseman, J. (1999), 'The continuing case for demo-optimism in Africa', *Democratization*, 6:2, 128–55.

Wright, E. O. (1999), 'Metatheoretical foundation of Charles Tilly's Durable Inequality', revised version of paper presented at Social Science History Conference, Chicago, IL., 20–23 November 1998.

Wu, C. (1998), 'Labor and democratization in South Korea and Taiwan', *Journal of Contemporary Asia*, 28:2, 185–202.

Young, I. M. (1990), *Justice and the Politics of Difference*, Princeton, NJ, Princeton University Press.

Youngs, R. (2001), *The European Union and the Promotion of Democracy*, Oxford, Oxford University Press.

Yuval-Davis, N. (1997), 'Women, Citizenship and Difference', *Feminist Review*, 57: Special Issue 'Citizenship: Pushing the Boundaries', 4–27.

Zielonka, J. (2001), 'Conclusions: foreign made democracy', in Zielonka, J. and Pravda, A. (eds), *Democratic Consolidation in Eastern Europe, Volume 2: Institutional and Transnational Factors*, Oxford, Oxford University Press, 511–32.

Zolberg, A. (1966), *Creating Political Order: The Party-States of West Africa*, Chicago, Rand McNally.

Zulu, L. (2000), 'Institutionalising changes: South African women's participation in the transition to democracy', in Rai (2000), 166–81.

Index